Abraham

Abraham

A Man Fearing God

SHAUL BAR

WIPF & STOCK · Eugene, Oregon

ABRAHAM
A Man Fearing God

Copyright © 2025 Shaul Bar. All rights reserved. Except for brief quotations in critical publications or reviews, no part of this book may be reproduced in any manner without prior written permission from the publisher. Write: Permissions, Wipf and Stock Publishers, 199 W. 8th Ave., Suite 3, Eugene, OR 97401.

Wipf & Stock
An Imprint of Wipf and Stock Publishers
199 W. 8th Ave., Suite 3
Eugene, OR 97401

www.wipfandstock.com

PAPERBACK ISBN: 979-8-3852-4461-4
HARDCOVER ISBN: 979-8-3852-4462-1
EBOOK ISBN: 979-8-3852-4463-8

08/06/25

All scripture quotations, unless otherwise indicated, are taken from the Jewish Publication Society TANAKH translation copyright © 1985, 1999 by the Jewish Publication Society.

Dedicated to the memory of
Rachel Finkelstein and
Lydia (Lidia) Armoni,
who were beloved and cherished

Contents

Acknowledgments		ix
Abbreviations		xi
Introduction		xvii
Chapter 1	Go Forth from Your Native Land	1
Chapter 2	Up, Walk About the Land	17
Chapter 3	He Mustered His Retainers	37
Chapter 4	To Your Offspring, I Assign This Land	57
Chapter 5	For I Make You the Father of a Multitude of Nations	72
Chapter 6	Will You Sweep Away the Innocent with the Guilty?	85
Chapter 7	For It Is Through Isaac That Offspring Shall Be Continued	102
Chapter 8	Take Your Son, Your Favored One, Isaac	119
Chapter 9	Please Say That You Are My Sister	136
Chapter 10	And He Circumcised the Flesh of Their Foreskins	154
Chapter 11	I Am YHWH; I Appeared to Abraham, Isaac, and Jacob as El Shaddai	167
Chapter 12	For Dust You Are, and to Dust You Shall Return	185
Conclusion		201
Bibliography		205
Scripture Index		217

Acknowledgments

To start with, I would like to thank my readers who read the early drafts of my manuscript and offered many perspectives and insightful comments: Anna S. Chernak, who read the initial manuscript offering valuable advice and continuous encouragement, and Dr. Dena Arendall who made many suggestions.

I want to express appreciations to the staff of the Harding School of Theology in Memphis, which was my second home for many years, and has sadly closed. To Don Meredith who was the head librarian for many years, associate librarian Sheila Owen and circulation assistant Tina Rogers, who helped with my research.

Special thanks to Yoram Bitton Chief, African, Middle Eastern and Hebraic Division (AMED) of the Library of Congress who provided me with help, wisdom and friendship.

Finally, a special thanks to the people of Wipf & Stock for their devotion and expertise in transforming my manuscript into this book.

Abbreviations

AASOR	Annual of the American Schools of Oriental Research
AB	Anchor Bible
ABD	*The Anchor Bible Dictionary.* Edited by David Noel Freedman. 6 vols. New York: Doubleday, 1992.
'Abot	'Abot
'Abot R. Nat.	'Abot de Rabbi Nathan
Ag. Ap.	*Against Apion.* Josephus.
AnBib	Analecta Biblica
ANET	*Ancient Near Eastern Texts Relating to the Old Testament.* 3rd ed. with supplement. Edited by James B. Pritchard. Princeton: Princeton University Press, 1969.
Ant	*Jewish Antiquities.* Josephus.
ASTI	Annual of the Swedish Theological Institute
AT	Alalakh Tablets
BA	*The Biblical Archaeologist*
BAR	*Biblical Archaeology Review*
BASOR	Bulletin of the Americans Schools of Oriental Research
BDB	Brown, Francis, S. R. Driver, and C. A. Briggs. *A Hebrew and English Lexicon of the Old Testament.* Oxford: Clarendon Press, 1975.
Ber	Berakhot
Beṣah	Beṣah

BethM	Beth Miqra
BHH	Biblisch-historisches Handwörterbuch: Landeskunde, geschichte, religion, Kultur. Edited by B. Reicke and L. Rost. 4 vols. Göttingen: Hubert & Co., 1962–1966.
Bib	Biblica
BibOr	Biblica et orientalia
B. Bab.	Baba Batra
B. Meṣ.	Bava Metziʿa
BR	Biblical Research
BZAW	Beihefte zur zeitschrift für die Älttestamentliche Wissenschaft
CAD	The Assyrian Dictionary of the Oriental Institute of the University of Chicago. Chicago: University of Chicago Press, 1956.
CBQ	Catholic Biblical Quarterly
COS	The Context of Scripture. 3 vols. Edited by W. W. Hallo. Leiden: Brill, 1997.
DDD	Dictionary of Deities and Demons in the Bible. Edited by K. van der Toorn, et al. Leiden: Brill, 1995.
EA	El-Amarna tablets. According to the edition of Jørgen A. Knudtzon. Die al-Amarna-Tafeln. Leipzig: Hinrichs, 1908–1915. Repr., Aalen: zeller, 1964. Continued in Anson F. Rainey, El-Amarna Tablets, 359–379. 2nd rev. ed. Kevelaer: Butzon & Bercker, 1978.
EMiqr	Encyclopedia Miqraʾit–Encyclopedia Biblica. 8 vols. Jerusalem: Bialik Institute, 1950–1982.
EncJud	Encyclopedia Judaica. 22 vols. Edited by Fred Skolnik. Jerusalem: Keter, 2007.
Exod. Rab.	Exodus Rabbah
Fast.	Fasti. Ovid.
Gen. Rab.	Genesis Rabbah
Giṭ.	Giṭṭin
Ḥag.	Ḥagigah

HALOT	*The Hebrew and Aramaic Lexicon of the Old Testament.* 4 vols. L. Koehler, et al. Translated and edited under the supervision of M. E. J. Richardson. Leiden: Brill, 1994–1999.
HSM	Harvard Semitic Monographs
HTR	*Harvard Theological Review*
HUCA	*Hebrew Union College Annual*
Ḥul.	*Ḥullin*
IBS	*Irish Biblical Studies*
IDB	*The Interpreter's Dictionary of the Bible.* 4 vols. Edited by G. A Buttrick. Nashville: Abingdon, 1962.
IDBSup	*Interpreter's Dictionary of the Bible: Supplementary Volume.* Edited by K. Crim. Nashville: Abingdon, 1976.
ICC	International Critical Commentary
IEJ	*Israel Exploration Journal*
Iraq	*Iraq*
ISBE	*International Standard Bible Encyclopedia.* 4 vols. Edited by G. W. Bromiley. Grand Rapids: Eerdmans, 1979–1988.
JAOS	*Journal of the American Oriental Society*
JBQ	*Jewish Bible Quarterly*
JBL	*Journal of Biblical Literature*
JCS	*Journal of Cuneiform Studies*
JEA	*Journal of Egyptian Archeology*
JJS	*Journal of Jewish Studies*
JNES	*Journal of Near Eastern Studies*
JNSL	*Journal of Northwest Semitic Languages*
JSOR	*Journal of the Society of Oriental Research*
JSOT	*Journal for the Study of the Old Testament*
JSOTSup	Journal for the Study of the Old Testament: Supplement Series
J.W.	*Jewish Wars.* Josephus

KAI	*Kanaanäische und Aramäische Inschriften.* H. Donner and W. Rölling. 2d ed. Wiesbaden: Harrassowitz, 1966–1969.
Ketub	Ketubbot
Kid	Kiddushin
KTU	*Dies keilalphabeticschen texte aus Ugarit.* Edited by M. Dietrich, O. Loretz, and J. Sanmartin. Alter Orient und Altes Testament 24/1. Neukirchen-Vluyn: Butzon & Bercker, 1976. *The Cuneiform Alphabetic Texts from Ugarit, Ras Ibn Hani, and Other Places.* 3rd ed. Münster: Ugarit, 2013.
L.A.B.	*Liber antiquitatum biblicarum*
Lev. Rab.	*Leviticus Rabbah*
Maarav	*Maarav*
Meg.	*Megillah*
Mid.	*Middot*
Moʿed Qaṭ.	*Moʿed Qaṭan*
NEAHEL	*The New Encyclopedia of Archeological Excavation in the Holy Land.* 4 vols. Edited by E. Stern. Jerusalem: Israel Society & Carta, 1993.
NICOT	New International Commentary on the Old Testament
Or	*Orientalia*
Od.	*Odyssey*
OTS	Old Testament Studies
PEFA	*Palestine Exploration Fund Annual*
Pesaḥ	*Pesaḥim*
Pesiq. Rab.	*Pesiqta Rabbati*
Pirqe R. El.	*Pirqe Rabbi Eliezer*
Praep. ev.	*Praeparatio evangelica.* Eusebius.
PRU	*Le Palais royal d'Ugarit*
RHR	*Revue de l'histoire des religions*
Roš Haš.	*Roš Haššanah*

Šabb.	Shabbat
Sanh.	Sanhedrin
SBLDS	Society of Biblical Literature Dissertation Series
Šebu.	Šebu'ot
Semeia	Semeia
Shnaton	Shnaton
Sifre Deut.	Sifre Deuteronomy
SJLA	Studies in Judaism in Late Antiquity
Soṭah	Soṭah
TA	Tel Aviv
Ta'an.	Ta'anit
Tanḥ. Gen.	Tanḥumah Genesis
Tarbiz	Tarbiz
TDOT	*Theological Dictionary of the Old Testament*. 14 vols. Edited by G. Johannes Botterweck and Helmer Ringgren. Translated by J. T. Willis et al. Grand Rapids: Eerdmans, 2004.
TLOT	*Theological Lexicon of the Old Testament*. Edited by Ernst Jenni, with assistance from Claus Westermann. Translated by Mark E. Biddle. 3 vols. Peabody, MA: Hendrickson, 1997.
TWOT	*Theological Wordbook of the Old Testament*. 2 vols. Edited by R. L. Harris and G. L. Archer Jr. Chicago: Moody, 1980.
TynBul	*Tyndale Bulletin*
UT	*Ugaritic Textbook*. Cyrus H. Gordon. AnOr 38. Rome: Pontifical Biblical Institute, 1965
UF	*Ugaritic-Forschungen*
VD	Verbum Domini
VT	*Vetus Testamentum*
VTSup	Supplements to Vetus Testamentum
Yebam.	Yebamot
ZAW	*Zeitschrift für die Alttestamentliche Wissenschaft*

Introduction

The patriarch Abraham is not mentioned in any of the extra-biblical documents. Thus, the inevitable question is whether Abraham was a real historical figure or a figment of the imagination, the product of a literary tradition. The fragmentary nature of the narrative in Genesis led scholars to the conclusion that the stories are a combination of oral traditions and written sources. Scholars who adhere to the documentary hypothesis identify sources J, E, and P in the stories but disagree about the time and the historical value of the material that was used. The usage of the biblical chronological data to place the patriarch in the framework of history raised more questions than answers. Examination of the Hebrew Bible shows that there are some chronological indications in the Bible itself, but this cannot be determined absolutely.[1]

The ambiguity within the text has led scholars to look outside the Bible for help in dating the patriarchal period.[2] Typically, scholars exam-

---

1. This hinges on the date of the exodus and the duration of slavery in Egypt. Based on 1 Kgs 6:1, Solomon began the construction of his temple in the fourth year of his reign, about 967 BCE, 480 years after the exodus from Egypt. According to Exod 12:40, the Israelites stayed in Egypt for 430 years, adding to this the total sum of 215 years that the patriarchs lived in Canaan, which is before the Israelites went down to Egypt; leading us to date Abraham's migration to Canaan around 2100 BCE. See Sarna, *Understanding Genesis*, 82–83; Finklestein and Siiberman, *Bible Unearthed*, 34–35.

2. There are some difficulties with the analysis for reconstructing the timeframe of the patriarchal narrative, such as the extraordinarily long life spans assigned to the patriarchs. The life of each of the patriarchs, Abraham, Isaac, and Jacob, exceeded one hundred years. In other words, the total life-span of the patriarchs covers a period of more than 300 years (Gen 21:5; 25:6; 47:28). Moses and Aaron were said to

ine the archeological findings, onomastics, and social and legal customs of the ancient Near East and compare them to the Hebrew Bible. To find parallels between the biblical and extra-biblical data would help set a timeframe for the period of the patriarchs.[3] However, this method of inquiry also leads to divergent conclusions where scholars followed their own beliefs and preferences.

Writing about the patriarchal period, Julius Wellhausen maintained that "we attain to no historical knowledge of the patriarchs, but only of the times when the stories about them arose in the Israelite people; this later age is here unconsciously projected, in its inner and its outward features, into hoar antiquity, and is reflected there like a glorified mirage."[4] And about Abraham, he said, "Abraham alone is certainly not the name of the people like Isaac and Lot: he is somewhat difficult to interpret. That is not to say that in some connection as this we may regard him as a historical person; he might with some more likelihood be regarded as a free invention of unconscious art."[5] Believing that writing was unknown in Syria and Palestine in the second millennium, Wellhausen concluded that an accurate description of the patriarchal period would not be possible. But ten years after the publication of Wellhausen's work, the Amarna letters were discovered in Egypt dating to the fourteenth century BCE. This proved the existence of writings in second-millennium Syria and Palestine. Although this discovery invalidated Wellhausen's conclusion, he did not modify his claims about the absence of literacy.

Following Wellhausen's lead, Gunkel saw the stories about the patriarchs as saga or legends. In his monumental work *The Legends of Genesis*,

---

be fourth-generation descendants of Jacob's son Levi (1 Chron 5:27–29). The period in which the Israelites were enslaved in Egypt was 430 years. This is too long for three generations from Levi to Moses and Aaron. In other words, this means it is 143 years per generation. Moreover, Joshua, who was the contemporary of Moses and Aaron, was a twelfth generation descendent of Levi's brother Joseph (1 Chron 7:20–27). If indeed this is the case, then eleven generations from Joseph to Joshua would average thirty-nine years each. There are apparently contradictions in calculating between years and generations and there is no satisfactory explanation for it. In addition, many of the figures appear to be round numbers—14, 20, 40, 60, and 100—which raises questions about the time frame of the Genesis narrative See Sarna, *Genesis Commentary*, 116; Wenham, *Genesis*, xxviii–xxx.

3. For an extensive study to date the patriarchal era see de Vaux, *Early History*, 257–66.

4. Wellhausen, *Prolegomena*, 342.

5. Wellhausen, *Prolegomena*, 343.

he pointed to the oral traditions that form the Hebrew Bible through its historical development. Speaking about Abraham he said,

> For even if there had once been a leader by the name Abraham, as is generally believed, and who conducted the migration from Haran to Canaan, this much is beyond question which everyone who knows anything of the history of legends, that a legend cannot be expected to preserve throughout so many centuries a picture of the personal piety of Abraham. The religion of Abraham is in reality the religion of the narrators of the legends, ascribed by them to Abraham.[6]

And for Gunkel: "Now it is in the nature of the legend that we do not catch sight of these old occurrences clearly by its means, but only as though a mist. Legends have woven a poetic veil about the historical memories and hidden their outline."[7] In other words, the legends about Abraham could not give us a real picture of him or his faith or the time of the events since they are the creation of the narrators. He recognized that some of the stories could contain historical data but given the inclusion of imaginative elements, there would be no way to distinguish between reliable history and fiction. According to his view, the patriarchs Abraham, Isaac, and Jacob were not individual humans but personified tribes. The names were simply retrojections of the first-millennium tribal names. But archeological discoveries suggest otherwise. The name Jacob was found in the eighteenth-century BCE site at Chagar Bazar in Iraq and in the fifteenth-century BCE list from Egypt compiled by King Thutmose III.[8] The name Ishmael was found in the eighteenth-century BCE text from Mari in Syria and the name Israel was found on the Merneptah stele dated to 1205 BCE.

Contrary to the views of Wellhausen and Gunkel, scholars such as Albright, Speiser, and Gordon showed that there is a kernel of historicity in the stories about Abraham. They accepted the diverse literary sources as traditions that were transmitted for different emphasis. The archeological excavations, their findings, and interpretation concur with the biblical story, which is trustworthy, even though the stories were put into writing long after the events took place. Focusing his attention on newly excavated material of cuneiform tablets from Mari and Nuzi, Albright

---

6. Gunkel, *Legends*, 122.
7. Gunkel, *Legends*, 122.
8. Sperling, *Original Torah*, 18; Thompson, *Historicity*, 49.

suggested that these sources contain family practices and customs that were also prevalent among the patriarchs.[9] He maintained that Abraham's stories fit the twentieth century BCE. In his evaluation of the book of Genesis Albright said, "The narratives of Genesis dealing with Abram (Abraham) may now be integrated into the life and history of the time in such surprising consistent ways that there can be little doubt about their substantial historicity."[10] Pointing to the archives that were found at Nuzi in northern Iraq that date to the fifteenth century BCE, Gordon suggested they are appropriate background for the patriarchs. He cited over twenty biblical passages that can be understood better considering the Nuzi material.[11] According to Gordon the time of Abraham and Jacob is the fourteenth century BCE (LB II).[12] Not all his comparisons to the Nuzi archives were valid, and some of the parallels were rejected by scholars.[13] And a late date does not coincide with the internal biblical chronology.[14] Speiser went further and proposed more than twenty examples where the Nuzi texts illuminate the book of Genesis. He believed those texts confirm the patriarchal era although they are not exact in every aspect. According to him, the authentic patriarchal tradition originated in Central Mesopotamia, and he set the time of the patriarchs in the second quarter of the second millennium BCE.[15]

Writing about Abraham, G. E. Wright said, "We shall probably never be able to prove that Abraham really existed, that he did this or that, said thus and so, but we can prove is that his life and times are reflected in the stories about him, fit perfectly within the early second millennium, but imperfectly within any later period."[16] A similar view was expressed by J. Bright's *History of Israel*: "One is forced to the conclusion that the patriarchal narratives authentically reflect social customs at home in the second millennium rather than those of later Israel." Furthermore, he added, "We can assert with full confidence that Abraham, Isaac, and Jacob were actual historical individuals."[17]

9. Albright, *Patriarchs*, 9.
10. Albright, *Patriarchs*, 10.
11. Gordon, *Customs*, 1–12.
12. Gordon, *Introduction*, 56–57.
13. Thompson, *Historicity*, 196–297.
14. Vaux, *Early History*, 262, 265–66.
15. Speiser, *Genesis*, xliii.
16. Wright, *Biblical*, 40.
17. Bright, *History*, 79, 91.

Introduction

In the 1970s, T. L. Thompson's *Historicity of the Patriarchal Narrative* and J. van Seters's *Abraham in History and Tradition* rejected the views of the historicity of the patriarchal narrative and challenged the archeological evidence for the existence of the historical Abraham in the second millennium BCE. According to Thompson, "'archeology' has not proven a single event of the patriarchal traditions to be historical . . . any such historicity as is commonly spoken of in both scholarly and popular works about the patriarchs of Genesis is hardly possible and totally improbable."[18] He suggested that some of the biblical text reflected the first-millennium conditions. The stories were created to describe the imaginary past to encourage the community for the present and hope for the future. In other words, it was the faith of the religious community that created Abraham; this is the opposite of what we read in the Bible, which says that it is Abraham who stimulates the faith of the religious community.[19] Van Seters maintained that too much was made of the parallel between the Nuzi text and the stories of Genesis. The stories in Genesis possess information of pre-Israelite times, but only to the time of their composition, which is late. He suggested the seventh to sixth centuries BCE as the time frame for Abrahamic stories.[20] These scholars failed to deal with all the evidence and did not review the patriarchal data against all periods. They neglected details from the third millennium and some evidence from the early second millennium, stressing the first-millennium data instead. As noted by scholars, some types of customs appeared in all periods, making them impractical for dating.[21]

Today, the leading scholars of the minimalist camp include Thompson, P. R. Davies, and N. P. Lemche. According to them, there were no "biblical Israelites." In Lemche's opinion, "the simple fact is that the ancient Near Eastern sources from the third and second millennium BCE do not contain a single direct reference to any features mentioned in the Old Testament narrative. There is not a single reference to Abraham the Patriarch, to Joseph and his brothers in Egypt, or Moses and the Exodus, or to the conquest of Canaan."[22] Moreover, according to Lemche, "Modern scholars invented ancient Israel, not because they wanted to

---

18. Thompson, *Historicity*, 328.
19. Goldingay, "Patriarchs," 29–30.
20. Van Seters, *Abraham in History*, 12–122.
21. Kitchen, *Bible*, 58.
22. Lemche, "Israel, History," 534.

invent something new but simply because of a rather naïve reading of the scripture."[23]

This is only a small sample of the different views that prevail among scholars. Our task is to evaluate the different views on the historicity or non-historicity of the Abrahamic stories and to draw a conclusion: Did a person by the name Abraham exist or is he a mythical figure? This endeavor is difficult because the stories were transmitted orally and only in a later period were they put into writing. At least a thousand years passed between the traditions that allegedly originated with Abraham and the written document. This raises questions about the validity and accuracy of those traditions and whether they reflect earlier times of the second millennium. Or were the stories a literary creation plaited from earlier sources that were created to fulfill the political needs of a later period? Writing about whether we can accept these traditions as evidence of the past patriarchal history, Lods pointed out,

> Considering all the facts, it is probable that many diverse elements have gone to the making of the patriarchal history: events and facts of the times of the Judges and Kings idealized or explained by popular imagination, historical reminiscences, Hebrew or Canaanite folk stories, fragments of mythology. The national consciousness has taken all this various material, fused and recast it, and produced therefrom a cycle of explanatory stories, accounting for the present state of Israel and its neighbors. Hence it follows that these traditions can only be used with great reserve as evidence for the pre-history of the Israelite tribes.[24]

Many works were written on Abraham in addition to exegetical commentaries on the book of Genesis. Thus, contemporary views will be considered. In addition, material found in the Talmud, Midrashim, and medieval commentators, which are less noted in the scholarly works on Abraham, will be studied. The synchronic method will be applied, analyzing the chapters in the book of Genesis as they appear. Epigraphic material from the ancient Near East that was discovered by archeologists in the cities of Ur, Babylon, Nuzi, Mari, Alalah, Ugarit, and Boğhazköy will be evaluated.

There are descriptions of the patriarch's journeys in the land of Canaan, his movement from a starting point, and his return to it. This itinerary can shed light on the lifestyle of the patriarch and his relations

---

23. Lemche, *Israelites*, 165.
24. Lods, *Israel*, 162.

with the different ethnic groups. Personal names and ethnographic and geographic names are useful for determining the historical and ethnic background of the stories and their timeframe. Another venue that can be helpful is the portrayal of the social and legal background of the stories such as adoption, circumcision, sacrifice, and death. Did these customs reflect the reality that is known to us from the first half of the second millennium? What were the religious beliefs of the patriarch? Is the description in Genesis a projection of later belief and the authentic religion of Israel or was it an animism or polydaemonism? In addition to YHWH and El Shaddai, Abraham worshipped El Olam, El Elyon, Elohim, and El Roi, which is mentioned in the story of Hagar. Later, the God of My Father with the name Abraham is mentioned. Thus, was Abraham a true monotheist, or did he worship many gods?

The rabbis of late antiquity pointed out that many events in the life of the patriarch foreshadowed the future: "R. Phinehas commented in R. Hoshaya's name: The Holy One, blessed be He, said to our father Abraham, 'Go forth and tread out a path for thy children.' For you find that everything written in connection with Abraham is written in connection with his children."[25] Similarly, "R. Joshua of Sikhnin thought that the Holy One, blessed be He, gave Abraham a sign that whatever happened to him would likewise happen to his descendants."[26] The rabbis termed it "the deeds of the fathers are signs to the sons." Two centuries earlier, Paul in his writings also noted, "Now all these things happened unto them for examples: and they are written for our admonition, upon whom the ends of the world come" (1 Cor 10:11). These assertions raise questions as to whether the descriptions of Abraham's journeys within the land of Canaan and to Egypt, his wars with the four kings, the mention of Melchizedek, the covenants with God, and the repetition of the wife/sister stories had additional meanings. The rabbis believed that these events took place in the past and alluded to future events that transpired.[27] If so, what was the purpose of linking the past to the future?

---

25. *Gen. Rab.* 40, 6.

26. *Tanḥ. Gen.*, "Get thee out of thy Country," 3:9.

27. Alternatively, Sperling suggested interpreting the Torah as a historical and political allegory. The characters of Abraham, Jacob, Joseph, Aaron, and Moses are wholly fictitious and allude to characters like Saul, David, and Jeroboam "who are firmly anchored in history." If Abraham is an allegory of David, it means that the writer approves of David's actions. The writers of the Torah targeted their message to a particular audience. "Their method was allegorical, and their goals ideological." Sperling, *Torah*, 136.

In addition to answering these and other questions, our goal is to rediscover Abraham so that we might have a better understanding of his personality, achievements, and failures. We will look at his personal growth and transformation from the time he left Ur of the Chaldeans to his death. We trust that this will provide a provocative and useful insight into the story of Abraham.

Chapter 1

Go Forth from Your Native Land

Abraham, at first called Abram, is the first of the Hebrew patriarchs and a figure revered by the three major monotheistic religions: Judaism, Christianity, and Islam. At his birthplace in Mesopotamia, he received a call from God to leave his country and people and go to an unknown land where he would become the forefather of a new nation. He obeyed the call and at the age of seventy-five took his wife Sarai, later named Sarah, his nephew Lot, and other companions for a long journey to the land of Canaan. So, who was Abraham, and what prompted him to obey the divine call from a God unknown to him? To answer this, we examine his family lineage and places of habitat to see if there is a shred of evidence in the extrabiblical sources that can support the biblical account. Although Abraham migrated to Canaan, there are open questions about the ties with his family that were left in Mesopotamia. The Bible repeatedly refers to the ancestors of Abraham and other patriarchs as Arameans. The earliest extrabiblical mention of the Arameans that scholars agree to is from the time of Tiglath-pileser I of Assyria (1116–1076 BCE). This led scholars to believe that the mention of the Arameans is an anachronism. Another question that was posed by scholars deals with the reasons for Abraham's migration and its time frame. Ignoring religious factors, scholars tried to link the migration to Canaan with the second millennium's larger movement to the east or linked it to the so-called "Amorite hypothesis." In this period the Canaanite urban culture collapsed, which was linked to invasion or migration from the north. Allegedly Abraham was part of this movement to the east, he was an Amorite merchant who came from the north and wandered in the areas of the central hill country of Canaan and the Negeb. Thus, in the following pages, we try to find if there is validity to these assertions.

IDOL WORSHIPERS

Abraham, the father of the Hebrew nation, started his spiritual journey in Haran where he received this divine command:

> The Lord said to Abram, Go forth from your native land and from your father's house to the land that I will show you. I will make of you a great nation, And I will bless you; I will make your name great, And you shall be a blessing. I will bless those who bless you, And curse him that curses you. And all the families of the earth Shall bless themselves by you. (Gen 12:1–3)

Ten generations passed from Adam to Noah and from Noah to Abraham when Abraham heard the divine command. He was seventy-five years old when God told him to leave Haran and go to Canaan. We are not told why God elected Abraham. This is quite puzzling since Abraham later received the promise of the land and the promise of many descendants. What made Abraham worthy of God's promises and blessings? Conversely, when God chose Noah, it says that Noah was a righteous man: "But Noah found favor with the Lord. . . . Noah was a righteous man" (Gen 6:8–9). When Moses was chosen to lead his people out of Egypt, the Bible recorded his righteous deeds when he protected the weak and stood up against evil. Not so with Abraham; his first seventy-five years are not documented. Nevertheless, a hint can be found in the book of Joshua, which provides an explanation:

> Then Joshua said to all the people, "Thus said the LORD, the God of Israel: In olden times, your forefathers Terah, father of Abraham, and the father of Nahor lived beyond the Euphrates and worshiped other gods. But I took your father Abraham from beyond the Euphrates, and led him through the whole land of Canaan, and multiplied his offspring. I gave him Isaac." (Josh 24:2–3)

Terah and Nahor were idol worshipers, but Abraham was not. At one point, he stopped worshiping idols and started believing in one God. For this reason, God singled him out and blessed him with many offspring and nationhood.

The conviction that Abraham was a monotheist and his forefathers were idol worshipers led to the creation of many legends and interpretations. In the Second Temple period (200 BCE–200 CE), many traditions were created to fill the "gap" as to the origins of Abraham and his beliefs. One of those traditions tells the following:

> Abraham's father, Terah, was an idol manufacturer. Once he had to travel, so he left Abraham to manage the shop. People would come in and ask to buy idols. Abraham would say, "How old are you?" The person would say "Fifty" or "Sixty." Abraham would say, "Isn't it pathetic that a man of sixty wants to bow down to a one-day-old idol?" The man would feel ashamed and leave. One time a woman came with a basket of bread. She said to Abraham, "Take this and offer it to the gods." Abraham got up, took a hammer in his hand, broke all the idols to pieces, and then put the hammer in the hand of the biggest idol among them. When his father came back and saw the broken idols, he was appalled. "Who did this?" he cried. "How can I hide anything from you?" replied Abraham calmly. "A woman came with a basket of bread and told me to offer it to them. I brought it in front of them, and each one said, 'I'm going to eat first.' Then the biggest one got up, took the hammer, and broke all the others to pieces." "What are you trying to pull on me?" asked Terah. "Do they have minds?" Said Abraham, "Listen to what your own mouth is saying. They have no power at all! Why worship idols?" (*Gen. Rab.* 38:13)

The Midrash portrays Abraham as the person who discovered monotheism. Abraham realized the futility of worshiping idols that are manufactured by human hands. Abraham believed in one God and rejected the worship of the sun, moon, and stars that was prevalent in polytheistic religious traditions. This idea is mentioned in the second century BCE in the book of Jubilees (12:1–4):

> And it came to pass in the sixth week, in the seventh year thereof, that Abram said to Terah his father, saying, "Father!" And he said, "Behold, here am I, my son." And he said, "What help and profit have we from those idols which thou dost worship, And before which thou dost bow thyself? For there is no spirit in them, For they are dumb forms, and a misleading of the heart. Worship them not: Worship the God of heaven, Who causeth the rain and the dew to descend on the earth, And doeth

everything upon the earth, And hath created everything by His word, And all life is from before His face."

Another interesting explanation for Abraham's belief in one God is mentioned in the writings of Josephus, a first-century historian:

> He [Abraham] thus became the first person to argue that there is a single God who is the creator of all things and that whatever any of these other things contribute to the good of the world, they are enabled to do so at His command, and not by inherent force of their own. He was able to figure this out by the changes that land and sea undergo, those that are connected with the sun and the moon, and all those occurring in the skies. For if these bodies had any power over themselves, they would surely have arranged for themselves to be regularly ordered; but since this is not so, it is clear that they come together for our benefit not by any authority of their own, but by the power of One who commands, to whom alone it is proper to give honor and thanks. Because of these ideas the Chaldeans and the other people of Mesopotamia rose up against him, and having resolved, in keeping with God's will and with His help, to leave his home, he settled in the land of Canaan.[1]

In his explanation, Josephus pointed out that Abraham knew that a solar year is 365 and a quarter days. But this is an awkward number, therefore he said that if the sun were a god, it would assign itself a more coherent number. The existence of a fraction is evidence that the sun cannot run things. As for the moon, its annual cycle is 354 days, which is not better. The fact that the sun and the moon cannot have the same annual cycle shows that they do not have their own abilities and they are subservient to the power that commands them. Thus, there is a Higher Power that assigned these irregular numbers that led Abraham to realize that there was a Mighty Power that had no link to anybody on Earth or in the heavens.[2]

That Abraham's ancestors were idol worshipers can also be inferred from their place of habitation. Ur of the Chaldeans and Haran, the places where they lived, were known as the centers of moon worshipers. Sin, a Mesopotamian moon god, was worshiped in those two sites. In addition, the names of Abraham's family members were also associated with moon worship. The name Sarah is based on the Akkadian *sharratu*, the female consort of the moon god Sin, the main god of Ur. The name of Nahor's

---

1. Josephus, *Ant.* 154–57.
2. Kugel, *How to Read*, 94–95.

wife, Milcah, stems from the Akkadian *malkatu*, which is the title of the goddess Ishtar who was known as the "Queen of Heaven," daughter of the moon god Sin. Laban, Jacob's uncle, is *leven* in Hebrew, which means white and the feminine form of the Hebrew word means moon. In addition, Terah, Abraham's father's name, could be connected to *yareach*, which means moon.[3] These details point to one conclusion: Abraham's family members were moon worshipers.

MIGRATION

No reason is given for the family migration from Ur of the Chaldeans to Haran. The city of Ur was an important city and a center of commerce with the countries of the Persian Gulf and the Indus Valley. The city is identified with el-Maqayyar in southern Iraq. As noted by scholars, the epithet "Chaldeans" is anachronistic since the Chaldeans did not arrive in Babylon until a later period. The earliest reference to them appears in a short statement of Ashurnasirpal II or III (883–859 BCE): "The fear of my dominion extended to the land of Karduniash [Babylon], and the calling fear of weapons overwhelmed the land of *Kaldu*."[4] In Gen 22:22 Kesed is one of the sons of Nahor and the eponymous ancestor of the Chaldeans (Kasdim); phonetically the names sound similar. He appears in the list with other Aramean tribes who roamed the desert between Aram-Naharaim and the Arabian Desert. Job preserves a tradition of their nomadic state when they are described as nomads, who attacked and murdered a settled population (1:17). The prophets Jeremiah and Ezekiel called Babylonia the Land of Kasdim (Jer 24:5; 25:12; 50:1, 8; Ezek 1:3; 12:13; 16:16). However, in Daniel, Kasda'e is a technical term for astrologers (2:5, 10).[5]

By 1960 BCE the city of Ur was destroyed. This was a result of the Elamite invasion in addition to the Amorites incursion. A strong Elamite dynasty arose about 2000 BCE that conquered several cities in Babylon, among them was the city of Ur. A poem that laments the destruction of Ur was found on tablets from the early post Sumerian period. This is the period between the fall of the Third Dynasty of Ur and the beginning of Kassite rule in Babylonia.

---

3. Dijkstra, "Abraham," 3–5.
4. Rainey, *Chaldea*, 330; Luckenbill, *Ancient Records*.
5. This usage is also found in Greek sources Herodotus 1:181, 5; Strabo 739.

Ur—its weak and (its) strong perished through hunger; Mothers and fathers who did not leave their houses were overcome by fire. The young lying on their mother's laps, like fish carried off by the waters.[6]

Abraham's family probably migrated from Ur before its destruction. The period is characterized as a time of chaos and economic decline that was the result of incursions from the eastern nomadic tribes. This tumultuous time more than likely led Abraham's family to migrate to Haran.[7] Originally the plan was to move to Canaan, but the journey came to a halt at the city of Haran, which was situated at the intersection of caravan routes from Mesopotamia to the Mediterranean Sea, 550 miles northwest of Ur and ten miles north of the present Syrian–Turkish border on the bank of the Balikh River, a tributary of the Euphrates. Haran in Akkadian (*harrānu*) means road and caravan; the name probably is derived from the city's location as an important station on the main international trade routes. The prophet Ezekiel spoke of the city as involved in trade with Tyre (27:23).[8] Speaking about Canaan, Van Seters asserted that "the name of the country or people is entirely unknown until the early fifteenth century BC."[9] But third-millennium texts from Ebla contain references to Canaan and Haran; more so, they also include the phrase "Ur in Haran."[10] This suggests that Ur was in upper Mesopotamia close to Haran, which is mentioned repeatedly in the patriarchal narrative. Indeed, Abraham's birthplace is in upper Mesopotamia (Gen 24:4, 7). Abraham's servant went to Aram-Naharaim, a place which is described as Abraham's birthplace. An identical place name in a different location appears in the Hebrew Bible.[11] It is possible that people from the southern side of Ur moved to the north and named it Ur. Similarly, the tribe of Dan moved to the north, conquered Laish, and named the town Dan. As noted above,

---

6. Kramer, "Lamentation," 459, lines 228–229.

7. Yelvin, "Ur," 75.

8. In 2 Kgs 19:12 it is mentioned with Gozan and Rezeph as one of the cities that were destroyed by the Assyrians.

9. Van Seters, *Abraham*, 47.

10 Gordon, *Abraham's Ur*, 52.

11. See for example Kadesh (Num13:26); also mentioned as Kadesh-Barnea (32:8); En-mishpat (Gen 14:7); Meribah (Num 20:13), or Meribah-Kadesh (24:17). Kedesh is a Canaanite city that Joshua conquered (Josh 12:22); in Josh 20:7 it is mentioned in the hill country of Naphtali in Galilee; Kedesh Naphtali (Judg 4:6); Kedesh Barnea (Gen 14:7); Kedesh a Levitical city in the territory of Issachar (1 Chr 6:57). Kadesh on the Orontes is a city located alongside the Orontes River in Syria.

the stories of the patriarch are linked to the Hurrians of Haran and not to the Sumerians and Babylonians in the south, which suggests the northern location of Ur.

Names that are part of Abraham's lineage such as Serug, Abraham's great-grandfather; Terah, Abraham's father; and Nahor, Abraham's brother, are also reflected in the geographical area of Haran and are mentioned in extrabiblical sources. Serug is a well-known city of Sarugi located north of Haran, in the Balik Valley, and is mentioned in neo-Assyrian texts.[12] Nahor is mentioned in cuneiform documents as a personal name and as a city. Akkadian sources from the beginning of the second millennium to the middle of the seventh century BCE speak of Nahor as a city in the Balikh valley. In twentieth- to nineteenth-century BCE Assyrian documents from Kanish, it is an important place in the Assyrian trade with Asia Minor.[13] Terah appears in Assyrian sources as a place named Til(ša) Turaḫi, the "ruin of Terah" located in the basin of Balikh River in upper Mesopotamia not far from Haran and Nahor.[14] All this suggests that the names were eponymous ancestors of towns on the Balikh River, near Haran. These names which are found in extrabiblical sources appear at the end of the third and beginning of the second millennium BCE, which is indicative of the antiquity of the Abrahamic stories.[15] More so, all three sites are in the vicinity of Haran, a place where Abraham's family stayed. The existence of names and sites in upper Mesopotamia and northern Syria shows that there was a population that was analogous to Israel's ancestors.

In extrabiblical sources, Haran is mentioned in a letter addressed to Yasmaḫ-Addu who was the Assyrian viceroy of Mari (1790 BCE). Another letter indicated that Haran was a center of the semi-nomadic "Benjamites." The letter warns the king of Mari of an alliance between Asdi-takim, the king of Haran, the kings of Zalmaqum, the sheik, and the elders of the Benjamites. This coalition was formed in the temple of the moon god Sin. It was Šamši-Addu (Shamshi-Adad) I of Assyria (1815–1782 BCE) who mounted a campaign against the land of Zalmaqum and

---

12. Schneider, "Patriarchennamen," 521–22.

13. On the city of Nahor, see Albright, "Western Asia," 27; Abright, "New Light," 29–30; Lewy, "Studies," 280–82; Malamat, "Nahor," 807–8.

14. Kareling, "Terach," 153.

15. Albright, *Stone Age*, 236–37; Bright, *History*, 70; Vaux, *Early History of Israel*, 196.

probably Haran. Following his death, the Old Assyrian Empire disintegrated, and Haran became independent.

The mention of nomadic groups from the first half of the second millennium BCE *Banū-śim l*, "son of the north," and *Banū-yamīna*, "son of the south," in the cuneiform text from Mari led scholars to associate the tribe of Benjamin with these nomadic groups.[16] As Rachel was dying giving birth to her son, she named him *Ben-oni*, which means "son of my sorrow." But Jacob changed the name to Benjamin, which could mean "son of my right hand." It could also mean "son of the south" (Ps 89:13) as he was the only one born in the south (Canaan); all the brothers were born in Aram-Naharaim. Or it could refer to the fact that the tribe of Benjamin was south of the tribe of Ephraim and Manasseh, which were referred to in the monarchial period as the "house of Joseph." Thus, the inevitable question is whether the name Benjamin comes from its geographical location or whether it is one of the oldest tribes that arrived at the land of Canaan after it was defeated by the kings of Mari.[17] Its arrival in Canaan coincided with the migration of other groups that was a result of the Horite's expansion. Here in Canaan, they joined their relatives, the sons of Eber, and kept their old name, but this is uncertain and there is no data to support it. More than likely the nomadic people of Mari and the tribe of Benjamin are only associated by name. Nevertheless, the similarities between the names and the fact that the patriarchal family originated from the same area lend more credibility to the biblical narrative.

FAMILY TIES

Abraham migrated from Haran to Canaan, but the ties between the patriarchs Abraham, Isaac, Jacob, and the family in Haran continued well after Abraham's migration. Abraham's brother Nahor and his wife Milcah stayed in Haran where Milcah bore eight children (Gen 22:20–22). Terah, Abraham's father, lived in Haran for another sixty years after Abraham's migration to Canaan (Gen 11:32; cf. 11:26). In subsequent chapters of Genesis Abraham and Nahor are depicted as ancestors of two clans that are intermarried. The Bible stresses that the Israelites were not of Canaanite origin and came from a foreign land, thus the nation of Israel was

---

16. Albright, "Northern," 150–55; Muilenburg, "Birth," 194–201; Kallai-Kleinmann, "Town List," 134–60; Schunck, "Benjamin," 671.

17. Yelvin, "Benjamin," 265.

formed not on its land. The patriarchs are described as wandering from one country to another, and they traveled between the great civilizations of Mesopotamia and Egypt.

The patriarchs are the relatives of the Arameans. Aram is the grandson of Nahor, Abraham's brother. Isaac marries Rebecca, the daughter of Bethuel the Aramean, and Jacob marries Leah and Rachel, the daughters of Laban the Aramean (Gen 31:47). The Bible repeatedly speaks of Laban the Aramean (25:20; 28:5; 31:20, 2 4). Deuteronomy 26:5 preserves a tradition in which Jacob is described as a fugitive of Aramean. The home of the patriarchs is recognized as Aram-Naharaim (24:10)[18] and Paddan Aram (Gen 25:20; 48:7).[19] Despite the recurrent mention of the family ties to the Arameans, their existence in earlier periods is not attested in extrabiblical sources. Egyptian and Akkadian sources of the fifteenth to twelfth centuries BCE just mention Naharin(a) or Naḫrima/Nārima but not Aram-Naharaim.[20] This led scholars to believe that the mention of Aram with Naharaim is an anachronism.[21] The Aramean roots of Israel were considered a fabrication. Other scholars tried to prove the opposite. Noth suggested a "Proto-Aramean" ancestry for Israel based on linguistics, but his arguments have been rejected.[22] De Vaux proposed an association of the Arameans and early Amorites. According to him, there was continuity between the Amorite of the patriarchal age and the Aramaean of the eleventh and tenth century BCE.[23] But nowhere are the patriarchs referred to as Amorites.

The earliest extrabiblical mention of the Arameans that scholars agreed on is from the time of Tiglath-pileser I of Assyria (1116–1076 BCE), who fought against the Ahalamu-Arameans. He led fourteen

---

18. Aram-Naharaim means "Aram alongside the River (Euphrates)." It is a region in eastern Syria and northern Iraq that was circled on its three sides by the Euphrates. The ending "*aim*" is not referring to the two rivers Tigris and Euphrates as was understood by the Greek translations, but it is a locative. Indeed, the ending "*aim*" is prevalent in names of cities like Jerusalem and countries such as Egypt.

19. Paddan is derived from Aramaic paddânâ, "a field, or plain," which means the "Plains of Aram" and is equivalent to *side Aram* (Gen 12:13). It is noteworthy that Abraham's servant went to Aram Naharaim to the city of Nahor to bring Rebecca (24:10), while in 25:20 Rebecca came from a Paddan-Aram, which might suggest that it is an alternate name for Aram-Naharaim.

20. O'Callaghan, *Aram Naharaim*, 131; Finkelstein, "Mesopotamia," 73.

21. Malamat, "Arameans," 140; de Vaux, *Early History*, 193–94; Mazar, "Historical Background," 78.

22. Noth, *Ursprünge des alten Israel*. For critical remarks, see Wagner, "Beiträgezur," 355.

23. Vaux, *Early History*, 209.

campaigns against them.[24] At that time the Aramaeans achieved historical significance; they already controlled large regions from the Bishri district, southeast of the Euphrates bend, as far west as the Tadmor (Palmyra) oasis, and to the foothills of the Lebanon mountains. This indirectly suggests that the Arameans existed in a much earlier period, and they were hardly mentioned before because they were not a force that had to be reckoned with.

Indeed, a place named Aram is mentioned as early as the twenty-third century BCE in the inscription of Naram-Sin of Akkad in his victory over Harsamatki, the lord of Aram and Am, in a region that is located on the upper Euphrates.[25] Tablets that were found in Derhem (2000 BCE) mentioned it as a city near Eshnunna on the lower Tigris.[26] It occurs as a personal name in Mari texts (eighteenth century BCE), which list people who are entitled to receive rations, and from Aalalah tablets in northern Syria (seventeenth century BCE).[27] The Rās Shamrah texts that are from a later period (fourteenth century BCE) mentioned the name Bn ʿArmi several times, which could be translated as "the Aramaean."[28] Aram is also mentioned in Egyptian texts as the name of a place (*p3–irm*) called "the land of Arameans," in the Syrian topographical list of Amenophis III (first half of the fourteenth century BCE), and from the time of Merenptah (1200 BCE) in a record of an official of the eastern frontier post of the Egyptian Delta telling of a colleague arriving from a town in "the district of the Arem."[29]

In spite of this data, there are scholars who maintain that these references are insufficient to indicate an early appearance of the Arameans.[30] The mention of Aram is found in personal names or place names never relating to a noun or adjective that denotes ethnic or national affiliation.[31] Malamat further says that Aram is mentioned "as an ono-

---

24. Luckenbill, *Ancient Records*, 99.
25. Vaux, *Early History*, 203.
26. Vaux, *Early History*, 203.
27. Malamat, "Arameans," 134.
28. Gordon, *Ugaritic Manual*, 22; Gordon, *Ugaritic Textbook*, 10.
29. Wilson, "Journal," 258–59.
30. Malamat, "Arameans," 135; Kupper, *Les nomads*, 113. On the other hand, there are scholars who accept the existence of the Arameans based on the cuneiform evidence and not using biblical passages; see Moscati, *Semites*, 67; Duppont-Sommer, "L'historie Araméenne," 40–49; McNamara, "De populi," 129–42.
31. Kupper, *Mésopotamie*, 112–14.

mastic and toponymic element even in non-Aramean contexts."[32] The geographically-scattered information also led to the dismissal of the existence of the Arameans in an early period. However, studies have shown that nomads infiltrated into and beyond Mesopotamia, from the fringe of the Arabian Desert, established themselves in one place or another, and then moved in other directions.[33] The same pattern applies to the Arameans.

It is strange that the Bible repeatedly mentions Israel's ancestors as Aramean, especially when the Arameans of Damascus became Israel's enemies in the ninth century BCE. This might suggest that the reference to the Arameans in the patriarchal narrative is of ancient origin, reflecting knowledge of an older situation or an ethnic or geographic location rather than political terminology, which is unknown to us.[34] Trying to explain the references to the Aramean, Van Seters suggested that the patriarchs were related to the Aramean of Haran and not the Syrian Arameans.[35] Only Laban is associated with Syria as indicated by the marking of the boundary with Jacob (Gen 31:47). However, Laban is also a resident of Haran, and he showed hostility towards Jacob.[36] Still, this does not explain the peaceful relations with the Arameans of Haran, especially when Van Seters maintained that the mention of Arameans in patriarchal stories is anachronistic. Another hypothesis that he proposed is the feeling of kinship between the Israelites and the Arameans of northwestern Mesopotamia. The Assyrians deported large numbers of Israelites to the Habur and Balih valley districts and swapped Arameans into the land of Israel, which led to a sense of kinship with the Arameans and the Haran region. This sense of identity occurred after the demise of the Aramean states in Syria.[37] Since the stories about the patriarchs were written in the exilic period as he suggested, it is hard to believe that the Israelites would feel a sense of kinship with the Arameans who were their bitter enemies in recent times. The sense of kinship could originate only at an early period.

Our knowledge of the cultures of the ancient Near East is incomplete and sporadic. What the patriarchal narrative conveys is that the

32. Malamat, "Arameans," 135.
33. Moscati, *Semites*, 67.
34. Millard, "Arameans," 348.
35. Van Seters, *Abraham*, 34.
36. Van Seters, *Abraham*, 34.
37. Van Seters, *Abraham*, 34.

Israelites originated from the region where the Arameans lived, and they share family ties. Aramean tribes lived in Mesopotamia during the time of the patriarchs, but they were powerless. They were small nomadic groups that were not considered a threat to settled communities in the Fertile Crescent. The lack of any extrabiblical evidence regarding the Arameans is not surprising. Only at the end of the second millennium and at the beginning of the first millennium did the Aramaeans attain historical significance. At that time, we find independent Aramaean states—in Syria the biblical Aram-Zoba, Aram Beth-Rehob, Aram-Maacah, and later Aram Damascus. Mesopotamian states were Bīt-Adini (Beth-Eden; Amos 1:5) Bît-Baḫyan, Bît-Ḫalupe, Bît-Zamani, Bît-Amukkani, Bît-Dakuri, and Bît-Yakin. It was the decline of the Mitanni Empire at the beginning of 1300 BCE, the limited influence of the Assyrian in areas where the Aramean tribes settled, the fall of the Hittite Empire about 1180 BCE that was splintered into several city-states, the decay of Egypt, and the weakness of Babylon that contributed to the spread of the Arameans. By the ninth century BCE, the entire area from Babylon to the Mediterranean coast was controlled by the Aramaean tribes known as Kaldu, the biblical Chaldeans. From that period the Arameans became an important political and economic factor: not surprisingly, we started to find epigraphic material that mentions them.

FROM UR TO CANAAN

Abraham received the divine call at Haran, but according to Gen 15:7, God brought Abraham out of Ur of the Chaldeans. This is repeated in the book of Nehemiah: "You are the Lord God, who chose Abraham, who brought him out of Ur of the Chaldeans and changed his name to Abraham" (9:7). It is also mentioned in the book of Judith (5:6), several times in the book of Jubilees (12 and 13), and in the New Testament in Stephen's speech (Acts 7:2). The narrator linked the wandering from Ur to Haran as part of the divine plan. Abraham's family made the detour to Haran and for unknown reasons the journey came to a halt. Medieval commentators such as Rashi (Rabbi Solomon ben Isaac, 1040–1105) and Ramban (Rabbi Moses ben Nahman, known as Nachmanides, 1194–1270) explain the discrepancy in the text by suggesting that the expression "brought you" refers only to his deliverance from Ur, but the divine call took place in Haran.

There are scholars who tried to link the migration of Abraham's family to Canaan with the migration of the Amorites of the second millennium.[38] During that period of time, different groups of people moved to the west, among them Abraham's family. William F. Albright claimed that Abraham was a wandering Amorite, a merchant who migrated from Mesopotamia to Canaan at about the time the Canaanite city-states collapsed.[39] Abraham entered Canaan as a part of the widespread Amorite movements that created disorder in the whole region during the early second millennium BCE. These invaders of the land of Canaan were called Amurru—the Amorites—literally Westerners of Mesopotamian texts. Albright identifies the patriarchs as Amorites and maintains that the story in Genesis suits the period between 2100–1800 BCE.

Texts that were discovered near Kayseri in central Turkey describe vibrant commercial ties between Mesopotamia and north Syria. Abraham, who was a merchant, took part in this commerce. Thus, Albright links it to the path that was taken by Abraham from Ur to Haran. At the same time, the caravan trade was also taking place between Transjordan and Egypt, which is a reminder of the Joseph story. Albright's theory was aided by the archeologist Nelson Glueck who pointed to hundreds of sites in southern Transjordan and the Negev desert. He believed that Abraham's journeys took place when these settlements flourished and identified these with MB I as the "Age of Abraham."[40] Albright connected the sites in the Negev with Abraham's movements there and to the destruction of the cities of the Dead Sea. However, Glueck's findings did not last long; following additional excavations, it appeared that the urban system did not come to an end, but it declined over many decades. The decline was a result of economic and social turmoil and not the result of outside invaders. In other words, studies showed that the so-called Amorite migration is erroneous.[41] Moreover, the biblical tradition does not associate the patriarchs with the Amorites, but rather with the Arameans, neither does it say that Terah and Abraham were part of this migration. That one family decided to move is not unlikely and therefore, not surprisingly, we do not find any details about it in royal or cultic records.[42]

38. Bright, *History of Israel*, 55; Albright, "Patriarchs to Moses," 5–19.
39. Albright, "Patriarchs to Moses," 5–19.
40. Glueck, "Age of Abraham," 2–9; Glueck, *Rivers*, 61–84.
41. Finkelstein and Silberman, *Bible Unearthed*, 35.
42. Mathews, *Genesis*, 8.

The migration of Abraham to Canaan was explained by the sages as the first test of the ten trials Abraham was tempted with. Abraham withstood them all, which shows great love and obedience to God.[43] The command "Go forth from your native land and from your father's house" (12:1) meant a break with family, a task which is very difficult, more so for a person who is seventy-five years old. Abraham embarked on a journey without knowing the exact destination. In the Midrash, we find an explanation for why God did not reveal it to Abraham: "In order to make it more beloved in his eyes and to reward him for every step he took."[44] The Midrash compares it to another incident where God did not reveal to Abraham the identity of the son to be sacrificed. According to the sages, "The Holy One, blessed be He, first places the righteous in doubt and suspense, and then He reveals to them the meaning of the matter."[45]

Although the Bible does not give us details about Abraham's journey from Haran to Canaan, we can still make some assumptions about the route that Abraham took. Abraham probably left Haran for Aleppo in the spring, which was part of a caravan route. The city existed during the patriarchal period. It was the capital of the kingdom of Yahmad in the period of the kings of Mari and relations existed between the two kingdoms.[46] An Arab legend tells us that Abraham passed through the city where he found its residents ill and underfed. He milked his white cow and gave its milk to the poor who, as a result, became healthy. Thus, the name of the city is Halab Shahba, which means "to milk the white cow." As noted previously, Ur and Haran were centers of the Sin cult. Interestingly, in the village of Nayrab located near Aleppo, two steles dedicated to Shahar (Sin) and Nikkal (Ningal) were discovered; this suggests that the patriarch's journey was marked with sanctuaries.[47]

From Aleppo, Abraham went southward to Qatna. The Mari tablets refer to relations between Aleppo and Qatna which suggests a route between the two cities. The first archeological finds at Qatna date to the mid to late third millennium BCE, but still this early period is not well represented. In the second millennium BCE, trade routes developed connecting Mesopotamia with Cyprus, Crete, and Egypt. Qatna was one of the important stops on this route. The first king of Qatna is mentioned

---

43. Pirke Abot 5:2; Jubilees 19:8.
44. *Gen. Rab.* 39:9.
45. *Gen. Rab.* 39:9.
46. Parrot, *Abraham*, 61.
47. Parrot, *Abraham*, 61.

in the Mari archives. His name was Ishi-Adad Ishi ("Haddad" or "Adad is my help"), an Amurru or "Amorite." He was succeeded by his son, Amutpî-el, who had been governor of Nazala. This was in the time of King Hammurabi of Babylon (1792–1750 BCE).

Abraham continued his travels to Damascus along the famous caravan route of Kings Highway. Ancient Damascus was an important stop on the trade routes linking the Fertile Crescent with Egypt. The city of Damascus is one of the oldest cities in the world. It is mentioned in the book of Genesis in association with the campaign by Abraham to rescue Lot (Gen 14:15). It is possible that when Abraham traveled to Canaan, he picked Eliezer of Damascus (Gen 15:2). The city of Damascus would later be an important station connecting the northern and western civilizations with Mecca and the Islamic kingdoms of North Africa. From Damascus, the caravan crossed the land of Bashan, first crossing the Jaboq and then the Jordan River at the ford of Damiya. This led them to the heartland of Canaan. We do not know how far down the Kings Highway Abraham traveled before crossing the Jordan River and entering Canaan. Most likely, he turned westward between the Sea of Galilee and the Dead Sea and entered the territory of what would become the promised land.

In summary, our study shows that Abraham was elected because he was a monotheist in contrast to his forefathers who were idol worshipers. The incursion of nomadic tribes from the east led Abraham's family to move from Ur to Haran. The city of Ur was an important city and was a center of commerce with the countries of the Persian Gulf and the Indus Valley. Similarly, the city of Haran was known as an important station on the main international trade routes from Mesopotamia to the Mediterranean Sea. Both cities were known as centers for moon worship. Not surprisingly, names that are found in the Abrahamic family, such as Sarah, Milcah, Terah, and Laban, are related to the worship of the moon. It appears that political, economic, social, and religious conditions were right for the Terahites to settle there for several generations. Terah, Abraham's father, Nahor, Abraham's grandfather, and Serug, Abraham's great-grandfather, are people with names of places found near Haran. Serug and Nahor are mentioned at the end of the third and the beginning of the second millennium BCE. This indicates that their names and the geographical setting of the Abrahamic stories fit the location in which they are set. The patriarchs maintained their family ties with their Aramean relatives in Haran for three hundred years. There are not many details about the Arameans who were nomadic or semi-nomadic people because only in a later period did they become important as well as an economic factor. Abraham's migration to Canaan should not be viewed as part of a larger movement to the east or linked to the so-called "Amorite hypothesis." It was one family who migrated, therefore there is no reason to find any testimony about it. Since Abraham migrated to Canaan, in the next chapter his travels within the land and his relationship with the local inhabitants of Canaan will be examined.

Chapter 2

Up, Walk About the Land

The biblical narrative portrays the patriarchal era as a period of wandering. Abraham is depicted as a nomad who travels to sites in the central mountain region and the Negeb, wandering back and forth between these two regions. He is constantly on the move searching for fresh pasture and water. The Bible relates that he lived in terebinth of Moreh, which is next to Shechem (Gen 12:6), the area between Beth-El and Ai (12:8; 13:3), the Negeb (12:9; 13:1; 20:1), Egypt (12:10), terebinth of Mamre, which is in Hebron (13:18; 18:1), the royal city of Gerar (20:1), and Beer-Sheba (22:19). He partially follows God's order "Up, walk about the land, through its length and its breadth, for I give it to you" (Gen 13:17). We will start our study by looking into Abraham's travels and places of habitation to see if there is any significance to it. This will lead us to see whether there are parallels between Abraham's and Jacob's travels and later the course taken by Joshua during the conquest of the land.

In addition, what kind of animals did he use in his travel, asses or camels? As a wandering shepherd he is described as living in tents, but there are scholars who maintain that the description of living in tents is more fitting for the first millennium than the second. Contrary to the view that Abraham was a wandering shepherd, it was suggested that he was a merchant who participated in international trade. We will see if there is any validity to this claim and try to give an answer as to his means of livelihood. When Abraham arrived in Canaan it was already inhabited by different people. The patriarch had to ensure the survival of his clan, so how did he protect his family and what kind of relationships did he have with the local inhabitants?

CENTRAL MOUNTAIN REGION

The first site where Abraham resided in the land of Canaan was the terebinth of Moreh, which was next to the city of Shechem. More than likely the terebinth of Moreh served as a landmark. In the ancient world land sale contracts included trees to specify the location of the property. The city of Shechem is forty miles north of Jerusalem and is located between Mount Ebal and Mount Gerizim. It is in the heart of the central hill country of the land of Israel in a fertile and well-watered valley. The city is identified with Tell al-Balāṭa, one mile east of modern Shechem. Excavations at Shechem show that the town already existed in the Middle Bronze Age II. Shechem is mentioned first in the Egyptian "execration texts" of the nineteenth century BCE. A stela describing a campaign by King Sen-User III (ca. 1880–1840 BCE) indicates that Shechem was a large and important city. In Egyptian texts, Shechem is referred to as a city and a region.[1] During the LB and Iron Ages, it served as a major crossroads for north–south and east–west highways.

The next stop in Abraham's wandering was between Beth El and Ai (12:8); both sites were known by previous names. Bethel earlier was called Luz (28:19) and Ai means a heap of ruins; no information is given about its original name before it turned out to be a heap of ruins. With the passing of time names were attached to places so people would be familiar with the sites even though the earlier names were different. Archeologists identify Bethel with modern Beitin, which is about 10.5 miles (17 kilometers) north of Jerusalem and 2,866 feet (880 meters) above sea level.[2] Signs of settlement in Bethel began at the turn of the third millennium. Plenty of springs are found in its vicinity and the area was suitable for pastoral nomads. Ai is identified with et-Tell 1.5 miles (2 kilometers) southeast of Bethel. Excavations reveal that it was a prosperous town during the early Bronze Age from ca. 3000 BCE. The city was destroyed no later than the twenty-fourth century BCE. Later it is mentioned as one of the cities that was conquered by Joshua. No remains were found between the Early Bronze Age and the Iron Age. Therefore, it was suggested that

---

1. Campbell, "Shechem," 1345–54.
2. Kelso, "Bethel," 192–94.

the city in Josh 8 is about another site[3] or it is fictional; it is an etiological story that explains the ancient ruins of the city.[4]

Following the dispute between Abraham's herdsmen and Lot's herdsmen, the patriarch settled in the terebinths of Mamre, which is in Hebron. In Gen 14:13, 24 Mamre is the personal name of an Amorite, one of the allies of Abraham. In 14:13 and 18:1 it is the name of a place where Abraham received the news about Lot's captivity and where he welcomed the three angels. According to Gen 23:17, Mamre was located near the land of Machpelah, elsewhere it is identified with Hebron (23:19; 35:27). Archeologists identify the place with Ḥaram Ramet el-Khalil, three kilometers (two miles) north of Hebron. Remains dating back to the Middle Bronze Age have been found at the site. A different location was suggested by scholars who believe the site is within the town of ancient Hebron (Tell Rumeideh).[5] A person's name and a site were sometimes linked as we noted already with Nahor and the city of Nahor. Thus, Mamre was the name of a clan that lent its name to one of the town's quarters. Eusebius, in *The Onomasticon*, says that Mambre is Chebron where Abraham's tomb is.[6] A similar view was expressed by Jerome who identified Mambre with Chebron; according to him it was called Mambre for one of the friends of Abraham.[7] Mamre is only mentioned in the book of Genesis. The mention of Hebron came to aid the later reader who was not familiar with Mamre. The area of Hebron has an abundance of water, wells, and springs that are suitable for pasture. There is evidence of settlement in the vicinity of Hebron as early as the third millennium BCE.

Dwelling at the terebinths of Mamre, which is Hebron, is the second time that Abraham is mentioned living next to trees. The Jewish historian Josephus mentioned a very ancient tree northwest of Hebron that was famous in the Second Temple times.[8] He calls this tree "Ogyges," who was the mythical king of Athens, said to have survived the flood that destroyed humanity. Josephus mentioned Ogyges to emphasize the antiquity of Abraham. In another statement, he said that about three-fourths of a mile from the city of Hebron stood a huge terebinth tree, which had been

---

3. Albright, "Kyle Memorial Excavation," 11.
4. Vaux, *Early History*, 617–20.
5. Magen, "Mamre," 939.
6. Eusebius, *Onomasticon*, 70.
7. Eusebius, *Onomasticon*, 70.
8. Josephus, *Ant.* 186.

there since the creation of the world.⁹ It is not clear, however, whether it refers to the same place.

The terebinth of Moreh, terebinth of Mamre, and later the tamarisk that Abraham planted at Beer-sheba (21:33) were landmarks that marked the place of habitat of the patriarch Abraham. In ancient times, trees were often used to mark the boundary between fields belonging to different owners. The rocky area with its woodland also provided good cover.¹⁰ Thus, Abraham lived in an area that had a considerable number of trees for safety reasons. In addition, trees also had some other practical uses such as shade, fuel for cooking, or food for the flock. People were also buried under trees, which served as a memorial to the dead, as a landmark, and as a sign of ownership. With the passing of time, and because of the association with important biblical figures, the places became sacred. A review of the book of Genesis shows that there is no trace of the patriarchs engaging in any religious rites at these trees. It is only in later periods that we read about the Israelites who worshiped YHWH on high mountains or on hills under any spreading tree (Deut 12:2; 1 Kgs 14:23; Jer 2:20). It was this late Bible reading and later traditions that associated Abraham with sacred trees. Thus, not surprisingly, the Aramaic translators avoided translating the word "tree" and instead translated it as "plain," giving it a different meaning in order to avoid any association of Abraham with paganism.

NEGEB

From the area between Beth-El and Ai, Abraham journeyed by stages toward the Negeb, the southern part of the land of Canaan. His movement from place to place towards the Negeb is not recorded in the text. The name Negeb is derived from a root meaning "dry." It is indicative of the lack of rainfall and dry conditions that exist in this area. It was suggested that since the Negeb is mentioned in Genesis (12:9; 13:1; and 20:1) the Negeb was the original home of the Abraham tradition. "It is the territory

---

9. Josephus, *J.W.* 4:533.

10. The fact that Abraham lived next to trees led Rowton to suggest that the warrior patriarch was a Ḫabiru (see chapter 3). The Ḫabiru warriors were known to dwell in scrub woodlands called "maquis forests." Abraham lived in the terebinths of Mamre and took part in the war against the eastern kings. Considering these factors raises the question of whether we can refer to Abraham as a Habiru warrior. This assertion is too speculative, even to this day guerilla fighters use the cover of trees. See Rowton, "Topological Factor," 375–87.

where Abraham really lived his life."[11] But he probably lived there only during the winter and spring. In this southern region, he lived between Kadesh and Shur, the royal city of Gerar, and Beer Sheba. Kadesh and Shur were the southern boundaries of Abraham's wanderings. Kadesh is located near ʿAin el-Qudeirat in the Wadi el-ʿAin.[12] ʿAin el-Qudeirat is the largest among the springs that are found in the area and flows all year. It is also close to pasturage land, so it was a natural place for Abraham to camp. Shur is the name for the desert in northwestern Sinai next to Egypt (Exod 15:22). It is mentioned several times in the biblical text as a place along the route to Egypt (Gen 16:7; 20:1; 25:18; 1 Sam 15:17; 27:8). In Aramaic (Ezra 4:12–13) and in biblical Hebrew (Gen 49:22; 2 Sam 22:30; Ps 18:30), Shur means "a wall." This may refer to the wall of fortification built by the pharaohs in the eastern Delta of the Nile, "the wall of the ruler." This line of fortresses was built to prevent the incursion of invaders from the east. Thus, we can assume that the road that led from the area of the Negeb and Beer-Sheba to the desert of Shur was called the road of Shur.[13]

According to Gen 20:1, "Abraham journeyed from there to the region of the Negeb and settled between Kadesh and Shur while he was sojourning in Gerar."[14] Both Abraham and later Isaac are mentioned as living in the royal city of Gerar. In the Table of Nations, Gerar is a landmark for the southern border of Canaan as far as Gaza (Gen 10:19). Isaac lived there because of the famine and the same is probably true for Abraham. Due to Abraham's oath to Abimelech, the land of Gerar was not included in the territory that was conquered later by the Israelites and was not part of the Israelite settlement (Josh 15).[15] Gerar was the home of the Philistines who originated from Casluhim; they were shepherds ruled by a king (about the Philistines, see more below). The city is not

---

11. Noth, *History of Israel*, 124–25.

12. Schmidt, "Kadesh-Berna," 62–71.

13. This was rejected by Naaman who located Shur between Gerar and Kadesh, at the site of Tell el-Farah. Others suggested that Shur begins in the east of Suez known as Jebel es-Sur or Rahah. See Naaman, "Shihor," 95–109; Mihelic, "Shur," 4:342; Thompson, "Shur," 4:497–98.

14. Gerar is not located between these two places. Therefore, some suggested that some details were omitted from the text. See Vawter, *On Genesis*, 245. Speiser proposed that verse 1c is temporal protasis to verse 2; "in the Negeb, Abraham ranged with his herds from Kadesh to Shur; in the course of that stay, he paid a visit to Gerar." See Speiser, *Genesis*, 148.

15. Gen 21:22–32; *Ḥul.* 60b.

mentioned in Egyptian or Assyrian sources, perhaps because it was not situated along the Via Maris or the north–south highway parallel to the coast that was used by the armies.[16] It was suggested to locate it in a valley known in Arabic as Wady Sheri'a, in modern Hebrew Nahal Gerar. But most archaeologists identify it with Tel Haror (Tell Abu Hureireh), which is located on the north bank of Nahal Gerar, twenty kilometers west of Beer-Sheba near the road from Gaza to Beer-Sheba.[17] Surveys that were conducted in the 1950s indicate that Tel Haror was occupied during the Bronze and Iron Age, which gives credence to its identification with the Canaanite–Philistine Gerar.[18]

Beer-Sheba is another site in the Negeb where the patriarchs Abraham (Gen 21:31–33; 22:19), Isaac (26:23, 33), and Jacob (46:1) made stops. In the patriarchal narrative, the place is associated with the well that was found there, and it was a cultic center, not a city. Abraham planted a terebinth there and invoked "the name of the Lord, the Everlasting God" (21:33). Isaac built an altar and invoked the Lord by name (26:25), and later the place was visited by Jacob (46:1). The ancient city is identified with Tell es-Sabaʽ, which is located on the peripheries of modern Beersheba. Excavation at the site of the ancient city suggests that there was no Canaanite settlement there. The earliest Israelite settlement is from the thirteenth to eleventh centuries BCE. These findings led to questions concerning the authenticity of the patriarchal traditions.[19] However, there is no need to find any settlement during the time of the patriarchs; the mention of the city of Beer-Sheba is a redactional note that explains how the place received its name (26:33).[20] Ahroni claimed that he discovered the well that Abraham dug, but this well can be dated only to the era of Joshua. This led him to conclude that the patriarchal narratives are collections of traditions from different periods.[21] However, he did not offer any conclusive evidence that the well that he discovered is the well that is mentioned in Gen 21:30. More so, some wells were discovered less than two miles west of Tell es-Sabaʽ.

---

16. Sarna, *Genesis*, 77.

17. Oren, "Gerar," 989; Aharoni, "Gerar," 26–32; Cross and Wright, "Boundary and Province Lists," 213. Dever does not accept the identification of this site with Gerar. See Dever, *History*, 100.

18. Oren, "Gerar," 989.

19. Van Seters, *Abraham*, 111–12.

20. Sarna, "Abraham," 9.

21. Aharoni, "Nothing Early," 71.

As nomads, the patriarchs depended on wells for their existence. They were digging and searching for new wells and were fighting for their ownership. These descriptions are typical of "small cattle nomads." One group of nomads tries to expel and harm the other group by blocking up their wells. This portrayal suits the patriarchal period and its lifestyle. In that period, the existence of a group and its herd relied on watering holes. Therefore, information about the wells was recorded. It included the location of the wells along with the route and the names of the wells; all of this was kept for the next migration.[22] Clearly, this is the case with Isaac: "Isaac dug anew the wells which had been dug in the days of his father, Abraham, and which the Philistines had stopped up after Abraham's death; and he gave them the same names that his father had given them" (Gen 26:18). Reading of feuds over wells in the Abraham and Isaac stories is not surprising since water has always been a very precious commodity in that part of the land, even today.[23]

EGYPT

Because of a famine, Abraham was forced to leave the promised land to Egypt. Each of the patriarchs would suffer from the reality of famine. There is no information about the length of his stay in Egypt, but the Bible indicates that it was a temporary residence, which is implied by the usage of the verb sojourn (*gur*). Egypt was dependent on the Nile, so the harsh conditions of the famine were not so severe, which led people to move into Egypt to ensure their survival. In a report of an Egyptian official on the eastern frontier of Egypt from the age of Ramses II to the scribe of the treasury, he describes the situation on the border. In his account, he mentions the passage of Edomite shepherds into the better pasturage of the Delta to whom permission was granted to enter Egypt "to keep them alive and to keep their cattle alive."[24] This description is parallel to the story of Abraham and reminiscent of the arrival of Joseph's brothers to Egypt during the famine.

What emerges from our study so far is that Abraham traveled between Shechem in the north and the Negeb in the south, and during

---

22. Westermann, *Genesis 12–36*, 426. See also Matthews, "Wells," 123; Bar, *Isaac*, 87.

23. A similar text from Mari deals with disputes over water. Accordingly, one group appeals to the king to intercede on its behalf against another group so the water and ownership will be returned to them. See Cornelius, "Genesis," 53–61.

24. Wilson, "Report," 259.

times of famine he sojourned in Egypt and Gerar, in areas which were suitable for pastoral nomads. He was constantly on the move in search of pasture and water. He avoided the northern part of the country—the coastal plain and the Jordan River—regions that were extensively populated with fortified urban centers. On the other hand, the central mountain area and the Negeb were less populated and, consequently, without a dominant power. Hence, we read about King Melchizedek of Salem, King Abimelech of Gerar, and later during the time of Jacob about Hamor the Hivite, which points to the distribution of power in these areas.

PARALLEL TRAVELS

Examination of Abraham's and Jacob's travels reveals that they are parallel, and both correspond to a later description of the conquest of the land in the book of Joshua.[25] Abraham entered the land from the north, and he arrived in Shechem at the terebinth of Moreh, there God appeared to him and promised him the land. To commemorate the theophany, he built an altar to the Lord (Gen 12:6–7). During his second journey, Abraham arrived at the hill country east of Bethel and pitched his tent, with Bethel on the west and Ai on the east. As in his previous stop, he built an altar to the Lord and invoked the Lord by name (12:8). On his third journey he traveled to the southern part of the land to the Negev (12:9). Later in Hebron he purchased the first piece of land which was the Cave of Machpelah (Gen 23).

Jacob's journeys have a similar route. He returns from Aram to the land of Canaan entering from the east. At first, he arrived at Shechem where he encamped before the city. There he purchased a parcel of land and set up an altar to *El-elohe-Yisrael* (Gen 33:20). Before leaving Shechem he ordered the members of his household to rid themselves of the alien gods and he buried them under the terebinth that was near Shechem (35:4). Later Jacob traveled to Bethel where he built an altar to God who revealed himself to him when he was fleeing from his brother (33:7). Jacob set up a pillar to honor his God (33:13–14). After burying Rachel, his next stop was Migdal-Eder (33:21), and from there he traveled to the south to Hebron (33:27).

The similar route taken by Abraham and Jacob is also manifested in parallel expressions describing the conquest of the land that is found

---

25. Casuto "Abraham," 65–66.

in the book of Joshua. One of the first cities that was conquered by the Israelites was Ai; in Genesis and Joshua, we find a comparable language: "east of Bethel" and "between Ai and Bethel–west of Ai" (Gen 12:8; Josh 7:2; 8:9, 12). Following the destruction of Ai, Joshua built an altar to the Lord, the God of Israel, on Mount Ebal, which is next to Shechem (Josh 8:30). From there the Israelites continued their march to the remaining areas from south of Ai-Bethel (Josh 10) and to the north of Shechem (Josh 11). These accounts are similar to what we read about Abraham and Jacob. Furthermore, at Shechem Joshua ordered the Israelites to remove the alien gods (24:23); his acts and the usage of language are identical to the words that were uttered by Jacob (Gen 35:2). In addition, Joshua took a great stone and set it up at the foot of the oak in the sacred precinct of the Lord (Josh 24:26). Again, this is a reminder of Jacob's act following his dream at Beth-El where he took the stone and set it up as a pillar (Gen 28:18).

What emerges from these parallel descriptions is that the deeds of the fathers are signs to the sons. This was already noted in the interpretation of Gen 12:6 by the Ramban: "And Abram passed through the land. I will tell you a principle by which you will understand all the coming portions of Scripture concerning Abraham, Isaac, and Jacob. It is indeed a great matter which our Rabbis mentioned briefly, saying: 'Whatever has happened to the patriarchs is a sign to the children.'[26] It is for this reason that the verses narrate at great length the account of the journeys of the patriarchs, the digging of the wells, and other events. Now someone may consider them unnecessary and of no useful purpose, but in truth, they all serve as a lesson for the future: when an event happens to any one of the three patriarchs, that which is decreed to happen to his children can be understood."

In other words, the conquest of the land symbolically took place during the period of the patriarchs. This was manifested by building altars and purchasing pieces of land. These actions by the patriarchs foreshadow the future and show that God's promises to the patriarchs were later fulfilled by their descendants.

---

26. *Tanḥ.* Lech Lecha, 9.

LIVING IN TENTS

From the dawn of history, people lived in tents. Jabal was the ancestor of those who dwell in tents and among herds (Gen 4:20). Noah became drunk and uncovered himself within his tent (Gen 9:21). This way of life is also mentioned in the stories of the patriarchs. Arriving in the land of Canaan, Abraham pitched his tent east of Bethel (Gen 12:8). When he returned from Egypt, he pitched his tent in its previous location between Beth El and Ai (13:3). On these two occasions he built a tent and an altar which signaled a symbolic possession of the land. Later he moved his tent to the terebinths of Mamare (13:18); and at the entrance of his tent, he greeted the three mysterious visitors (18:1, 6, 9). It was on this occasion that Sarah was listening at the entrance of the tent (18:10). After parting from Abraham, Lot pitched his tents near Sodom (13:12). Isaac brought his bride Rebecca to the tent of his mother Sarah (24:67). Jacob, in contrast to Esau, was a mild man who stayed in camp (25:27).[27] During his flight from Laban, the tents and camels are mentioned (Gen 31:25, 33, 34). Following the death of Rachel, Jacob pitched his tent beyond Migda-eder (35:21).

Van Seters does not accept the Genesis stories as a reliable source of the pre-Israelite times but only to the time of their composition, which is late. He believed that the description of the patriarchs living in tents is more fitting for the first millennium than the second. "It is a curious fact that tents are not mentioned in the Mari archives at all and only rarely in other second millennium sources. This is in contrast to the tent encampments of the Bedouin, which are most distinctive features by the mid-first millennium BCE."[28] But examination of texts from the first millennium reveals that the mention of tents is less than in earlier periods. Assyrian kings' lists dating to the reign of Samsi-Adad I (ca. 1750 BCE) mention seventeen kings who lived in tents. The Sumerian Myth of the god Martu describes the Amorite as a "tent-dweller [buffeted?] by wind and rain . . . who in his lifetime does not have a house," and a similar reference is found in the administrative texts of the Ur-Isin-Larsa periods (ca. 2000–1800 BCE).[29] The Egyptian Sinuhe (twentieth century BCE) who fled to Syria lived in a tent; after combat said, "I took what was in

---

27. In contrast, in Succoth he built a house for himself (Gen 33:17).
28. Van Seters, *Abraham*, 14.
29. Wiseman, "Abraham," 92.

his tent and stripped his encampment."[30] Ugaritic epics from the second millennium mention tents and use the Hebrew word *ohel* as do Egyptian sources.[31] The West Semitic word is mentioned by Ramesses III (1192–1161 BCE) who describes the looting of tents in Edom: "I destroyed the people of Se'ir among the Bedouin tribes. I razed their tents, their people, their property, and their cattle as well, without number, pinioned and carried away in captivity, as a tribute of Egypt."[32]

Van Seters's view that the mention of tents and other nomadic details all point to the social and political circumstances of the first millennium BCE cannot be supported.[33] Tents are found in all periods; it is unwise to date the patriarchal period based on tents. Abraham, Isaac, and Jacob were tent dwellers. They did not build cities; they were semi-nomadic people who were constantly on the move. They did not own any land, and they purchased plots to bury their dead (Gen 23; 33:19; 50:5). In times of famine, they dwelt among the Philistines and the Egyptians. They depended on the goodwill of the local population. They also spent most of their lives outside the promised land. Abraham was born in Ur of the Chaldeans and spent some time in Egypt during a famine (Gen 12:10–20); later he lived in Gerar (Gen 20:1). The same holds true for Jacob who spent most of his life in Haran, and in his sunset years lived in Egypt. The wandering of the patriarchs suits the condition of the early second millennium. They moved freely from Mesopotamia to Canaan, back and forth; there are no barriers that limit their movement. The fact that they did not own land and constantly were on the move gives more credence to the belief that they lived in tents.

SMALL SCALE TRADE

Observations of the path of the patriarchs' journeys offer interrelating data. The patriarchs stayed close to the cities, but they did not enter the cities or live in them unless they were forced to by famine. The only person who lived in the city was Lot. Pastoralist and agricultural villagers lived close, balancing each other as a part of a dimorphic society.[34]

30. Wilson, "Story," 20.
31. Kitchen, *Bible*, 59.
32. Wilson, "Ramses III," 262. Wiseman, "Tents," 198.
33. Van Seters, *Abraham*, 121.
34. Gottwald, "Pastoral Nomads," 2–7, 223–55.

The patriarchs stayed close to urban centers so they could barter for the domestic necessities they required. They probably participated in small-scale trade. This assumption is based on the verb "*sahar*" in Gen 34:10, 21, and 42:34. The main meaning of this root is "go around," or "turn-about/away."[35] The Shechemites invited Jacob and his sons to dwell and trade "*sahar*" with them (Gen 34:10). The verb "*sahar*" denotes grazing rights but could also by extension be explained as trade, to barter, which was the way it was understood in the ancient versions.[36] Joseph allegedly told his brothers that if they could show that they were honest they could trade "*sahar*" in the land (42:34). The description of the purchase of the cave of Machpelah by Abraham from Ephron the Hittite looks like a bill of sale although it was by verbal consent. Abraham paid out to Ephron four hundred shekels of silver at the going merchants' rates (Gen 34:16).[37] He paid in silver, which was the mode of payment, but that probably also included gold and probably payments of animals.[38]

Gordon suggested that Abraham was not a wandering shepherd but a merchant from Ur of the Chaldees in Hittite land. Abraham was a *tamkârum* merchant prince who was engaged in international trades.[39] He comes from the Euphrates, trades in Canaan, goes to Egypt, deals with the Hittites, makes treaties with the Philistines, and forms an alliance with the Amorites. Abraham was engaged in importing silver to Egypt and gold to the Hittite land. A similar path was taken by Albright who suggested that Abraham took part in caravan activity between 2000 and 1800 BCE. Abraham came from Ur, which was a trading center and went to Haran, a caravan city. He went to Damascus where he adopted a merchant; at that time property was not allowed to be sold to outsiders. This act allowed him to "obtain credit in order to buy donkeys, equipment, and supplies for caravanning or related activities."[40] From Damascus, he went to the major centers of trading in the land of Canaan, which are

---

35. The same meaning is also found in Akkadian, "saḫāru," and Old Akkadian, "siḫrum," or "rim."

36. Targums, LXX, Vulg. have "trade." See also, Albright, "Some Remarks," 28.

37. Later we read of the king's weight which is mentioned only in 2 Sam 14:26. This was probably a royal standard that was used at the time of the monarchy. See Rainey, "Royal," 35; Scott, "Weights and Measures," 34.

38. In Gen 13:2 and 24:35, we read that he was rich in gold and silver as well as cattle (see also 20:16).

39. Gordon, "Abraham," 28–31.

40. Albright, *YHWH*, 66.

mentioned in Genesis. He lived in the Negeb between Kadesh and Shur where he could survive only if he were engaged in trade with Egypt.

Reading the biblical text shows otherwise. When Abraham left Haran, he took with him all the wealth that he amassed (Gen 12:5). This verse anticipates the following account that describes Abraham acquiring sheep, oxen, assess, and both male and female slaves (12:16). Abraham's prosperity is mentioned again when he returned from Egypt; he is rich in cattle (13:2). Sheep and oxen are cited when Abraham signed a pact with Abimelech (21:27). Speaking to Rebecca's family the servant described Abraham's wealth, which included sheep, camels, and asses (24:35). The repeated mention of Abraham's cattle shows that he was a wandering shepherd. There is no evidence that he participated in international trade. Abraham went to Egypt to sojourn there because of the famine. Later he went to the city of Gerar, probably for the same reason—famine. In Gerar, he traded pastoral products for supplies to ensure the survival of his clan. He lived next to the Canaanite cities so he could trade with them, he participated in small-scale trade within the land of Canaan. Buying and selling does not make one a professional merchant.[41]

ASSES VERSUS CAMELS

The patriarchs were breeders of sheep and cattle, and their beast of burden was the ass, which limited their wandering. Abraham went to Mount Moriah on an ass (Gen 22:3, 5); Simeon and Levi seized flocks, herds, and asses in the town of Shechem (34:28); Joseph's brothers journeyed to Egypt with asses to buy food (42:26; 43:18; 44:3, 13); and Joseph sent asses to bring his father to Egypt (45:23). Nevertheless, camels are mentioned with Abraham, Jacob, and Joseph.[42] Pharaoh gave Abraham camels (Gen 12:6), and Abraham's servant traveled to Haran with ten of his master's camels (Gen 24). Jacob put his children and wives on camels (31:17), and among his gifts to his brother Esau were thirty lactating camels with their colts (32:16). Rachel hides the household gods in the camel cushion (31:34). In the Joseph story camels are used by the Ishmaelites and Midianites (37:25). The consensus among scholars is that the domestication

---

41. Kitchen, *Ancient*, 49.

42. Israel's neighbors were known to use camels: Ishmaelites (Gen 37:25); Midianites (Judg 6:5); Amalekites (1 Sam 15:3; 27:9); Queen of Sheba (1 Kgs 10:2; 2 Chr 9:1); Aram (2 Kgs 8:9); Sons of Kedar and Hazor (Jer 49:29); Hagrites (1 Chr 5:21); Zerah the Cushite (2 Chr 14:14); even Job had camels (1:3; 42:12).

of camels did not take place before the twelfth century BCE, and the mention of the camels in the patriarchal stories is an anachronism.[43] The mention of camels does not reflect the period of the patriarchs, but it reflects a later period when the traditions became established.[44]

Camel remains from the early second millennium from Syria-Palestine are very rare. It is difficult to determine whether the remains are of wild or domesticated camels based on morphological change of the skeleton.[45] Evidence of the domestication of the camel is found in eastern Iran in 2700 BCE and Indus Valley in 2300 BCE; thus it is possible that from these regions it spread to North Arabia and South Levant in the later part of the second millennium.[46] Camel bones were found in Mari dating to the middle of the third millennium. The hindquarters of camels were recognized on a jar.[47] A tablet from the city of Alalakh in Syria (eighteenth century BCE) mentioned camels in a list of domesticated animals where it reads, "1 SA. GAL ANŠE. GAM.MAL, one (measure of) fodder-camel."[48] But evidence has been disputed by Lambert who suggested that the ideogram means "stag," not a camel.[49] He instead shows evidence of camels from the old Babylonian period (nineteenth century BCE) in a text from Ugarit.[50] A bilingual Sumerian Akkadian text (ca. 2000–1700 BCE) associated the domesticated animal with a dromedary. Interestingly, the scribes distinguished between the dromedary humped camel—which they called "amše-a-ab-ba," or "a donkey of the sea-land"—and a Bactrian two-humped camel which they call "am-si-ḫar-ra-an-na," or "elephant of the road."[51] In a more recent study from Arad from EB I (2900 BCE), few bones were found.[52] From Bir Resisim in the North Negeb EB IV (1900 BCE), several remains have been reported.[53] This is not necessarily proof of the domestication of the camels, but we

---

43. Van Seters, *Abraham*, 17; Albright, *Stone Age*, 164–65; Bright, *History*, 80–81. For further study on this subject, see Sarna, *Understanding*, 108n42.

44. Vaux, *Early History*, 225.

45. Hakker-Orion, "Role," 209.

46. Zarins, "Camel," 824–26.

47. Parrot, *Abraham*, 100–101.

48. Wiseman, "Rations," 19–33.

49. Lambert, "Domesticated," 42–43.

50. Lambert, "Domesticated," 42–43.

51. Sarna, *Genesis*, 96.

52. Lernau, "Remains," 83–113.

53. Hakker-Orion, "Role," 207–12.

cannot dismiss it. The domestication of the camel was a slow process that lasted for a long period and isolated occurrences of its taming took place. A wealthy man could acquire camels as a symbol of wealth or to use the milk, hair, and skin. This might explain the mention of camels in Abraham's servant entourage as a show of Abraham's wealth to impress the girl and her family.[54] This leads us to believe that the domestication of camels was already known in the third millennium BCE.

Even if the patriarchs had several camels, they were not great nomads like Bedouin sheiks. Abraham's journeys were mostly a short distance from Shechem to Bethel (50 kilometers), Bethel to Hebron (21 kilometers), Hebron to Beersheba (42 kilometers), and Hebron to Gerar (45 kilometers). Domesticated asses can travel 40 kilometers a day and carry between 40 and 80 kilograms. In ancient times camels were used as the main means of transportation of goods and of people, especially on long journeys. Camels, by comparison, could cover between 100 and 150 kilometers per day and carry between 200 and 250 kilograms; they can travel for much greater distances than donkeys without water. Asses were domesticated before Israel's patriarchal age. Tamed onagers appear in Mesopotamia in the third millennium BCE and domesticated Nubian wild asses in Egypt during the same period. Asses were used for carrying burdens (Gen 42:26; 1 Sam 16:20; 25:18; Neh 13:15), agricultural purposes (Isa 30:24), and for riding. Possession of an ass was a sign of wealth (Gen 12:16; 24:35). Donkey caravans are known from the nineteenth century BCE from Babylon to Egypt. Caravans were traveling between Assyria and Cappadocia. From Cappadocia and Mari, merchants used asses for their traveling from Anatolia and Syria to Mesopotamia. The famous portrayal on the walls of the tomb at Beni Ḥassan includes two grayish-brown donkeys. In the painting from Egypt, asses are also depicted in agricultural environments.

ABRAHAM AND THE INHABITANTS OF THE LAND

No major confrontation between Abraham and the local inhabitants of the land is recorded. The patriarch was the head of a small clan, and he maintained peaceful relations with the native people of the land. Later, the Israelites are instructed to destroy the seven nations of Canaan and not to intermarry with them. On the eve of their entrance to the land of

---

54. Sarna, *Genesis*, 96.

Canaan, the Israelites are warned, "Beware of making a covenant with the inhabitants of the land against which you are advancing, lest they be a snare in your midst.... You must not make a covenant with the inhabitants of the land, for they will lust after their gods.... And when you take wives from among their daughters for your sons, their daughters will lust after their gods and will cause your sons to lust after their gods" (Exod 34:12–16).[55] The fear against intermarriages, emulating the practices of the land, and following their laws were behind the orders the Israelites received in the book of Deuteronomy: "When the Lord your God brings you to the land that you are about to enter and possess ... you must doom them to destruction: grant them no terms and give them no quarter" (Deut 7:1–2). The Israelites were instructed to drive out the natives (Exod 33:2; 34:11); dispossess them (Deut 11:23); dislodge (7:1); to annihilate (Exod 23:23); and doom them to destruction (Deut 7:2).

By contrast, Abraham maintained a peaceful relationship with his neighbors. He formed an alliance with Mamre, the Amorite kinsman of Eshkol, and Aner, who joined him in the battle against the four kings from the east. Later, as noted above, the Amorites were among the people that the Israelites had to destroy. When God revealed to Abraham his plan to destroy the cities of Sodom and Gomorra, Abraham pleaded with God to save its people who were complete strangers to him. There was no animosity towards the Egyptians. The land of Egypt was a place of refuge for Abraham and the patriarchs during the time of famine. When Abraham stayed there with his wife, he was treated well. Only after Pharaoh realized that Abraham deceived him, was he sent away. The depiction of Egypt as a place of refuge ultimately would be reversed in the book of Exodus where the Israelites were enslaved and oppressed by the Egyptians. Still, there is no hatred toward Egypt and the biblical narrator remembered the hospitality of the Egyptians; thus we read, "You shall not abhor an Egyptian for you were a stranger in his land" (Deut 23:8).

In the book of Judges and in the book of Samuel, the Philistines are described as the archenemies of the Israelites. They terrorized the Israelites for hundreds of years. Saul, the first king of Israel, fought against the Philistines' domination throughout his life. It was only later that King David defeated the Philistines, and they served in his army.

On the other hand, the book of Genesis portrays peaceful relations between Abraham and the Philistines. Abraham dwelled in the Philistine

---

55. This warning against intermarriages will be repeated later in Deut 7:3–4.

city of Gerar and signed a covenant with Abimelech the king of the Philistines. More so, it was the Philistine king who demanded a covenant that was sealed by an oath, a covenant that included future generations (Gen 21:23). This suggests that the patriarch was not powerless. Similarly, Isaac dwelt in Gerar where he was treated with respect by the Philistines. Reminiscent of the Abraham story, Abimelech the Philistine king came with his councilor and Phicol, chief of his troops, and asked Isaac to sign a pact of non-aggression (Gen 26:29).[56]

Scholars maintain that the mention of the Philistines in the patriarchal period is anachronistic.[57] They believed that the Philistines arrived at the land of Canaan in a later period. The earliest reference to the Philistines comes from the time of Ramses II at the beginning of the twelfth century BCE, however, we should point out that there are major differences between the Philistines' portrayal in Genesis and later descriptions in the Bible. The Philistines in Genesis are not organized into five city-states led by Seranim. In Genesis, they live around Beer Sheba in the city of Gerar and are ruled by a king. Later, in the books of Judges and Samuel, we read about the five coastal cities. To explain the differences between the Philistines in Genesis and those who are mentioned in Judges and Samuel, Van Seters suggests a later exilic date. At that time the Pentapolis had dissolved.[58] He also pointed out that the text speaks of a king of Gerar without ethnic qualification. It is a later writer who identifies Gerar as the land of the Philistines. But as Kitchen pointed out there is evidence of Aegean culture and people who migrated to Canaan in the early second millennium. Accordingly, Abimelech and his retainers, especially Phicol, might have been Kaphtorians or even Kerethites. The name Philistines "became a blanket term for non-Canaanite, Aegean people," who lived in the southwest of Canaan.[59] In other words, there was an earlier migration of Aegean people, and the description in Genesis reflects an early era when the relationship between the patriarchs and the Philistines was a peaceful one.

Peaceful relations existed also with the Hittites. When Abraham approached them for the purchase of the cave of Machpelah, they referred

---

56. The mention of Abimelech's general made him part of the treaty; he will fight in case of a covenant breach. Muffs, *Love and Joy*, 79.

57. On the Philistines in the patriarchal period, see Kaufmann, *Toldot*, 2, 304; Grintz, *Genesis*, 73; Abramsky, "Origin," 103.

58. Van Seters, *Abraham*, 54.

59. Kitchen, *Reliability*, 341.

to him as "the elect of God"; they treated him with respect. Ironically, Abraham had to negotiate the purchase of this burial site, which was a part of the land that God already promised Abraham. They sold it to him despite being a resident alien. In ancient times, resident aliens could not purchase real estate. The Hittites originally were people who lived in central Anatolia and are referred to as natives of the area of Hebron, while Abraham calls himself a resident alien. However, the Hittite's existence in the patriarchal period in Hebron appears to be problematic. There is no evidence of Hittite expansion to this vicinity before the destruction of the Hittite empire. Nevertheless, the Bible consistently mentions the Hittites. In the Table of Nations, Heth is the second son of Canaan (Gen 10:15); and Esau's wives were Hittites (26:34; 36:2) who were rejected by Rebecca (27:46). There are twenty-two references that list the Hittites as one of the pre-Israelite original inhabitants of the land of Canaan.[60] In those lists, the Hittites are mentioned six times in the first place and nine times in the second, which is indicative of their importance. The biblical stories indicate that at the time of Abraham and Esau, the Hittites lived in Hebron and Beer Sheba, while Ezekiel preserves a tradition of Jerusalem as their place of habitat (16:3, 45). Adding more to the puzzle, the Hittites' names in Genesis are Semitic, such as Ephron, Zohar, Judith, Beeri, Basemath, Elon, and Edah (Gen 26:34; 36:2).[61] This implies that their arrival to Canaan was earlier, and they were fully assimilated into the Semitic population. Indeed, Abraham spoke freely with them without the aid of an interpreter.

One of the main problems for the identification of the origin of the people so-called Hittites is that the term "Hittite" was applied to at least four groups in antiquity.[62] However, there are some indirect testimonies about the migration of Hittites from Anatolia to southern Syria and to the land of Israel. A plague prayer of Mursilis ^{I} (1343–1295 BCE) speaks of a treaty between the Hittites and Egypt that deals with the settlement of the population of Kurustama, a city in Asia Minor in the land of Egypt.[63] At that time the city of Hebron was under Egyptian control. It is possible that these immigrants kept their national ethnicity until the time of the conquest. The account of their existence was kept in the biblical

---

60. See Exod 3:8; Deut 7:1; Josh 3:10; 9:1; Judg 3:5; 1 Kgs 9:20; 2 Chr 8:7; Ezra 9:1; Neh 9:8.
61. Hoffner, "Contributions," 32.
62. Hoffner, "Hittites," 213.
63. Goetze, "Prayer," 395.

tradition. Another explanation might be that individual merchants migrated to the vicinity of Hebron; this can be assumed based on Gen 23:16 and the phrase "at the going merchant's rate."[64] Also, it is possible that the "son of Heth" of the land of Israel and the "men of Ḥatti" of Anatolia and northern Syria are two different groups. It was the similarity between the two names which led to the identification of these people. We can see that there is no clear-cut answer to the existence of the Hittite in Abraham's time. What is clear, however, from the biblical text is that Abraham had a peaceful relationship with the inhabitants of Hebron who are called Hittites.

As we pointed out already in chapter 1, from the time of David, the Arameans were the enemy of Israel; they were military rivals. On the other hand, in the patriarchal narrative there is a peaceful relationship with the Arameans. The patriarchs marry and live with their kin the Arameans (Gen 24 and 29). Isaac marries Rebecca the daughter of Bethuel the Aramean and Jacob marries Leah and Rachel the daughters of Laban the Aramean (31:47). The Bible repeatedly speaks of Laban the Aramean (Gen 25:20; 28:5; 31:20, 24). Deuteronomy 26:5 preserves a tradition in which Jacob is described as a fugitive Aramean. It is unlikely that the Israelites would emphasize that their origin was Aramean and trace their ancestral homeland as the native habitat of their enemies unless it had a kernel of historicity.

In conclusion, from a geographical point of view, it appears that Abraham's places of habitat are between Shechem in the north and the Negeb in the south and during times of famine he sojourned in Egypt and Gerar. He wandered back and forth between the same sites. He avoided the northern part of the country, the coastal plain, and the Jordan River, which were regions that were extensively populated with fortified urban centers. On the other hand, the central mountain area and the Negeb were less populated and, consequently, without a dominant power. His journeys in the land of Canaan are parallel to Jacob's travels and correspond to a later description of the route of the conquest of the land in the book of Joshua; in other words, it foreshadows the future that came to establish Israel's right to the land. Throughout his travels, Abraham stayed close to urban centers so he could participate in small-scale trade for essential products to ensure the survival of his family. When he camped or was on the move he stayed in a tent. He used the ass for his travels. Camels were

---

64. Cowley, *Hittites*, 9; Gordon, "Abraham," 29.

used for long journeys, and wealthy men like Abraham could acquire camels as a symbol of wealth or for their milk, hair, and skin. Being the head of a small nomadic clan, Abraham had to avoid military confrontation and keep peaceful relationships with the local inhabitants of the land. During a famine he lived in Gerar and Egypt. He signed a covenant with Abimelech, and he formed alliances with Mamre, Eshkol, and Aner. He purchased a burial site, the cave of Machpelah, from the Hittites. The Arameans were his kin and not his enemies. These peaceful relationships contrast with a later period when the Israelites would be instructed to destroy the seven nations of Canaan. The stories in Genesis are not retrojections of a later period but represent an earlier period when there was no hostility between the patriarch and the local population. In the next chapter, we will examine the story of Abraham's rescue of Lot to see if there is any historical validity to the story and its purpose within the biblical narrative.

Chapter 3

He Mustered His Retainers

Genesis 14 is the first biblical account of warfare. It describes a punitive expedition of a coalition of four eastern kings against five rebellious Canaanite kings. Lot, Abraham's nephew, was taken captive. Abraham, with the aid of three allies, fought against the invading forces. In a surprise night attack, Abraham defeated the kings and freed Lot. On his way back he was greeted by Melchizedek, the priest-king of Salem, to whom he gave a tithe of spoils. There are scholars who maintain that the chapter is a historical report from ancient times that took place in the early second millennium BCE around the nineteenth to seventeenth centuries BCE.[1] Others suggested that it is not historical, a legend, or Haggadah,[2] but a late composition any time between the Deuteronomistic school to the end of the fourth century BCE.[3]

No other chapter in the book of Genesis contains such vast information of geographic and ethnic data. Of the vocabulary in this chapter, 4.5 percent is exceptional and does not reappear in the Bible and 6.5 percent is rare in usage. In other words, 11 percent is rare, which attests to its antiquity.[4] It is the only chapter where Abraham is portrayed as a military hero. In addition, God does not speak to Abraham or anyone else. The

---

1. Albright, "Third Revision," 33–36; Albright, "Background," 231–69; Kitchen, *Ancient*, 43–47; Sarna, *Understanding*, 111–15.

2. For the view that it was not historical, see Seters, *Abraham*, 296–308. Thompson, 175; Soggin, "Genesis 14," 283–91.

3. Astour, "Symbolism," 65–112. For a later date, see Van Seters, *Abraham*, 296–308.

4. Sarna, *Genesis*, 102.

theme of promise that is prevalent in the Abrahamic cycle is also missing. Thus, the questions that arise are whether there is a kernel of historicity to the chapter. Did a military voyage take place, and what is behind the title "Abraham the Hebrew" and the reason for the inclusion of Melchizedek's story?

STRUCTURE

According to von Rad, Gen 14 breaks the flow of the previous and the next chapter. He further argues that it is isolated and was incorporated by the redactor. It cannot relate to one of the Hexateuchal sources.[5] Westermann divided the chapter into three parts: (1) the report of the campaign (14:1–11 or 12), (2) the liberation narrative (14:12–17, 21–24) and (3) the Melchizedek episode (14:18–20).[6] The report of the campaign is paralleled in the ancient world in kings' chronicles describing their victories.[7] The second part is a narrative of liberation which is reminiscent of the stories in the book of Judges where a hero delivers his people from foreign oppression; according to Westermann one can read Gideon for Abraham.[8] The verses that mention Lot (14:11–12, 16) were added later to link them to the Abraham–Lot tradition in Gen 13:18–19.[9] The Melchizedek episode is not original to the chapter and was added at the time of David to legitimize new cultic practices. Originally the story was about Abraham's defeat of Chedorlaomer and the rescue of Lot. The campaign of the Eastern kings was only added later to the text (14:1–11).[10] What arises from these explanations is that the three parts emerged at different times and settings in Israel's history.

Examination of Gen 14 shows otherwise. It is a whole literary unit that is part of the Lot–Abraham traditions that is found in Genesis chapter 13 and 18–19. Removing parts of the narrative would break the logical order of the chapter. Even Van Seters pointed out that the removal of the reference to Lot implies "a radical emendation of the entire story-not

---

5. Rad, *Genesis*, 175.
6. Westermann, *Genesis 12–36*, 190.
7. Westermann, *Genesis 12–36*, 190–91.
8. Westermann, *Genesis 12–36*, 191; Emerton, *Riddle*, 432–34.
9. Emerton, "Riddle," 407, 438.
10. Westermann, *Genesis 12–36*, 191–92; Emerton "False Clues," 24–47; Emerton, "Riddle," 407–29.

just of this text-would be necessary."[11] There is continuity between Gen 14 and the previous and next chapters.[12] The chapter continues the theme of evil that was attributed to Sodom in Gen 13. It is exemplified here by the behavior of the king of Sodom; the names of the kings of Sodom and Gomorrah allude to evil. Their wickedness is fully exhibited in Gen 18 and 19. Our chapter (Gen 14) foreshadows future events. The seeming breakup between Abraham and Lot (13:5–11) is forgotten and instead, Gen 14 shows the virtues of Abraham as a compassionate man who risks his life to save his nephew. That Abraham was dwelling near the oaks of Mamre (14:13) connects the story back to 13:18 and forward to 18:1. In addition, Gen 14 is linked verbally to Gen 15 and this is not coincidental.[13] Both Gen 14 and 15 deal with issues such as family inheritance and land.[14] In both, the enemies are defeated by Abraham or his descendants.[15] The description of Abraham as a military hero versus a nomadic clan leader who plays a role on the world stage led Westermann and Van Seters to think that this could only refer to a later period. They point to Jewish popular stories about Daniel and Judith who were confronted by the world empire,[16] but the comparison between Abraham, Judith, and Daniel is unfitting. Abraham was not a Jew who lived in exile under imperial rule. More so, the other part of Genesis shows that Abraham dealt with Pharoah (Gen 12), Abimelech treats him with respect (Gen 21), and the Hittites refer to him as the elect of God (23:6). His dealings with the king of Salem and the king of Sodom are in line with his portrayal as a major political figure.

PUNITIVE EXPEDITION

The head of the eastern coalition was Chedorlaomer, king of Elam, however, no name of such a king was found among Elamite records.[17] The name encompasses two separate Elamite components. Laomer is a divine name that relates to the Elamite "Lagamar," while Chedor is derived

11. Van Seters, *Abraham*, 298.
12. McConville, "Horizons," 93–118.
13. Sarna, *Genesis*, 112.
14. On the comparison between Gen 14 and 15, see Carr, "Reading," 164–65.
15. Gen 14:13–16; 15:16, 19–21.
16. Westermann, *Genesis 12-36*, 192; Van Seters, *Abraham*, 305.
17. Elam was east of Mesopotamia from the Caspian Sea to the Persian Gulf and was a powerful nation in the early second millennium BCE.

from Elamite "Katir, Kutir," which means "servant." In other words, the name can be interpreted as "servant of [the god] Lagamar." The second monarch, Amraphel the king of Shinar, is also not mentioned in any extrabiblical sources.[18] Arioch, the third king on the list, has a name that resembles Arriyuk/Arriwuck, which is mentioned in the Mari records from the eighteenth century BCE, or Ariukki of the Nuzi documents from the fifteenth century BCE.[19] According to Speiser, "Its appearance in the present context thus presupposes an ancient and authentic tradition."[20] The fourth king was Tidal; a royal name Tudhalia is found among Hittite kings who lived between the eighteenth and thirteenth centuries BCE.[21]

The description of Chedorlaomer leading a coalition of kings suits the history of Mesopotamia. Power alliances between different kings were well known in the ancient world. A coalition of city-states that are mentioned in Gen 14 must refer to the thirteenth century BCE or earlier.[22] The coalition between Mesopotamian and neighboring kingdoms could take place between 2000 BCE, the fall of the Third Dynasty of Ur, and 1750 BCE, the victory of the Babylonian king Hammurabi. During that period unions between different kings were common. A Mari letter describes an association of ten, fifteen, and twenty kings. Coalitions of Mesopotamian kings are known from the nineteenth and eighteenth century BCE.[23] No extrabiblical sources were found that can corroborate the biblical account of a military expedition that reached the land of Canaan during the second millennium BCE. This, however, does not exclude the possibility that an excursion took place and it was mentioned in a

18. The attempt to identify him with Hammurabi the king of Babylon presented philological difficulties. Therefore this view was abandoned and it is unlikely. Also, the association between Amarphel and Shinar is also uncertain. In Gen 11:2 and Zech 5:11 Shinar is a land around Babylon

19. Arioch is mentioned in Dan 2:14 as captain of the guards in Babylonia in the days of Nebuchadnezzar and Daniel. A king of Elymaeans (Elamites) is mentioned in Jdt 1:6 and an angel in 2 En. 33:11.

20. The name Arioch appears also in Dan 2:14, 15. But according to Zadok the etymology of this name is different. See Zadok, "Five Iranian Names," 246.

21. Tidal was the king of Goiim, which is the Hebrew word for "nations." Speiser suggested a derivation from "Ummah-Manda," a name used since the Babylonian times and even earlier to describe barbarian people who destroyed the empire of Akkad. These people are associated with the Elamites, which could be relevant to our chapter. Conversely, Goiim was the name of the town, or as Onkelos interpreted Goiim, not as a proper noun but as a descriptive noun. In other words, Tidal was king of nations, he was the head of the confederacy of people. See Speiser, *Genesis*, 107; Sarna, *Genesis*, 104.

22. Kitchen, *Bible*, 72.

23. Kitchen, *Bible*, 72.

document that was lost. There is an ancient tradition behind the story of Gen 14. The text preserves a memory of an event that describes an end to settlements during the twentieth century BCE. The narrator probably had at his disposal a manuscript that originated from the archive of one of the Canaanite kings that was translated and revised.

THE NAMES OF THE DEFEATED KINGS AND PEOPLE

The names of the five Canaanite kings who fought against the monarchs from the east appear as a midrash. Evil and wickedness are synonymous with the kings of Sodom and Gomorrah.[24] Shinab, which can be translated as "Sin (the moon god)," is "(my) father, Shemeber," "Shem is a powerful," or "powerful name."[25] The name of the fifth king is missing. Instead, we read of a king from a place called Bela, which is Zoar.[26] As noted by Sarna, "Had the whole episode no historical foundation, the writer would surely not have been at a loss for a name."[27] The fact that the narrator mentioned the current place named Bela and its previous name Zoar shows that we have here an earlier tradition. This information was furnished for the reader who was not familiar with the previous name of the place.

The names of the people who were defeated are also recorded: Rephaim, Zuzim, Emim, Horrites, Amalekites, and Amorites. The Rephaim are mentioned in the list of the pre-Israelite residents of the land (Gen 15:20; Josh 17:15). Rephaim is a generic name or an epithet of gigantic people (Deut 2:11, 20; 3:11). They were called by different names in different locales; therefore, the Moabites called them Emim and the Ammonites called them Zamzummim.[28] The Zamzummim are more than likely identical to the Zuzim, which are mentioned only in Genesis, while in 1QapGen 21:29 and Deut 2:20 they are equated to the Rephaim.

---

24. Bera is linked to the verb "to be evil," and Birsha is probably related to "be wicked." This interpretation is found in the midrash. See *Gen. Rab.* 42:5

25. Hamilton, *Genesis*, 401. In *Gen. Rab.* 42:5 we find a different interpretation to the names: "Shinab, that he amassed with wealth Shemeber, that he flew. Reading the name, he made himself wings."

26. In Gen 36:32 Bela is the name of a king.

27. Sarna, *Understanding*, 111.

28. The Targums and midrash explain the name Emim as an epithet that means "the fearsome ones."

The original inhabitants of Seir were the Horites (Deut 2:12) who were evicted by the Edomites in the thirteenth century BCE. An Egyptian text referred to Canaan as "the land of Hurru." Other biblical references (Gen 36:20; Deut 2:12, 22) link them to the area southeast of the Dead Sea. Only the Amalekites and Amorites were present at the time of the Israelite occupation. The Amalekites were nomadic people who roamed the Sinai Peninsula and northern Negeb. Their clashes with the Israelites are recorded following the Exodus. They perceived the appearance of the Israelites as a threat to their control of their oasis and trading routes (Exod 17:8; Num 13:29).[29] The Amorites appear in all the lists of the pre-Israelite inhabitants of the land of Canaan and Transjordan. In Deut 1:44, the hill country of the Amorites is described as the whole country of the promised land, and the Amorites were its entire population. The territory of Syria-Palestine was sometimes called the Land of Amurru and its people Amorites.[30]

THE LOCATIONS OF THE BATTLES

The geographical locations of the battles are also recorded, which includes six sites. These places are identifiable and are found along Kings Highway along the length of Transjordan from north to south. The first site was Ashteroth-Kernaim. Ashteroth was a Canaanite city in the Bashan that received its name after the goddess Ashtoreth. A place named Ashtaroth is mentioned in the book of Deuteronomy (1:4; 3:1, 10) and it has been identified with Tell Ashterah in Syria. Karnaim is a place near Ashtaroth, therefore the expression means "Ashteroth near Karnaim."[31] Ashtaroth is mentioned in Egyptian Execration Texts (nineteenth to eighteenth centuries BCE) in the list of Thutmose III and the El-Amarna tablets (EA 197, 256).[32]

The next site was Ham, which is south of Ashtaroth along Kings Highway. It is identified with Tel Ham located eight kilometers (five

---

29. These feuds with the Amalekites continued until the early-monarchial period (1 Sam 15:2–8; 30:17–19). Later, the Amalekites became the hereditary enemy of Israel (Exod 17:14; Deut 25:17–19).

30. Mazar, "Emori," 440–46; Altmann, "Question," 3–22.

31. Amos 6:13.

32. Wilson, "List," 242; Albright, "Amarna Letters," 486; Ahituv, "Ashtarot," 404–406; Ahituv, *Canaanites*, 72–73; Avi-Yonah, "Ashtaroth," 737.

miles) south of modern Irbid in the Bashan.[33] At Tel Ham, evidence of settlement of the Bronze and Iron Ages and remains of a triple wall were found. But no remains from the patriarchal age have been found so far.[34] The next battle took place at Shaveh-Kiriathaim; its location has not been identified. Since Shaveh is defined by Kiriathim, more than likely it is a city the Israelites conquered from the Moabites, which was included within Rueben's territory near the northern edge of the Moabite plateau.[35]

The Horites were defeated at the hill country of Seir as far as El-Paran. Seir is the hill country east of the Arabah between the Dead Sea and the Gulf of Akaba. As for "El-Paran which is by the wilderness" (Gen 14:6) it is mentioned only here. Its exact location is uncertain. It is suggested that it may be another name for Elat (Deut 2:8) or Eloth (1 Kgs 9:26) on the Gulf of Akaba or a place west of Kadesh.

The kings returned to En-mishpat, which is Kadesh, and subdued the Amalekites. En-mishpat means "the spring of judgment." The name occurs only here, and it is the older name of the place. Based on its name, the site served nomads to air their complaints to solve their disputes. Kadesh, also known as Kadesh-bernea, was a well-known oasis that included several springs, and it is identified with Ein-el-Quedeirat in eastern Sinai. This site is mentioned with Abraham's wanderings. Later it was an important site where the Israelites settled during their wandering (Deut 2:14).[36] The last people who were defeated on the route to Sodom were the Amorites at Hazazon Tamar. More than likely, Hazazon was the earlier name of Tamar.[37] The place is associated with En-Gedi on the west bank of the Dead Sea (2 Chr 20:2). But according to Gen 14:7, Hazazon Tamar was between Kadesh and Sodom, which precluded the identification with En-Gedi. Scholars are divided about the locations of Hazazon Tamar.[38] A convincing argument was aired by Ahroni who suggested

33. A place named Huma is mentioned in the list of Thutmose III, no. 118 but its identification with the biblical Ham is doubtful. See Astor, "Ham," 32.

34. Glueck, "Explorations," 165–66.

35. For the different sites of Kiriathaim, see Mattingly, "Kiriathaim," 4:85.

36. The name Kadesh implies that this site was a cultic center for the nomads of the Negev and the Sinai Peninsula.

37. According to 1 Kgs 19:8, Solomon built "Tamar in the wilderness" but the parallel verse in 2 Chr 8:4 has Tadmor (Palmyra).

38. The prophet Ezekiel mentioned Tamar as a boundary point of the land of Israel together with Meribath-Kadesh (47:19; 48:28). In *The Onomasticon* (8:6), Eusebius mentions Asasonthamar, a village with a fortress and Roman garrison, which was a one-day journey from Mampsis (Kurnub) on the road from Hebron to Elath. The site

identifying Tamar with ʿAyn al-Ḥuṣb, forty kilometers southwest of the Dead Sea, a site where remains of a Roman fort and pottery from the Iron Age were discovered.[39] The site was probably intended to protect the trade routes to Elath.

The final battle was against the five Canaanite kings, which was the objective of the expedition. It took place at the "Valley of Siddim now the Dead Sea" (Gen 14:3). This place existed before it was flooded by the waters of the Dead Sea. There is no detail of the battle itself, only that the kings of Sodom and Gomorrah in their flight threw themselves into bitumen pits while the rest escaped to the hill country. This might imply that they died, but the king of Sodom met Abraham later. Therefore, it means that they threw themselves into the pits to save their lives. As for the eastern kings, they withdrew after they took the booty.

The route and the six sites that are mentioned in the path of the invasion from north to south coincide with Kings Highway in Transjordan that served for the transfer of goods from south Arabia to the Red Sea (Num 20:17; 21:22). Studies have shown the existence of a flourishing civilization between the twenty-first and nineteenth-century BCE, but then there is an end to settled life in Transjordan and the Negeb, which points to some catastrophe such as invasion. Transjordan remained in ruin for six hundred years until the founding of Edom and Moab in the thirteenth century BCE, while the Negeb was desolate for a thousand years.

There is a parallelism between the route that the four kings took and the route that the Israelites took when they came out of Egypt in reverse order. The Rephaim, Zuzim, Eimim, Horites, and Amorites and their place of habitat that is mentioned in Gen 14 are also cited in Deut 2–3 when Moses started the journey to conquer the land of Israel. We might explain that the Israelites took an identical route by suggesting that people in the ancient world tended to use the same roads that were convenient for passage. But more than likely this is not a coincidence, and it has a symbolic meaning. By Abraham defeating the eastern kings, the patriarch acquired his own rights to the land and his descendants. His acts legitimized later generations of Israelites to conquer and claim the land. The right to the land is God's will and has its roots in the patriarchal period, which foreshadowed future events.[40]

---

of Mampsis was never identified.

39. Aharoni, "Tamar," 30–42.

40. Cassuto, *"Quaestio" of Genesis,* 311–13.

Trying to explain the purpose of Gen 14, Sperling maintains that "tales of Abraham/Abram are an allegorical representation of specific Israelite leaders of the historical period."[41] He pointed to parallels between Gen 14 and the tales of David.[42] Abraham's chase after the kings for the retrieval of the captives and possessions is like David's pursuit of the Amalekites and the recovery of the captives. In addition, there are many phrases that are common to Gen 14 and 1 Sam 30. According to his interpretation, the story was composed to glorify David and Solomon. It came to justify Israel's possession of the land on both sides of the Jordan in the Davidic period. We believe that the similarity between Abraham's tales and David's is not a coincidence, and as we mentioned in the previous chapters it is what the sages meant when they said, "The deeds of the fathers are signs to the children." Many events in the life of the patriarch Abraham are repeated with the other patriarchs and are signs to future generations. The phrases that are common to Gen 14 and 1 Sam 30 are an indication of the period in which Gen 14 was composed, namely the monarchial period. The similarity between David and the ancestral figure of Abraham came to legitimize the Davidic monarchy. Specifically, the possession of the land was one of the main concerns that is mentioned in the covenant between God and Abraham and is also the subject of the covenant between YHWH and David (see the next chapter). The repetition of the covenant with David signals that it remains forever. As noted above, Abraham's defeat of the kings indicates his ownership of the land and justified the possession of the land in the monarchial period.

ABRAHAM THE WARRIOR

When Abraham received the news that Lot was taken captive, he went in pursuit of the four monarchs from the east and he was supported by his allies Mamre,[43] Eshkol,[44] and Aner. According to the text, they were Amorites, which testifies to the antiquity of the story. In a later period, the

---

41. Sperling, *Original Torah*, 80.

42. For more on Genesis reflecting a Davidic background, see Muffs, *Love and Joy*, 78.

43. Mamre is a personal name (Gen 14:13, 14) but also the name of a place where Abraham dwelled, which is in Hebron (Gen 13:18).

44. Eshkol is a personal name (Gen 13:24), which means "cluster of grapes." It is also the name of a wadi near Hebron (Num 13:23, 24), an area that was known for its groves.

Israelites are ordered to eradicate these people (Deut 7:1). The Amorites are among the seven nations that are not given the opportunity to surrender, but their whole population must be destroyed (20:17). The invention of a story that suggests that Abraham had Amorite allies is unlikely and is against the spirit of legislation in the book of Deuteronomy.[45]

Abraham mustered his forces, which numbered 318 men and chased the invading armies. The low number of combatants reflects his courage; he stood against a large army without fear. His act here served as an example to the next generations. To explain Abraham's victory in leading a small group of warriors against large armies, Josephus pointed to the courage of the soldiers in *Antiquities of the Jews*.[46] But in *Jewish Wars*, he maintained that Abraham had 318 captains under him and an immense army under each of them.[47] However, reading the Amarna tablets implies that a fighting force consisting of three hundred men was considered a large army.[48] Gideon, for example, defeated the Midianites with a force of three hundred men (Judg 7:8, 16). It is also possible that the description in Genesis is an exaggeration, and the campaign by the eastern king was not a large one but a description of a small raid.

Referring to Abraham's forces, the Hebrew Bible employs the term Ḥanikh, "retainer," which occurs only here (Gen 14:14). The Egyptian Execration Texts of the nineteenth-eighteenth centuries BCE mention *ḥnk*, which refers to armed retainers of Canaanite chieftains.[49] The term has an Egyptian origin (*ḥnk.w*) from an earlier period.[50] A cuneiform text from Taanach, Israel from the fifteenth century BCE mentions *ḫanâku*, an armed retainer of a local chief. Abraham pursued the invading armies as far as Dan. The mention of Dan is anachronistic (Gen 14:14). The previous name of Dan was Laish; the Danites captured it and renamed it Dan. Laish is mentioned in the Egyptian text of around 1850–1825 BCE. It is also mentioned in the royal archives of Mari.[51] The place was part of the international trade routes. The final defeat to the armies took place in Hobah, which is north of Damascus. The prophet Ezekiel mentions the

---

45. Sarna, *Genesis*, 102–103.
46. Josephus, *Ant.* 1:10:1.
47. Josephus, *J.W.* 5:9:4.
48. Albright, "Amarna Letters," 485.
49. Hamilton, "ḥānîk," 301.
50. Lambdin, "Loan Words," 150; Reif, "Dedicated," 495–501.
51. Malamat, "Canaan," 164–77.

famous wine of Helbon (27:18).[52] The place is identified with the modern village of Khalbun, 15.5 miles (25 kilometers) north of Damascus.[53]

What emerges from this description of Abraham is completely different from Gen 12. Before, Abraham feared for his life and needed to use deception to save his life. Here, without hesitation, he comes to the aid of his nephew Lot. In a night attack with the aid of his allies, he defeated the coalition of the eastern kings. The story stresses the importance of family ties and it serves as an archetype for the deed of releasing the captives; Abraham intervened and rescued his nephew Lot.[54] Referring to the subject of redemption of the captives, Maimonides says, "The redemption of captives takes precedence over the feeding and clothing of the poor. There is no commandment as great as that of redeeming captives, for they are among the hungry, the thirsty, and the naked, and are in danger."[55] Delay in fulfilling it is considered as bloodshed.

As mentioned previously, just as Abraham was depicted as a military hero, so was David. Not surprisingly, there are numerous parallels between Gen 14 and the tales of David. In 1 Sam 30, David is depicted as a military hero like Abraham. The city of Ziklag, which was the seat of David and his people, was attacked when David was not present. David's wives and the families of his warriors were taken captive. David fought back and retrieved the captives. "David rescued everything the Amalekites had taken; David also rescued his two wives. Nothing of theirs was missing—young and old, sons or daughters, spoils, or anything else that had been carried off—David recovered everything" (30:18–19). Returning to Ziklag, David sent a share of the spoil to the elders of Judah. This is a clear reminder of the battle that Abraham fought against the kings when he rescued Lot: "He brought back all the possession; he also brought back his kinsman Lot and his possession, and the women and the rest of the people" (Gen 14:16). Like Abraham, David is depicted as a military hero; he enforced the division of booty between combatants and noncombatants. Abraham defeated the kings north of Damascus (Gen 14:15); similarly, David struck down twenty-two thousand of the Aramaeans

---

52. In 1QapGen 22:10, the name *hlbwn* is mentioned, which is Helbon.

53. In Jdt 4:4; 15:5 (and maybe 15:4), Choba is mentioned in a list that includes Samaria, Jericho, and Jerusalem. This would imply a Judean or Israelite site, possibly el-Marmaleh between Beth-Shan and Tubas. But in Jdt 15:5 we read that the Israelites pursued the enemy as far as Hobah even beyond Damascus, which is like what we read in Gen 14:15. See Thompson, "Hobah," 235; Moore, *Judith*, 149.

54. Sarna, *Genesis*, 379.

55. Maimonides, *Yad, Hilkhot Zeraim*, 8:10.

and installed a garrison in Aram of Damascus. The Arameans became tributary vassals of David (2 Sam 8:5–6). It was suggested that the chapter "was composed for the aggrandizement of David and Solomon."[56] But as we mentioned before, Abraham's acts foreshadow the future.

ABRAM THE HEBREW

In Gen 14:13, Abraham is called "Abram the Hebrew." This title is never employed again with reference to Abraham. Scholars tried to connect the designation "Hebrew" with Ḫabiru or ʿApiru, which led to various scholarly conclusions. As Speiser noted, the evidence remains ambiguous. Genesis 14 corresponds more closely than any other chapter with the data on the Western Ḫabiru. He especially points to the date formula in Alalakh Tablets 58 (eighteenth/seventeenth centuries BCE), which speaks of a treaty with Ḫabiru warriors and the state of Idrimi (fifteenth century BCE) that describes how the royal fugitive found asylum among the Ḫabiru warriors.[57] The Ḫabiru lived during the second millennium BCE in the Fertile Crescent. They were a class of displaced people who originated from urban and tribal sedentary populations. In the eighteenth and seventeenth centuries BCE, they appeared in Cappadocia, Babylon, and Mari; they are referred to as mercenaries who served the local rulers. These people who appeared in different places and periods had several things in common. They were considered outsiders in the places where they lived, were fugitives from their original societies, and shared a common inferior status. They are not considered to be a single ethnic group, but a mixture of other people, which is clear from their names; most of them were Semites. Their description as fugitives from authority resembles bands in Israel during the biblical period (Judg 9:4, 26; 11:3), especially David's band (1 Sam 22:2). Migration of tribes and people to Canaan in the first half of the second millennium BCE is well known. Therefore, it is possible that among the Semitic tribes who migrated were people who were called *Hapiru*/Apiru.

The question of whether the Ḫabiru can possibly be identified with the word "Hebrew" remains very complicated; any conclusion must be tentative. As noted above, the designation of Abraham as a Hebrew appears only once when he went on a military campaign to aid his nephew

---

56. Sperling, *Original*, 83.
57. Speiser, *Genesis*, 103.

Lot and the king of Sodom. Abraham was never labeled as a warrior before. He is described as an outsider like the Ḫabiru Apiru who were on the fringes of society. Speaking of Abraham, Cazelles said he is a "typical hapiru of the Amarna type."[58] This raised questions among scholars whether Abraham was like Ḫabiru who was known to be engaged in military activity. But a closer examination of the terms "Ḫabiru" and "Hebrews," reveals that there is no basis for identifying Ḫabiru and Hebrews, on both historical and philological grounds. The development of *hapir* or *ʿpir* to *ʿibr* is without parallel, more so, the difference between the p and b is unlikely considering the Ugaritic evidence that *ʿapiru* was of Northwest Semitic origin.[59] More so, Abraham is not attacking and robbing communities and creating chaos like the Habiru who were known for their savagery. Their vicious attacks are described in Mari letters and the El-Amarna documents (fifteenth–fourteenth centuries BCE), which describe chaotic situations where bands of the Ḫabiru robbed and destroyed everything. Abraham's involvement in a military expedition was forced on him because Lot was taken captive, which left him with no alternative but to try to rescue him from captivity.

An alternative solution to explain the term Ḫabiru would be that the name Hebrew *ʿivri* is related to *ʿever*, "to cross over from the other side," as we read in the book of Joshua: "In olden times, your forefathers Terah, father of Abraham and father of Nahor lived beyond [*ʿever*] the Euphrates and worshiped other gods" (34:3). So, when the people are referred to as Hebrews, it is simply another way of calling them "the ones who came from beyond the river." But this geographical suggestion should be discounted since Abraham's family in Mesopotamia who lived beyond the river are not called Hebrew but Aramean.[60]

Another possibility suggests that the name Hebrew comes from *ʿEber*, which appears in the Table of Nations (Gen 10:21, 25) and Abraham's genealogy (Gen 11:6; 1 Chr 1:18–19). In other words, Abraham is a descendant of Eber from the line of Shem. The suggestions that Abraham came from beyond the river and that he is a descendent of Eber are found in the midrash:

> R. Judah said: "[Ha- ʿIBRI signifies that] the whole world was on one side (*ʿeber*) while he was on the other side (*ʿEber*)." R.

58. Cazelles, "Hebrews," 22.
59. Astour, "Habiru," 384; Beitzel, "Habiru," 589.
60. Sarna, *Genesis*, 378.

Nehemiah said: "[It denotes] that he was descended from Eber."
The Rabbis said: "It means that he came from across the river; further, that he spoke in the language of the dwellers across the river."[61]

The term "Hebrew" is found in the stories about Joseph and Moses when the Israelites were in Egypt. Later, it appears in the first half of the book of Samuel when Saul is fighting against the Philistines. In these contexts, the term is used by non-Israelites when speaking about an Israelite. The term is found for the last time in the book of Jonah and used by non-Israelites (1:9). In some instances, the term is used by the editor to distinguish the Israelite from a foreigner. In the laws dealing with emancipation the term 'eved 'ivri, "Hebrew Slave," is used. The term comes to distinguish an Israelite slave from a slave of foreign origin. This leads us to the conclusion that the term "Hebrew" in the Hebrew Bible designates an ethnic term while, "Ḫabiru" (Ḫapiru) is a social element. Since the Israelites did not describe themselves as Hebrews it is possible that a non-Israelite source is behind the account, which describes Abraham as Hebrew.[62]

MELCHIZEDEK

Following Abraham's victory against the kings and rescuing Lot, there is a description of Abraham's meetings with a mysterious person by the name of Melchizedek, the king of Salem. Melchizedek is a king and a priest, but the Bible does not reveal anything about his background. The nature of his priesthood is not clear, and he worshiped the same God as Abraham. He is also the king of Salem, which is believed to be Jerusalem, the future capital of the nation of Israel. This episode appears in Gen 14:18–20 and it was suggested that it was inserted into Abraham's tale.[63] It breaks the continuity of 14:17 and 14:21–24, which describes the meetings between Abraham and the king of Sodom. Genesis 14:17 and 14:21 follow easily from one to another and there is no conceivable reason to separate them. But as we mentioned before, we believe that verses 18–20 are original parts of the chapter, and it comes to show the difference between Melchizedek and the king of Sodom; it came to give the reader

---

61. *Gen. Rab.* 42:8.
62. Cazelles, "Hebrews," 1–28; Wenham, *Genesis 1–15*, 313.
63. Westermann, *Genesis*, 189.

a glimpse into the character of the king of Sodom. The Torah does not describe people directly. Instead, we learn about them indirectly through their actions or lack of actions. The cunning aspect of the king of Sodom is exhibited here. As Abarvanel (Isaac ben Judah, 1437–1508) noticed according to the laws of that time, all that Abraham rescued belonged to him. But when the king of Sodom saw Abraham's generosity—he gave a tenth of everything to Melchizedek—he seized the moment and asked Abraham to share the booty with him. The disparity between the righteous Melchizedek and the wicked king of Sodom is displayed here. The king of Sodom came to welcome Abraham empty-handed although he was obligated to repay him for rescuing him. On the other hand, Melchizedek, who did not have any obligation towards Abraham, came out and welcomed Abraham with bread and wine; he showed generosity towards Abraham. Beckor Shor (Joseph ben Isaac, twelfth century) pointed out that this act of kindness is similar to the acts that were taken by David's supporters during the Absalom revolt (2 Sam 17:27–28).[64] For the misconduct of neglecting the elementary duty of bringing food for the weary, the Transjordanian neighbors of Israel Moab and Amon were forbidden to enter the congregation of the Lord "because they did not meet you with food and water on your journey after you left Egypt" (Deut 23:5). These people reacted with hostility when the Israelites passed through their territory on the way to the land of Israel. Their behavior is an example of wickedness, a conduct that is exemplified by the king of Sodom. Although the king of Sodom suffered a defeat, this did not change him. His actions here serve as an introduction to the wickedness of the Sodomites that would be displayed on a larger scale in Gen 19.[65]

Melchizedek means "King of Righteousness." The name is mentioned in our text (Gen 14:18–20), and in Ps 110:4 it is written as two separate words, Melchi-zedek, linked by *maqqēp* that implies it is a title and not a personal name. A similar formation is found in the title Adoni-Zedek, the name of the Canaanite king of Jerusalem (Josh 10:1). The element *ṣdk* is attested in West Semitic names. A Canaanite god Ṣidqu, is referred to in later sources as "Sydyk," which is associated with the sun god, the patron of justice.[66] Kings in the ancient Near East were given the title "righteous king." King Yehimilk (ca. 950 BCE) of Byblos was called a

---

64. Nebo, *Perushe Rabbi Yosef Bekhor*, 124; Sperling, *Original*, 82.
65. Leibowitz, *Studies*, 132.
66. Sarna, *Genesis*, 380.

righteous upright king.⁶⁷ Another king from Byblos is Yehawmilk (fifth–fourth centuries, BCE) who requested prolonging his days and years to come because he is a righteous king.⁶⁸

Melchizedek is identified as the king of Salem. In the Ps 76:3, Salem appears as a place name parallel to Zion, which is Jerusalem. The 1Qap-Gen (22:13), Josephus (*Ant.* 1:181), and the Targums identify Salem with Jerusalem.⁶⁹ Jerusalem is mentioned in Egyptian Execration Texts (ca. 1850 BCE) as Urushalimu and in the El-Augarna texts (fourteenth century BCE) as Urusalim. King of Salem means literally "king of peace." The association between the king of righteousness and the king of peace appears together in the Hebrew Bible (Ps 85:11; Isa 9:6; 32:17; 48:18; 60:17).

In addition to being king, Melchizedek is also a priest (Gen 14:18). In Ps 110:4, this dual role of kingship and priesthood is mentioned again: "You are a priest forever, a rightful king by My decree." The Hebrew Bible prohibited the dual role of priest-king, nevertheless, we find that some of the early kings of Israel such as Saul, David, Solomon, and Jeroboam participated in cultic activities. In the ancient world, kings were perceived as god's priests and the notion of a king-priest was very common. The king of Tyre Ethbaal, who was Jezebel's father (1 Kgs 16:31), was a priest-king of Astarte and according to Josephus "he was slain by Ithobalus, the priest of Astarte, who reigned thirty-two years, and lived sixty-eight years."⁷⁰ Tabnit the king of Sidon was a priest-king of Astarte: "I, Tabnit priest of Ashtoreth and King of Sidon."⁷¹ His son, Eshmun'azar, inherited the title priest-king and his mother, Amoashtart, was a priestess of Astarte.⁷²

Melchizedek is the embodiment of a king-priest, he blesses Abraham by El-Elyon (God Most High), maker of heaven and earth, and attributes Abraham's victory to El-Elyon. The divine title "God Most High" is found again only in Ps 78:35. Phoenician sources mention two deities, El and Elyon, called Most High.⁷³ In an Aramaic treaty from the eighth cen-

---

67. Rosenthal, "Building," 653.

68. Rosenthal, "Yehawmilk," 656.

69. A different tradition suggests that Salem is the Samaritan city of Shechem. This is based on Gen 33:18—"and Jacob came to Salem, a city of Shechem"—which means that Melchizedek was a priest at the temple of Mount Gerizim. The grammatical structure of the verse is awkward; RSV and JPS translated the word Salem as "safe," which makes more sense. See Astour, "Salem," 905.

70. Josephus, *Ag. Ap.* 1:123.

71. *KAI* 13:1.

72. *KAI* 14:13–15.

73. *Praep. ev.* 1:10.

tury BCE near the village of Sfire, the gods "El and Elyon" are mentioned in addition to "Heaven and Earth, Abyss and Sources, Day and Night."[74] It appears that El and Elyon were two separate deities, but the Hebrew Bible united them. By Abraham making an oath to "YHWH, El-Elyon, Creator of heaven and earth," he placed YHWH before El-Elyon, making the latter an epithet.[75]

Following his victory against the kings, Abraham gave tithe to Melchizedek. It was suggested that our story points to the virtues and privileges of the priests of Jerusalem. The tithe that Abraham gave to Melchizedek attests to the rights of the priests and what is displayed here is an etiological story that comes to justify it.[76] But an examination of the biblical text reveals that what Abraham gave to Melchizedek is a one-time payment comparable to what we read in Num 31:25–41, which speaks about the distribution of the spoils. It is different from the later annual tithing that supported the religious institutions (Deut 14:22–29; 26:12–15). The one-time payment that Abraham gave to Melchizedek is related to the blessing that the king-priest bestowed on Abraham: "Blessed be Abram of God Most High, Creator of heaven and earth" (Gen 14:19).

Van Seters suggested the story of Melchizedek belongs to the postexilic times. He pointed to the Hasmonaeans who desired to be kings and "high priests of God Most High." The title "priest of El Elyon" is not used in the history of the priesthood in the Hebrew Bible. It is only in the Maccabean period that the Hasmonaeans used the title of "high priests of God Most High." The title did not originate with the Hasmonaeans but more likely with a late Persian or Hellenistic period when syncretism became common. By the time of the Hasmoneans, it was a fixed title whose origin was unknown.[77] Emerton did not think that the divine names or the name Melchizedek suggest a postexilic period, neither was there an indication of postexilic priest-king before the Maccabees. He suggested that preexilic kings could fulfill priestly functions. He points to the monarchial period and to David who chose Jerusalem as his capital, a place that was the center of Canaanites' worship. By his act, David united the cults of YHWH and El and ruled over Israelites and Canaanites alike.[78] A different view is expressed by McConville who believes that the episode

---

74. Rosenthal, "Treaty," 659–61.
75. Hundley, *YHWH*, 210.
76. Liver, "Melchizedek," 1154–57.
77. Van Seters, *Abraham*, 308.
78. Emerton, "Riddle," 414–19.

of Melchizedek in Gen 14:18–20 is an integral part of the Abrahamic stories and does not belong to any work of a later period that came to establish a religious or political purpose.[79] Genesis 14, as we noted already, shows continuity to the previous and later chapters and there is no need to find an explanation for its purpose that is not related to the patriarchal narratives.

In addition to Gen 14:18–20, Melchizedek is also mentioned in Ps 110:4. It is suggested that it was written in the Davidic era to legitimize the pre-Israelite Jebusite priesthood of Zadok and the kingship of David. Accordingly, Zadok was the priest of the Jebusite sanctuary in Jerusalem. When David captured the city, he allowed Zadok to continue his priestly function in order to enlist the support of the inhabitants of the city.[80] Another suggestion is that Zadok was the pre-Davidic king of Jerusalem.[81] The notion of kingship and priesthood that received its legitimation from a Canaanite king or a priest of Jerusalem is alien to the Bible and the Second Temple period. The high priest and the priesthood have their legitimation as the descendants of the priesthood of Aaron.[82] David's kingship was divinely ordained. Psalm 110 does not speak about the status of the priests but deals with the priestly rights of the king, the privileges of the king as God's elected one. David is a forever priest as the son of God. The views about the early kingship concepts are presented here. The style of the Psalm is archaic; it is probably based on Canaanite hymns that were chanted to glorify the kings that were later adopted by Israel. The link between Israelite kingship and the previous kingship of Jerusalem attests to the earlier form of the psalm, which belong to the Davidic period and the early stages of Israelite monarchy.[83]

Besides showing the difference between the righteous king and the wicked king of Sodom, the story of Melchizedek had other objectives. One of its goals was to point to the early sanctity of Jerusalem, which was a foreign city until the Davidic era. The narrator attributed our story to the time of Abraham, the father of the Hebrew nation. Abraham was blessed by the king-priest of Jerusalem. His meeting with the king-priest of Salem following the battle had a symbolic meaning; it foreshadows the city's role as a city of peace. Later, speaking about Zion and Jerusalem, the

---

79. McConville, "Horizons," 111–16.
80. Rowley, "Zadak," 113–41; Rowley, "Melchizedek," 461–72.
81. Bentzen, "Geschichte," 173–76.
82. Liver, "Melchizedek," 1155.
83. Liver, "Melchizedek," 1155.

prophets Isaiah and Micah said that the city was a symbol of peace (Isa 2:1–4; Mic 4:1–4). And in the book of Psalms where Salem is mentioned, we read: "There He broke the fiery arrows of the bow, the shield and the sword of war. Selah" (Ps 76: 3–4).

Jerusalem was the seat of an ancient Jebusite kingship of the order of Melchizedek under the patronage of the deity of El-Elyon. It's mentioned in Genesis foreshadowing the Davidic kingship who was a king and fulfilled priestly functions as did Melchizedek. David and Solomon transformed a Jebusite city into a cult center. David even appointed his own sons as priests (2 Sam 8:18). The account of Genesis was written during the monarchial period, it could not ignore the Canaanite background that had some influence on the courts of David and Solomon. The old tradition from Genesis and the current tradition from the monarchial period were fused in Ps 110:4, displaying the dual functions of kingship and priesthood, thus equating David and Melchizedek.

In conclusion, Abraham's portrayal in Gen 14 is different from the previous chapters. He is no longer a timid person but a warrior who fought against the four eastern kings and defeated them. He came to the aid of his nephew Lot and rescued him. His act stresses the importance of family ties, and it serves as an archetype for the mitzvah of *pidyon shevuyim*, redemption of the captives. For the first time, Abraham is called Hebrew. In the Hebrew Bible, it designates an ethnic term, while Ḫabiru (*Ḫapiru*) refers to a social element. Although the punitive expedition of the four eastern kings is not attested in the extrabiblical sources, the cumulative information points to the existence of a kernel of historicity in the text. Genesis 14 contains names of sites and people's personal names that are consistent with the earlier period. The route of the invaders—Kings Highway—and the usage of archaic place names that are supplemented by current names and locations of the battlefield adds more credibility to the story. Abraham's defeat of the four kings foreshadows future events. The Israelites later took the reverse route of Kings Highway; they conquered the land to claim it. Similarly, David defeated the Arameans and rescued the captives; he is a military hero like Abraham. Melchizedek is the king-priest of Salem; later David became the king-priest of Jerusalem. The resemblance between Gen 14 and some of David's tales is not coincidental. The aim was to create a link between Abraham and David to further legitimize David's kingship. The story of Melchizedek is an integral part of Gen 14 and does not belong to a later period that came to establish a religious or political purpose. Its inclusion stresses the difference between Melchizedek's righteousness and the wickedness of the king of Sodom and prefigures the story of Sodom and Gomorrah. It comes to emphasize the sanctity of Salem and its role as a city of peace, a Jebusite city that David transformed to his capital. In the next chapter, we will examine the covenant between God and Abraham, which entails the promise of many descendants and the promise of the lands.

Chapter 4

To Your Offspring, I Assign This Land

A covenant is an agreement between two parties in which one or both make an oath and promise to abide by it. Genesis 15 describes a special covenant (*bᵊrit*) between God and Abraham. The Sinaitic and Deuteronomistic covenants included imposing obligations on both parties: God and Israel. Not so in Gen 15. The "covenant between the pieces," between God and Abraham, were promises made by God alone. No obligation is imposed on Abraham. It is only God who takes it upon himself to fulfill his promises to Abraham, the promise of descendants, and the promise of the land. Following God's promises, a ceremonial slaughtering of animals is described. God instructed Abram to take a three-year-old heifer, a three-year-old she-goat, a three-year-old ram, a turtledove, and a young bird. Abraham cuts them into pieces (except for the bird) and places the pieces in parallel rows. The covenant was sealed by a ritual form: a smoking oven and a flaming torch passed between the parts of the animals that were cut, representing the presence of God. Hence, the meaning of the animal's slaughter and its equivalent in the ancient Near East will be examined. In addition, the promises of descendants and the land that are recurring motifs in the book of Genesis and the purpose of the covenant will be evaluated. Parallels in the Abrahamic covenant with God can also be found in the Davidic covenant. Therefore, is there any significance to these parallels?

STRUCTURE

In Gen 15:1, God appears to Abram in a vision. The traditional commentators differed as to whether the word "vision" in 15:1 refers to the entire chapter (Radak, acronym for Rabbi David ben Joseph Kimhi, 1160–1235) or whether two separate but consecutive divine revelations are described here (Abraham Ibn Ezra, 1089–1164). Rashbam (Rabbi Samuel ben Meir, ca. 1080–1174), by contrast, held that the promises to Abram were made at different times and the chapter recounts two different events that did not take place one after the other. Many modern scholars believe that the chapter combines two different sources.[1] However, the multiple-source thesis is untenable for this chapter, as shown by the extreme variation of scholarly opinions as to the assignment of its parts to the various sources.[2]

Regarding the content, the Gen 15 clearly has two parts.[3] The first part, 15:1–5, comprises the promise of a son and the promise of many offspring. The second, 15: 7–21, adds the promise of the land. The revelation in the first part certainly takes place at night: "He took him outside and said, 'Look toward heaven and count the stars, if you are able to count them.' And He added, 'So shall your offspring be'" (15:5). In the second part, the revelation takes place at sunset or twilight: "As the sun was about to set, a deep sleep fell upon Abram, and a great dark dread descended upon him" (15:12); and subsequently, "when the sun set and it was very dark" (15:17). Hence, the promise of offspring took place at night, when Abram was awake, whereas the promise of the land took place when Abram was asleep or in a deep trance.

Van Seters, Hoftijzer, Snijders, Rendtorff, and Westermann have all noted the unity of the chapter,[4] as did Sarna, who noted the intimate

---

1. Gen 15:1–6 E, 15:7–21 J (cf. Wellhausen) or interwoven E in 15:1b, 3a, 5, 11, 12a, 13a, 14, and 16 with the rest. See Wellhausen, *Composition*, 21; Noth, *History of Pentateuchal Traditions*, 28, 200–201; Speiser, *Genesis*, 114–15; Skinner, *Genesis*, 276–77; Emerton, "Origin," 17.

2. Lohfink, *Landverheissung*, 24, 27; Anbar, "Abrahamic," 34–52. According to Anbar, the chapter is the end product of the merger of separate stories, the first in 15:1–6 and the second in 15:7–21. He holds that each story is an independent creation inspired by ancient sources. Their original date of composition is evidently the end of the First Temple period; their merger took place at the start of the exile in order to blend into a single text, the ceremonial promises of a son, many offspring, and the land.

3. Sarna, *Genesis*, 111–12.

4. "There seems to be no need to dispute any longer that the text, in spite of a certain awkwardness of style, is a unity" (Van Seters, *Abraham*, 249–50). For the literary unity of Gen 15, see also Hoftijzer, *Verheissungen*, 17–55; Snijders, "Genesis 15," 261–79;

connection between its two parts—especially the motifs of the promise of offspring and the promise of the land, which are associated and interwoven through the end of Genesis.[5] A close reading of the chapter reveals that the two sections have a parallel structure and that each consists of three parts: (1) a promise by God (15:1, 7-8); (2) Abram's expression of doubt and worry (15:2, 8); and (3) another promise by God, expressed in words and a symbolic act (15:4, 9, and 21). In both sections, God begins his speech with the words "I am" (15:1, 7), and Abram replies, "O Lord God" (15:2, 8)—a rare conjunction of the divine names in the Bible. In addition, the keywords "offspring" (15:3, 5, and 13), "inherit" (15:3, 4 [twice], 7, and 8), and "take/bring out" (15:5, 7) appear in both parts of the chapter. The same applies to many of the idioms that appear in both Gen 15 and the previous chapter. All of this strengthens the argument for the unity of chapter 15.[6]

THE PROMISE OF OFFSPRING

The opening of the chapter—"The word of the Lord came to Abram in a vision"—is a typical introductory formula for divine messages to prophets.[7] It is followed by a dialogue between Abram and the Lord, the latter promises Abram both an heir and many offspring.[8] The interchange here is a reminder of the dialogue in Abimelech's dream: God's opening

---

Rendtorff, "Genesis 15," 74-81; Westermann, *Genesis 12-36*, 250-57; Ha, *Genesis*, 43-57.

5. On the promise of offspring and the land, see Gen 12:2, 7; 13:14-16; 16:6-7; 24:7; 26:3-4; 28:3-4 and 13-14.

6. Gen 15 is full of words and idioms that appear in the previous chapter, which strongly suggests a link between the two chapters. "Fear not" (15:1) links up with the previous chapter in which Abram overcame the four kings, a victory for which he may perhaps fear revenge. The Lord's statement, "I am a shield [*magen*] to you" (15:1) reminds us of Melchizedek's "And blessed be God Most High, Who has delivered [*miggen*] your foes into your hand" (Gen 14:20). The Lord concludes a covenant (*berit*) with Abram, while in the previous chapter (14:13) we were introduced to Abram's allies (*ba'lei berit*). The Amorites who, in chapter 14, are Abram's allies (14:13), are to be dispossessed of the land (14:16 and 21). Abram's slave is the Damascene Eliezer (15:2), while in chapter 14 we read about how Abram pursued the four kings north of Damascus (14:15). For other linguistic echoes that point to the link between the two chapters, see Sarna, *Genesis*, 112.

7. Cf. 1 Sam 15:10; 2 Sam 7:4; 1 Kgs 12:22, 16:1, 17:2 and 8, 18:31, and 21:17.

8. The motif of the promise of a son also appears in Judg 13:2-5; 1 Sam 1; 2 Kgs 4:8-17; and Luke 1 and 2. It is also found in the Ugaritic stories of Keret and Aqhat, where we read about childlessness, the promise of a son, and the birth of a son.

statement (15:1b), the address to God as a question that is really a complaint (15:2–3), and the divine reply that explains his position (15:4–5). Abraham speaks here for the first time to God; he complains that he is childless. Many years passed by and the promises of "I will make you a great nation" (Gen 12:2) and "I will make your offspring as the dust of the earth" (13:16) remained unfulfilled. Since he does not have an heir, it is his servant Eliezer who would inherit him. Some suggest that, based on Abram's request for a son and heir, this is an incubation dream.[9] A similar petition is found in Ugaritic texts that are considered to describe incubations. In the story of the dream of King Keret, the deity appears and asks why he is weeping. Keret replies, "What need do I have of silver and gold? . . . Let me beget sons."[10] In reply, the god tells him how he can find a woman who will bear him sons. Some compare Keret's petition with Abram's request here: "What can You give me, seeing that I am childless?" (Gen 15:2). In another story in the Aqhat saga, Daniel provides the gods with food and drink for six days; on the seventh day he is vouchsafed a response from Baal, who in turn petitions El who conveys to Daniel his blessing of the birth of an exemplary son.[11] Note, however, that in contrast to Daniel's ritual preparations and Keret's tears, Abram does nothing. The Lord appears to Abram at his own initiative. The text in Genesis does not specify the location of this epiphany.

But God assured Abraham that his servant will not be his heir, only his own offspring will inherit him. The suggestion is that Abraham will father a son in the future. To affirm his commitment, the Lord took him outside and told him to look up and count the stars.[12] His offspring would be as countless as the stars. God had already compared them to the dust of the earth (13:16); thus, the sages tried to explain the difference by suggesting that the nation of Israel, "when they descend, they descend to the dust, and when they rise, they rise to the stars."[13]

---

9. Obermann, "Daniel," 28.

10. "What need (have) I (of) silver and yellow metal, (even) gold, a share of his estate perpetual, slaves, three horses (and) chariots) from the stables of the son of the slave-girl? So do thou give (me) what is not in my house: Give me the wench Hury (the most) gracious progeny of thy first-born." See Driver, *Canaanite*, 33.

11. Obermann identifies this as an incubation. See, however, Margalit's criticism of this interpretation. Obermann, "Daniel," 10; Margalit, *Ugaritic*, 260–66.

12. The stars as representing an immense number can be found in the promises in Gen 22:17 and 26:4; cf. Exod 32:13; Deut 1:10, 10:22, and 28:62; Neh 9:23.

13. *Meg.* 16a.

Abraham is wide awake. This revelation is both visual and aural. Direct and unmediated, it is typical of the age of the patriarchs.[14] Sarna, discussing the topic of revelation, says that it is difficult to know whether the scene described here is a real event or a dream theophany.[15] Those who opt for the latter option note the nighttime setting of the vision, which can be inferred from Gen 15:5.[16] According to them, the stars are seen during the dream. Radak, in his commentary on 15:5 and 12, writes that "he took him out of his tent in a prophetic vision.... This is like 'He brought me in visions of God to Jerusalem' (Ezek 8:3).... Everything was in a prophetic vision, for it was all one vision on a single occasion." Nevertheless, we should note that the examples he cites took place in "visions of God" and by "the spirit of the Lord."

THE PROMISE OF THE LAND

The second dialogue between the Lord and Abram occupies Gen 15:7–21.[17] This colloquy focuses on the promise of the land to Abram's descendants, a promise accompanied by a ceremonial slaughtering of animals. God instructs Abram to take a three-year-old heifer, a three-year-old she-goat, a three-year-old ram, a turtledove, and a young bird. Abraham cuts them into pieces (except for the bird) and places the pieces in parallel rows. The animals listed in 15:9 were precisely those offered in Israelite sacrifice.[18] Moreover, according to Lev 1:17 a sacrificial bird is not cut up or separated into pieces, but merely torn open.[19] According to the retelling of this scene in the book of Jubilees (chapter 14), Abram built an altar, offered sacrifices, and sprinkled the blood on the altar. A ceremony parallel to that in Gen 15 is found in Jer 34:17–19, but only a calf is used.[20] As noted, cutting up the animals connotes a sacrificial offering and so does

14. Westermann, *Promises*, 120; Westermann, "Way of the Promise," 200–24.

15. Sarna, *Genesis*, 113.

16. Skinner, *Genesis*, 278; Ehrlich, *Traum*, 36 and 39. On page 36, Ehrlich refers to this as a vision, but on page 39 he calls it a dream.

17. Verse 7 begins with "Then He said to him" in order to provide continuity between the two halves of the chapter.

18. See Lev 1.

19. There is disagreement about the word *gōzāl*. In addition to our verse, it appears only in Deut 32:11 where it refers to a young eagle. Apparently, here the reference is to a dove because we also have the common idiom blank. *Gen. Rab.* 44:17, Targum Onkelos, and Septuagint have a pigeon. For a parallel, see Lev 1:14; 5:7, 11.

20. On the Jeremiah text, see Miller, "Sin and Judgment," 611–13.

the age of the animals. A three-year-old animal was the most desirable offering in ancient Israel and the Near East.[21] In Greece, too, it was the custom to offer three-year-old animals at covenant ceremonies.

In contrast to the view that Abram's actions allude to the offering of sacrifices, some argue precisely the opposite.[22] Here we have no altar and no mention of the sprinkling of blood, as is found in Exod 24:8. Furthermore, the "sacrificial" animals are neither eaten nor burned. Their carcasses serve only to define an alley through which God passes. Linguistically, too, the terminology of this chapter is not the same as that of the sacrificial regulations of the Priestly Code. There, the term "carcass" (*pāgar*) does not appear, and the second type of bird is specifically a pigeon (*ben yonah*), not a "young bird" (*gōzāl*). Neither does the Priestly Code emphasize a requirement for three-year-old animals. Nevertheless, several questions remain such as: Why precisely are the animals of the Israelite sacrificial ritual involved here, and why dit Abram not rend the bird?

The fact that Abram cut apart the animals that were used in sacrifice and that he slept while the Lord conveyed a message to him has led a number of scholars to conclude that the text describes incubation.[23] But this conjecture must be rejected. It is the Lord who tells Abram to slaughter and split the animals; in incubation ceremonies, the sacrifice is offered at the dreamer–petitioner's initiative. Eichrodt, on the other hand, believes that here Abram is depicted as a seer in quest of divine guidance. This is why he offers sacrifices and follows the flight of birds. These actions have ancient Babylonian origins. The author of Genesis himself no longer understands their full significance; evidently, with the passage of time, these customs had been forgotten or sunk into oblivion.[24]

Parallels to the covenant ritual described here can be found in treaties from the second and first millennia BCE. In one of the Mari letters, the idiom whose literal meaning is "kill a donkey foal" actually has the

---

21. Where the Masoretic (MT) text of 1 Sam 1:24 reads "with three bulls," the Septuagint (and 4qsam[a]) have "with a three-year-old bull." The Septuagint version seems to be preferable because we subsequently read that only one bull was slaughtered (verse 25). See Cross, "New Qumran," 15–26. Rattner, however, thinks the MT is correct. See Rattner, "Three Bulls," 98–102.

22. Sarna, *Genesis*, 114; Jacob, *First Book*, 101; Levine, *Presence*, 37.

23. Jirku, "Ein Fall," 153; Gordon, *Ugarit and Minoan Crete*, 25; Obermann, *Daniel*, 28; Wellhausen, *Text*, 21–22.

24. Eichrodt, *Theology*, 1:302.

sense of "conclude a covenant."[25] When the donkey foal was slaughtered, a dog and she-goat were also brought, reminiscent of the three animals cut apart by Abram. The extrabiblical texts indicate that in addition to the slaughter of animals, there was also an imprecation. In a treaty of the seventeenth century BCE from Alalakh, between Yarimlin and Abban, Abban conveyed the city of Alalakh to his vassal Yarimlin. The text reads (11:39–42), "Abban placed himself under oath to Yarimlin and had cut the neck of a sheep (saying): '(Let me so die) if I take back that which I gave thee.'"[26] With our chapter in mind, note not only the slaughtering of animals but also that it is the stronger party that binds itself under the threat of punishment. The implication is that God binds himself by sanctions if he does not fulfill the conditions of his promise to Abram.

The cutting apart of animals is also found in two treaties of the eighth century BCE. We will cite one of them here.[27] The well-known Sefire inscription reports on a treaty between Bir-Gayah, king of KTK, and Mati'el, king of Arpad. The treaty alludes to a violation by Mati'el and adds, "[Just as this calf is cut in two, so may Mati'el be cut in two, and may his nobles be cut in two! And just as a [ha]r[lot is stripped naked], so may the wives of Mati'el be stripped naked." According to the treaty, the slaughtering of an animal when the covenant was concluded was a magical act accompanied by imprecations that threatened one party with dire punishment should it violate the conditions of the pact.[28]

---

25. Cutting up animals was an integral part of the covenant ceremony, as we find in the Mari letter: "I went to Ašlakka and they brought me a young dog and a she-goat in order to conclude a covenant [literally, 'kill a donkey foal'] between the Ḫaneans and the land of Idamaraṣ. But, in deference to my Lord, I did not permit [the use of] the young dog and the she-goat, but (instead) had a donkey foal, the young of a she-ass, killed, and thus established a reconciliation between the Ḫaneans and the land of Idamaraṣ." See Held, "Philological Notes," 33. Weisberg points to the similarity between the splitting of Tiamat and the biblical "covenant between the pieces" as recorded in Gen 15 and Jer 34. See Weisberg, "Loyalty and Death," 264–66.

26. Wiseman, "Abban and Alalakh," 129; Weinfeld, "Covenant," 196; Weinfeld, "Loyalty Oath," 400–401. Compare the translation by McCarthy who believes that slaughtering animals was part of the treaty but not an imprecation: "Abba-An is under oath to Yarimlim and also, he cut the neck of a lamb. (He swore): I shall never take back what I gave thee." See McCarthy, *Treaty*, 185.

27. The second example comes from the curses in the vassal treaty of Esarhaddon, king of Assyria: "Just as male and female kids and male and female lambs are slit open and their entrails fall down upon their feet, so may the entrails of your sons and daughters roll down over your feet." See Wiseman, "Vassal Treaties," 69–72.

28. Fitzmeyer, *Aramai*, 14–15, 56–57. See also Rosenthal, "Treaty," 660.

A biblical parallel to the "covenant between the pieces" appears in the book of Jeremiah.[29] There, according to the text, during the Babylonian siege of the city, the nobles of Jerusalem set their slaves free, only to force them back into servitude later. The prophet complains bitterly about this: "I will make the men who violated My covenant, who did not fulfill the terms of the covenant which they made before Me, [like] the calf which they cut in two so as to pass between the halves: The officers of Judah and Jerusalem, the officials, the priests, and all the people of the land who passed between the halves of the calf shall be handed over to their enemies, to those who seek to kill them. Their carcasses shall become food for the birds of the sky and the beasts of the earth" (Jer 34:18–20). We may infer that someone who passes between the pieces subjects himself to the punishment of being rent in two should he violate the agreement.[30] A comparison of the extrabiblical texts reviewed above with the passage from Jeremiah indicates their affinity because all include both imprecations and the slaughter of animals. On the other hand, the element of the curse is absent from Gen 15. Another difference is that in the "covenant between the pieces," it is the Lord who passes between the halves of the carcasses, whereas in Jeremiah he is the guarantor of the covenant. Finally, in contrast to the self-imprecation of the ancient Near Eastern treaties, Gen 15 concludes with a divine promise to Abram.

The fact that the curses of the vassal treaties are replaced by a divine promise to Abram has led scholars to conclude that this chapter is modeled on a second type of treaty known to us from the ancient Near East—the grant treaty. In grant treaties, the ruler took upon himself a unilateral obligation toward his servant, granting land to him and his offspring in return for their loyal service. There are no curses against either party in this kind of treaty. Instead, the imprecation is directed at anyone who violates the treaty and deprives the servant of what the king has granted him. The treaty is meant to protect the rights of the servant who received the grant, while the curse is directed against any third party who might try to violate the treaty. This model is found in Abraham and David; both are granted land and a dynasty.[31]

After all the preparations for the covenant ceremony—this must have taken some time—Abram stands and waits. Birds of prey swoop

---

29. On this Jeremiah text, see Miller, "Sin," 611–13.

30. In Genesis, God is a party to the covenant, as shown by the fiery furnace that passes between the pieces. In Jeremiah, by contrast, he is the guarantor of the covenant (34:18).

31. Weinfeld, "Covenant," 184–203; Loewenstamm, "Divine," 509–10.

down on the carcasses and Abram chases them away.[32] The appearance of the birds may be a sign that forebodes evil, as we find later (Gen 15:13–16); here Abram chases away the evil sign. In Egyptian art, the falcon was the totem bird of, among others, the god Horus, with whom the pharaoh was identified.[33] The fact that Abram chases the bird away may allude to the future conflict in Egypt. The Israelites will be enslaved in Egypt but will depart from that country with vast possessions. Another possibility is that the descent of the birds of prey is a warning sign that the corpse of anyone who violates the covenant will be left as carrion for beasts and fowls. It may also be meant to inform Abram that foes will indeed attempt to prevent the fulfillment of the covenant, but the Israelites will be able to overcome them if they hold firm to the covenant. In this reading, the slaughtered animals symbolize the Israelites, and Abram is defending his offspring against attacks by their enemies.[34]

The biblical author proceeds to describe how the sun was about to set; as night approached, a deep sleep fell upon Abram.[35] Moreover, when the deep sleep falls on Abram, the verse also notes the "dark dread" that besets him (15:12b). His fear is the same as that which plagues Eliphaz when the Lord appears to him in a deep sleep: "A word came to me in stealth; my ear caught a whisper of it. In thought-filled visions of the night, when deep sleep falls on men, fear and trembling came upon me, causing all my bones to quake with fright" (Job 4:12–14). The message to Abram relates to the future; its theme is both national and personal. For four hundred years his offspring will be aliens, enslaved and persecuted, for God has decreed that the Israelites will be subjugated in Egypt. Only after three generations in that country will the fourth generation return to Canaan. On the personal level, Abram is told, "You shall go to your fathers in peace; you shall be buried at a ripe old age" (Gen 15:15); that is,

---

32. The Hebrew word "'*ayit*" does not indicate a species of bird but is a generic term for birds of prey; in the Bible, birds of prey can symbolize the gentile nations. See Ezek 17:3 and Zech 5:9.

33. Sarna, *Genesis*, 117.

34. Wenham, "Symbolism," 61–78; 134–37.

35. For *terbemah* as "deep sleep," see Gen 2:21; Job 4:13 and 33:15–16. In the last of these, the word is associated with dreams: "In a dream, a night vision, when deep sleep falls on men, while they slumber [*betenumot*] on their beds. Then He opens men's understanding, and by disciplining them leaves His signature" (Job 33:15–16); cf. Isa 29:10. See also *BDB*, 922. Hartley suggests that "*tenumah*" refers not to a deep natural sleep but to a "stupor that God causes to fall upon a person, blocking out all other perceptions, in order that the person may be completely receptive to the divine word." See Hartley, *Job*, 112.

he will not witness the start of their servitude with his own eyes, nor even its incipient causes. His descendants, however, will have to wait outside the land until the fourth generation, when the sin of the Amorites reaches its full measure. After Abram hears this message, the text returns to the present time: the sun has set and the darkness of night begins; in this blackness, Abram sees a smoking furnace or oven[36] and a flaming torch that passes between the pieces of the slaughtered animals. These symbols are the emissaries of the Lord and signs of his presence. As mentioned before, "the deeds of the fathers are signs to the sons." The signs of God's presence in Gen 15 foreshadow future events. At the revelation on Sinai, smoke and fire appeared with the Lord (Exod 19:18 and 20:18). During the journeys of the Israelites in the wilderness, a pillar of cloud by day and a pillar of fire by night accompanied their camp (Exod 13:21).[37] The passing of God between the pieces ($g^ez\bar{e}r\bar{\imath}m$) is an allusion to God splitting apart ($g^ez\bar{e}r\bar{\imath}m$) the Red Sea and the Israelites passing through it (Ps 136: 13).

The covenant included the promise of the land to Abraham's descendants. It gives the ideal boundaries of the land from the river of Egypt to the great river Euphrates. The river of Egypt is not the Nile, but it is modern Wadi el-Aris in the northeastern Sinai. It is full of water only after substantial rain, which creates a barrier between the Negev and the Sinai Peninsula (Num 34:5; Josh 15:4; 2 Kgs 24:7). The other river boundary in the northeast is the Euphrates. But even at the height of Israelite hegemony during David's and Solomon's empire (1 Kgs 5:1, 4), these borders never actualized; it is unlikely that they extended as far as the Euphrates.[38] The geographical details are supplemented by a list of ten non-Israelite people who occupied the promised land, which includes the Kenites, Kenizzites, Kadmonites, Hittites, Perizzites, Rephaim, Amorites, Canaanites, Girgashites and Jebusites. This is the most comprehensive list, which includes ten different ethnic groups.[39] There are

---

36. The idiom "smoking furnace" has no parallel elsewhere in the Bible. Parallels are found, however, in a series of oaths against witches from Maqlû, where we read, inter alia, "I sent out against you repeatedly a going [i.e., lighted oven (*āliku timūru*)], a fire that has caught"; cf. Maqlû II, line 19. See also Soden, "Wörterbuch," 127. It is possible that here, too, we have an ancient oriental image that had been forgotten by other biblical authors.

37. On the links between the revelation at Sinai and the "covenant between the pieces," see Van Seters, "Confessional," 448–59.

38. Malamat, "Aspects," 1–17.

39. Later we read that God gave Israel the territory of only seven nations (Deut 7:1).

seventeen such lists in the Hebrew Bible; some of the lists include seven ethnic groups, some include six or five, and one only has three.[40] Strangely, the Kenites, Kenizzites, Kadmonites, and Rephaim who do not appear in another list are mentioned here, while the Hivites who appear in all other lists are missing from our list. The Kenites and Kenizzites are tribes of the Negev and were absorbed in Judah, which solidifies our belief that the list is from an earlier period. The Kadmonites are mentioned only here, probably identical to the Kedemites, or "easterners" (Gen 29:1), the inhabitants of the eastern desert. The Jebusites appear last on the list; they were the residents of Jerusalem prior to its conquest by David. It was from Arauna the Jebusite that David bought the land on which the temple was built. Thus, it appears the narrator foreshadows here the possession of the city by David.

AN ANCIENT STORY

Speaking about Gen 15, Westermann wrote that it "not only stands at the center of external structure of the Abraham narratives, but also regarded in the history of exegesis right down to the present as the very heart of the Abraham story. God's covenant with Abraham and Abraham's faith appears as the kernel of which the Bible says about him."[41] The origin and the time of Gen 15 is fiercely debated. It is suggested that it is a late composition, a combination of royal court, cult, prophetic narrative conventions, and legal spheres.[42] Alternatively, it is an ancient story of a covenant between God and Abraham, covenant where God promised Abraham offspring and the promise of the land. Nehemiah understood the covenant as a response to Abraham's act of faith and Gen 15:6 served as a link between the two parts of the chapter (Neh 9:8. Van Seters suggested that the Abrahamic tradition is from a late-exilic period and the words of Gen 15 are addressed to the exilic community.[43] According to him, 15:7–21 tells the Jew of exile "exactly where he stood and what his future was if he would exercise faith in this word

---

The Kenites, Kenizzites, and Kadmonites—identified as Edom, Moab, and Amon—will become Israel's passion in the future (Isa 11:14).

40. Sarna, *Genesis*, 359.

41. Westermann, *Genesis*, 230.

42 Van Seters, *Abraham*, 260.

43. Van Seters, *Abraham*, 264.

of salvation from the God of Abraham."[44] In that period, the image of Abraham was the ideal for the people in exile. But in the late-exilic period, what distinguished Jews was the observance of the Sabbath, circumcision, and dietary laws that cannot be applied to Abraham.[45] More than that, it is strange that there is not a single word in the chapter that mentions salvation and deliverance from exile, which was the main concern of that period.

The oracle to Abraham came after his battle with the kings. It came to assure him of God's protection: "Fear not, Abram, I am a shield to you."[46] "Fear not," in its various grammatical forms, appears some eighty times in the Bible as a formula of encouragement and comfort. Its sense is made clear by the expressions that accompany it: "I am a shield to you" (Gen 15:1); "for I am with you" (Gen 26:24).[47] Similar formulas are known from the ancient Near East. The prophecies to Esarhaddon begin with the expression "fear not," after which we find "I will go before you," "I will protect you," and so on.[48] Similarly, the god appears to King Zakir of Hamath and Lu'ath and says, "Do not fear, for I have made you a king, and I shall stand by you and deliver you from all these kings who set up a siege against you."[49] The assurance to Abraham appears in the form of a covenant that includes the promise of many descendants and the promise of the land. These promises, in particular the promise of the land, could not be from a later date that was projected by the narrator back into the patriarchal period. The covenant and the animal rite are modeled on a concept of a land grant from the second millennium; it took place after Abraham's battle with the kings.[50] The promise of the land was part of the pre-Mosaic religion that was given to each of the patriarchs Abraham, Isaac (26:3–4), and Jacob (28:13–15). It was the first stage in the development of the promise motif. In Genesis, God is associated with each of the patriarchs. He revealed himself to them and protected them. In Gen 15

---

44. Van Seters, *Abraham*, 269.

45. Mathews, *Genesis 11:27–50:26*, 159.

46. The image of a shield is common in Psalms. Particularly close to our verse is Ps 3:4 where we read, "But You, O Lord, are a shield about me."

47. Similar language is found in the book of Isaiah: "I will be your help" (Isa 41:13); "for I will redeem you" (Isa 43:1). See Conrad, "Fear," 143–45.

48. "(15)[Esarhad]on, king of the countries, fear not!"; "(20) I shall lie in wait for your enemies, I shall give them to you. I, Ishtar of Arbela, will go before you and behind you." Pfeiffer, "Akkadian Oracles and Prophecies," 449–50.

49. Rosenthal, "Zakir of Hamat and Lu'ath," 655; Greenfield, "Zakir," 182–83.

50. Weinfeld, "Covenant," 184–203.

the promise of the land is sealed by a covenant. The assurance of ownership of the land only makes sense when the patriarchs were present in the land and not in exile. The promise of offspring started to be materialized in the following chapters (Gen 16, 21). Abraham is depicted as one of the prophets that God tells the future. The future of his descendants encompasses exodus and conquest (15:13–16), which is linked to the promise of the land.

ABRAHAMIC AND DAVIDIC COVENANTS

The covenant between God and Abraham has its parallel with the covenant between God and David (2 Sam 7:4–16; Ps 89:4). Both Abraham (Gen 15:6; 22:12, 16; 24:40; 26:5) and David (1 Kgs 3:6; 8:23) showed their loyalty to God. The covenants were unconditional and everlasting. Therefore, the Israelites in time of distress asked God to remember his covenant with the patriarchs, to be mindful, to pay heed, and to be active (Exod 2:24; 6:5; Lev 26:42, 45); the same is true with David (Isa 55:3; Ps 89:3). The Abrahamic and Davidic covenants share similar ideas, especially the continuation of offspring. This is expressed in analogous language: "But your very own issue shall be your heir" (Gen 15:4); and "one of your own issue, and I will establish his kingship" (2 Sam 7:12). The verses use the same verb and noun to convey the idea of the emergence of the issue of one's own body. The growth of Abraham's descendants into a nation came to its full fruition in the Davidic age when Israel became a state among the nations.[51] Similarly, as noted before, the promise of land to Abraham was never actualized; the closest it reached was during David's and Solomon's empire. This promise referred to the future of the conquest under Joshua and King David. It came to legitimize David's empire, which was achieved by military force. It is not a coincidence that there is a geographical link between David and Hebron, the place where Abraham was buried and the site of the shrine of Mamre.[52] The fact that, at first, Hebron was David's capital came to cement the connection between David and the ancestral figure of Abraham. More so the blessing that was given to Abraham that all the nations will be blessed by him was transferred by the Psalms to the David-Solomonic empire: "May his name be eternal; while the sun lasts, may his name endure; let men invoke

51. Clements, *Genesis 15*, 58.
52. Clements, *Genesis 15*, 58.

his blessedness upon themselves; let all nations count him happy" (Ps 72:17). Despite the similarities between the covenants, we should point out that there is a difference between them. In the Abrahamic covenant, the promise of the land is for all descendants, while to David it is a promise of a dynasty for one family. God and Abraham were witnesses to the covenant; David, on the other hand, received from the prophet Nathan a message from God. The similarities in idea and language between the covenants lead us to believe that the Abrahamic covenant is a product of the united monarchy. The three motifs—many descendants, settlement of the land, and the destruction of its inhabitants—suit this era. According to Mendenhall, "The tradition of the covenant with Abraham became the pattern of a covenant between YHWH and David.[53] The chosen Abraham became the chosen David, the 'seed of Abraham' became 'David and his descendants.'" Since the covenant promises were not fulfilled during the Abrahamic period, the covenant with Abraham was the "prophecy" and the covenant with David was the "fulfillment."[54]

Genesis 15 is a product of a later period, but the author used earlier material. This is evident from the description of the ritual to seal the covenant, which can be found in the treaties from the second millennium. An earlier period is also attested in the promise of the land, which is modeled on grant treaties in which the ruler took upon himself a unilateral obligation toward his servant, granting land to him and his offspring in return for his loyal service. The twofold promise of land and many descendants are recurring motifs in Genesis.

In conclusion, the intimate connection between the two parts of the chapter that contains offspring and the land promises suggests the unity of Gen 15. The "covenant between the pieces" followed Abraham's battle with the kings; it came to assure the patriarch of God's protection. It included the promise of the land and many descendants, themes that appeared already in previous chapters and are repeated later in the "covenant in the flesh." The promise of the land was accompanied by a ceremonial slaughtering of animals. The implication is that God binds himself by sanctions if he does not fulfill the conditions of his promise to Abraham. The twofold promises were of immediate concern to the patriarch and could not be from a later date that was projected by the narrator back into the patriarchal period. Assurance of ownership of the

---

53. Mendenhall, "Covenants," 72.
54. Mendenhall, "Covenants," 54; Freedman, "Commitment," 427.

land only makes sense when the patriarchs were present in the land and not in exile. The promises of land and descendants are intertwined and repeated to each of the patriarchs. The ritual ceremony in which the land was promised to Abraham has its parallel in the ancient world from the second millennium. There are similarities between God and Abraham's covenant and God and David's covenant. This is exemplified by the usage of equivalent language and ideas. This is not a mere coincidence, but it stems from the belief that Gen 15 was composed at the time of the united monarchy, and the narrator had at his disposal, ancient material that he inserted into the chapter. The covenant between God and David was modeled after the covenant between God and Abraham. It displays continuity between Abraham and David, thus further legitimizing the house of David.

In the next chapter, we will examine another covenant—"the covenant in the flesh"—its meaning and link to "the covenant between the pieces."

Chapter 5

For I Make You the Father of a Multitude of Nations

The second covenant between God and Abraham is the "covenant in the flesh." At least eleven years passed from the first announcement of the "covenant between the pieces," and Sarai was still barren. This raised questions about whether the promises of the first covenant were still intact. To remove any doubt, God reconfirmed his promises and oath to Abraham. He changed Abram's name to Abraham and Sarai's name to Sarah. Abraham was promised to be a father of a multitude of nations. God will keep an everlasting covenant with Abraham and his offspring, which will entail the possession of the land. The matriarch Sarah is designated as the mother of Isaac. Nations and people shall issue from her. The twofold promises—descendants and land that are mentioned in Gen 17—are a recurring motif in the Abrahamic story and run throughout the rest of Genesis. Like the "covenant between the pieces," this covenant is also sealed by a ritual, the ritual of circumcision that marked the recipient of the promise. The law of circumcision is mentioned in the legislation of Lev 12:3, but according to Gen 17:9–14 God already ordered Abraham to circumcise every male in his household. The antiquity of the practice of circumcision is also attested among different cultures of the ancient Near East. Considering the purpose of this rite and its significance in later periods, it is suggested that the composition of the chapter occurred in the exilic period, which came to answer concerns over kings, land, and the practice of circumcision. In addition, there are questions about the literary make-up of the chapter. Von Rad, for example, had argued that Gen 17 belongs to the Priestly document, and it does not have a unified structure and continuity.[1] On the other hand, McEvenue maintained that the chapter is a "completely original literary unit" and the repetitions within the narrative stem from style and structure and not from different sources.[2] These views raise further queries about whether Gen 17 is a double of Gen 15—in other words, it is presupposing and supplementing it in various ways—or whether it is an independent composition based on earlier sources. We start our study of Gen 17 by examining its structure.

STRUCTURE

The chapter can be divided into four parts: (1) Abraham would become the father of many descendants, and his name is changed (Gen 17:1–8); (2) the law of circumcision is set (17:9–14); (3) Sarah would become the progenitrix of nations and kings, and her name is changed (17:15–22); and (4) the law of circumcision is implemented (17:23–27). The first three parts are set within God's speech. He appears to Abraham in 17:1a and leaves in 17:22. The last part, 17:23–27, describes the enactment of God's command. God's speech contains a promise (17:3b–8), a command (17:9–14), and a promise (17:15–21). The promises are directed to Abraham and Sarah and include a change of their names. In other words, the promise is the main motif of Gen 17. The acceptance of the promises was sealed by the rite of circumcision. It is God who is mostly speaking in the text, which is one-sided and resembles divine discourse. There are five speeches by God to Abraham: (1) 17:1b–3a; (2) 17:4–8; (3) 17:9–14; (4) 17:15–16; and (5) 17:19–21. The speeches are counterbalancing each other. Therefore, speeches one and two (17:1c–8) report the promise of many descendants and speeches four and five (17:15–21) specify that Sarah will be the mother of Abraham's heir. The third speech, the central one (17:9–14), includes instruction on circumcision, which is carried out after the conclusion of the divine address.[3] McEvenue pointed out that each speech is similarly introduced, each is of comparable length, and each must be considered as a unit dealing with circumcision.[4]

1. Rad, *Genesis*, 197.
2. McEvenue, *Narrative*, 146, 147–48.
3. Van Seters, *Abraham*, 286.
4. McEvenue, *Narrative*, 157.

A Abraham ninety-nine years of age (17:1a)

B YHWH appears to Abraham (17:1ba)

C God speaks (17:1bb)

D First speech (17:1bc–2)

E Abraham falls on his face (17:3a)

F Second speech (name-change, nations, kings) (17:4–8)

G THIRD SPEECH (17:9–14)

F' Fourth speech (name-change, nations, kings) (17:15–16)

E' Abraham falls on his face (17:17–18)

D' Fifth speech (17:19–21)

C' God ceases speaking (17:22a)

B' God goes up from him (17:22b)

A' Abraham ninety-nine years of age and Ishmael thirteen (17:24–25)[5]

The exchange between God and Abraham is very limited and Abraham's response to God is laconic. He threw himself on his face when God appeared to him (17:3a, 17); he laughed and raised doubt that Sarah would have a son (17:17b). He speaks only twice—once to himself (17:17) and once to God, when he fears for the life of Ishmael (17:18). The analysis by McEvenue ignores major themes such as circumcision and oath. As he himself admitted, presenting the structure of the chapter in these terms alone "would be to treat it too extrinsic or formal a point of view."[6] So, he also suggested that Gen 17 be arranged as two parallel panels.

A YHWH's intention to make an oath about progeny (17:1–2)

B Abraham falls on his face (17:3a)

C Abraham the father of nations (17:4b–6)

D God will carry out his oath forever (17:7)

E The sign of the oath (17:9–14)

A' God's intention to bless Sarah with a progeny (17:16)

B' Abraham falls on his face (17:17–18)

C' Sarah mother of a son, Isaac (17:19)

---

5. McEvenue, *Narrative*, 158.
6. McEvenue, *Narrative*, 158.

D'	God will carry out his oath forever (17:18b, 21a)
E'	The sign of the oath (17:23–27)[7]

This parallelism includes the oath and its contents, the birth of Isaac, and the circumcision. It combined the command of circumcision and its fulfillment, elements that are not found in the palistrophe. The chapter is set with the introductory and concluding statement of chronology. Abraham's age, ninety-nine years old, is mentioned in the first part of the chapter (17:1a) and it seals the last section of the chapter (17:24a). Also included is a statement about God appearing to Abraham (17:1b) and God leaving Abraham (17:22).

In addition to parallel structure, the Hebrew word "*b'rīt*" served as a leitmotif of Gen 17, and it occurs thirteen times in the chapter.[8] It appears with the promise of many descendants (17:4) and as a covenant between God and Abraham and his descendants (17:7). The theme of the *b'rīt* is mentioned in the second section of the chapter that deals with the law of circumcision (17:9, 14). Since Isaac is singled out as the future heir of the covenant, the theme of the *b'rīt* recurs in 17:19 (twice) and in 17:21. By repeating the word *b'rīt*, the author created a link between the different parts of the chapter. It stressed the importance of the covenant between God and Abraham and Isaac and the act of circumcision that serves as a sign of the covenant. It connects the promise with the command. Not surprisingly, the Hebrew word for circumcision and covenant became identical in Late Hebrew.

CHANGE OF NAME

God changed the patriarch's name from Abram to Abraham and his wife's name from Sarai to Sarah. Names were given by parents at birth, but here God changes the patriarch and matriarch names at midlife. A name in the ancient world was not just for identification, but it conveyed the essence of the man and who he was. To name a person meant to know him and to have power over him.[9] When a name was changed, it signaled a change, the person outgrew his old status: Jacob–Israel; Joseph–Zepanath-paneah; Joshua–Hosea-Joshua; Chananiah, Mishael, and Azeriah

---

7. McEvenue, *Narrative*, 159.

8. Westermann, *Genesis*, 256.

9. A person who gives a name has power over the object; therefore, Adam gave names to all the cattle, birds, and beasts to illustrate his dominance over them (Gen 2:20).

to Shadrach, Meshach, Abed Nego. A new era or a new state policy in the ancient world was marked by a new name. A king who acquires a new throne receives a new name. King Amen-hotep IV of Egypt was noted for ending Egyptian traditional polytheism; when introducing the worship of Aten, his name was changed to Akh-en-aten. When Pharaoh Neco appointed Eliakim son of Josiah in place of his father, he changed his name to Jehoiakim (2 Kgs 23:34). Similarly, when the king of Babylon appointed Mattaniah, Jehoiachin's uncle, as a king, he changed his name to Zedekiah (24:17). Even in our times, when the inauguration of a new pope in Rome takes place, the pope receives an additional name. In Jewish tradition, the name Haim is added to a person who is very ill to confuse the angel of death so that he will not find the home of the sick person.

The change of Abraham and Sarah's name marked a change in their destiny. The longer form of the name Abraham is only a variation in dialect. It is explained as the insertion of *h-* in a weak root or a long syllable. This phenomenon is attested in the Hebrew Bible in the name Yoseph to *Yhoseph* (Ps 81:6) and is found in Ugaritic[10]—*bhtm*, from *bt*, the feminine plural *umht, amht, qrht, ilht*—and occurred in Aramaic[11] and Phoenician.[12] Abraham's name is changed since he would be a father of a multitude of nations. This was already conveyed to Abram when God elected him: "I will make of you a great nation" (Gen 12:2). The Gemara explains that "initially he became a father, a minister, and a prominent person, only to Aram, so he was called Abram, father [av] of Aram, and ultimately with God's blessing he became the father of the entire world, so he was called Abraham, father of the masses [*av hamon*], as it is stated: "I have made you the father of a multitude of nations" (Gen 17:5).[13] Ibn Ezra suggested that the name is derived from the "strong one" (*Abir*) of the multitude (*Hammon*) of nations (*goyim*). The name Abraham as well as the other patriarchs Isaac and Jacob are part of onomastic types that existed before Israel emerged as a nation; they were transmitted by a very early tradition. No person was given the name of Abraham, Isaac, or Jacob in all scriptural literature. The names are found in every region that the patriarchs lived in. Since the editors of Genesis could not understand the meaning of these names, they used popular etymology. Therefore, as

---

10. Gordon, *Ugaritic Manual*, 7, 8.
11. Albright, "Names," 203.
12. *KAI* 18:3; 122:2.
13. *Ber.* 13a.

mentioned above, Abraham was given this name because he was to be the "father of multitudes" and because of the assonance with "multitude."[14]

Sarai's name was changed to Sarah. The ending ׳ _ (*ay/ya*) was widespread in West Semitic feminine names from the second millennium BCE mainly from Ugarit where names such as *Pidray*, *Ṭallay*, and *ʾArṣy* are found.[15] From the first millennium, the ending ה ָ (*ah*) became more common. The change of Sarai to Sarah signifies her new, universal status. The Gemara explains, "Initially she was a princess only to her nation: My princess [*Sarai*], but ultimately she became Sarah, a general term indicating that she was a princess for the entire world."[16] Since Abraham had a new status as a father of a multitude of nations, his wife also had to take a more universal status which is embodied by her new name as princes not only for Abraham. Sarah's name foreshadows her role as the progenitrix of the future Israel.[17] The sages maintained that a change of name brings a change of man's fate.[18] And according to Ralbag, after Sarai's name was changed, she was blessed with a child. It is at this stage that God promised Abraham that he would have a son through Sarah: "I will give you a son by her" (Gen 17:16), and kings of peoples will rise from her. This promise is parallel to the promise that was made to Abraham: "And kings shall come from you" (17:6).

Reacting to God's announcement, Abraham threw himself on his face and laughed (17:17). This is the second time that Abraham reacted in this manner. He threw himself on his face when God appeared to him (17:3) in reverence of God and gratitude for the good news. But here he also laughed, which is a result of joy and surprise. Ramban explained that Abraham was surprised since he did not have a child with Sarah when they were younger; now when he is one hundred years old and she is ninety it seems unreal. He did not express surprise when God told him (17:6) that nations would descend from him, but only when God told him that his descendants would be from Sarah was he was astounded. It was his laughter that is linked to the name Isaac; later it would be repeated with Sarah's laughter when she doubted that she could bear a child (18:13). Sarah's laughter would turn to a joyous laugh after she gave birth to Isaac (21:6). Three times the Bible refers to the birth of Isaac, and

---

14. Vaux, *Early History*, 199.
15. *UT* 62; Cross, "YHWH," 246–47.
16. *Ber.* 13a.
17. Sarna, *Genesis*, 126.
18. *Roš Haš.* 16b.

in these three occurrences the name relates to human laughter (17:17; 18:12; 21:6).[19]

THE PROMISE MOTIF

God promised Abraham that he would make him exceedingly numerous (Gen 17:2). The promise is repeated in verses 4, 6, 16, and 20. According to Malbim (Meir Leibush ben Yehiel Michel Wisser, 1804–1879), repeated assurance comes to remove any doubt from Abraham that the circumcision will prevent his potency. The covenant between God and Abraham includes Abraham's descendants. It is the first time that they are part of the covenant, an everlasting pact. It recalls the covenant between God and Noah (Gen 9:16) and the Sinai covenant (Exod 31:16). The patriarch will be a father of a multitude of nations, which is usually understood as referring to the nations that are derived from Abraham: the descendants of Ishmael and Keturah (Gen 25:1) and Esau (Gen 36). But the language used here is figurative; Abraham will become the spiritual father of many nations. In addition, there is a promise by God that "kings shall come forth from you, (17:6), which is repeated with Sarah (17:16) and later with Jacob (35:11). The mention of kings alludes to the future Davidic dynasty. In a message to David by the prophet Nathan, the promise of everlasting kingship is promised to him (2 Sam 7:16, 24–29). The book of Psalms repeats that promise (Pss 89:29–30, 37; 132:12). David's kingship was considered the high point of national development.

God also promised Abraham and his descendants an everlasting holding of the land of Canaan. The promise of the land reflects an early form of tradition (Gen 12:6). Ramban, in his commentary, pointed to the difference between the current promise of the land and the previous one. The present promise states that although the Israelites would be exiled from the land, it would be their possession and they would return to it. The idea of everlasting possession of the land is repeated later to Jacob and conveys that only God can give it. The promise of many descendants and the promise of the land of Canaan is repeated with each of the patriarchs, and is one of the original elements of the Hebrew Bible.[20] These promises were eventually fulfilled. God also promised to be God to

---

19. There is a wordplay with the name Isaac. Ishmael played with Isaac (Gen 21:9), and Isaac fondled Rebecca (Gen 26:8; "to play" and "to fondle" are two other meanings of the root *s.h.q*).

20. Noth, *History of Israel*, 121.

Abraham and to his offspring, which is stated twice (Gen 17:7–8). Being God to Israel and dwelling in their midst is repeated many times in the Hebrew Bible (Exod 29:45; Lev 11:45; 22:33; 25:38; 26:45; Num 15:41). It expresses the idea that God chose Abraham and his descendants as his people, which distinguishes them from other people. There is an unbreakable bond between the Jewish people, the land of Israel, and God. The promise of the land is bounded by the promise of the divine presence. What we have is threefold promises: many descendants, the land of Canaan, and the promise to be Israel's God.

Like Abraham, Sarah also received a promise of progeny, a promise of childbearing. But the message was not delivered to her directly; it was Abraham who was the recipient of this message from God. The message about Sarah in Gen 17:16 is the counterpart to 17:6. Before, Abraham was the receiver of the promise of nations and kings; now, it is Sarah by nursing her own child who will give rise to nations and kings. In other words, the promises to Abraham will be realized through Sarah. God is blessing her; it is the first time that the word bless appears in Gen 17. Sarah will be blessed with a son (17:16a) and numerous progeny (17:16b), which points to the significance of the two blessings. The promise of a son is repeated in 17:18, but here God gives him the name Isaac. This promise of a son to Sarah is repeated for a third time (17:21); a time limit is set "at this season next year," which foreshadows Gen 18:10, 14. More importantly, God will maintain his covenant with Isaac and his offspring, an everlasting covenant. To remove any doubts, God declares it twice: "Sarah your wife shall bear a son, and you shall name him Isaac, and I will maintain My covenant with him as an everlasting covenant for his offspring to come" (Gen 17:19). It is repeated in 17:21 where He declares, "My covenant I will maintain with Isaac whom Sarah shall bear to you at this season next year."

CIRCUMCISION

Inserted between the promises to Abraham and Sarah is the law of circumcision. The appearance of the law in our chapter seems to be derived from a collection of laws. The declaration, which opens God's order, is typical of laws in ritual texts. It is in second person plural, which suggests that it was addressed to the whole community and not to an individual. Every male at the age of eight days should be circumcised. These include homeborn slaves and the one that Abraham bought. Eight days is significant because the newborn completed seven days, which corresponds to seven days of creation.[21] According to Exod 22:29, the firstborn of an animal is dedicated on the eighth day after birth and the text in Lev 22:27 states that an animal may not be sacrificed until the eighth day after birth. The rite of circumcision is a law, but the reason for it is not given in the Torah. Jewish philosophers tried to give a rationale for it. Among the different explanations, Maimonides's (1108–1204; also known as Rambam) interpretation stands out; he said that the commandment was not given "as a complement to a deficient physical creature, but as a means for perfecting man's moral shortcomings . . . for circumcision counteracts excessive lust."[22] Circumcision was originally commanded only to Abraham. The patriarch circumcised his son Ishmael and every male in his household. Ishmael was circumcised as an example to others. According to the rabbinic legend, the practice of circumcision was known before.[23] Abraham knew exactly what to do although no instruction was given to him. The usage of a flint-blade knife for circumcision points to the antiquity of this custom (Exod 4:25; Josh 5:2).

The act of circumcision serves as an external sign of the covenant like the rainbow was with Noah (Gen 9:13); the blood of the paschal lamb (Exod 12:13); the tefillin (Exod 13:9, 16; Deut 6:8; 11:18); and the Sabbath (Exod 31:12, 17; Ezek 20:12, 20).[24] It is a symbol of dedication and commitment to live life according to the covenant, a constant reminder for the Israelites that they are God's people and he is their God who chose them. Performing the act of circumcision links every generation to the covenant between Abraham and God. It shows the commitment of every Jew to God, a mark of his identity that distinguishes him from other people. Neglecting to perform the ritual meant a break of the covenant. The punishment for it was *karet*, which is carried out by divine execution. In Rabbinic literature, it indicates premature death and childlessness (Lev 20:18–20).[25]

---

21. Sarna, *Genesis*, 125.
22. Maimonides, *Guide for the Perplexed*, 3:49.
23. Gen. Rab. 42:8.
24. Fishbane, "'Sign,'" 213–34.

25. *Sifra Emor.* 14:4; *Moʿed Qaṭ.* 28a; *TJ Bik.* 2:1. For further study on the subject of circumcision, see chapter 10.

According to Van Seters, Gen 17 "represents a movement toward reconstituting the religion of Israel for the condition and needs of the post-exilic period."[26] If this is the case as we discussed in Gen 15, it is strange that there is not a single word in the chapter that mentions salvation and deliverance from exile. Scholars believe that Gen 17 is a work of P's account. Circumcision was of priestly concern and was important at the time of the exile. From the Second Temple period, circumcision was a distinctive sign of Judaism. The book of Judith mentions that Achior, after "seeing all that the God of Israel has done, believed firmly in God. He circumcised the flesh of his foreskin, and he has been united with the house of Israel to the present day" (Gen 14:10). At the exilic period, circumcision was a sign of religious distinctiveness in contrast to earlier periods when it was a rite that symbolized entrance into the community. But if this assumption is correct, then how could we explain the mention of Ishmael's circumcision in a later period? As Weinfeld observed, "Who would be interested in the time of the exile, when circumcision became the badge of Jewish distinctiveness, to share this very symbol of devotion with the Ishmaelites?"[27] The command of circumcision that was given by God to Abraham is tied to the covenant between God and Abraham to give him and his descendants everlasting possession of the land. For the first time, the chapter mentioned the future birth of Isaac (17:15–22), and that Abraham carried God's command and circumcised himself, his son Ishmael, and all the males of his household. The covenant between God and Abraham, its fulfillment to Isaac and his descendants, and the command of circumcision are all tied together. As previously mentioned, the act of circumcision served as an external sign just as the rainbow did for the Noachian covenant and the Sabbath did for the Mosaic covenant; they are a constant reminder of God's promises that Israel belongs to God. This link between circumcision and the election of Israel is mentioned in the book of Jubilees (15:30). Other nations also practice circumcision but there is a difference between them and Israel. For Israel, circumcision had a religious meaning—it was a sign of a covenant with God. Circumcision and covenant became identical and the Late Hebrew term b°rīt has the same meanings. For the other nations, it had different meanings such as a sign of unity.

---

26. Van Seters, *Abraham*, 293.

27. Weinfeld, "Covenant," 203; Haran, "Religion," 42–43; Hamilton, *Genesis Chapters 1–17*, 480.

GENESIS 15 VERSUS GENESIS 17

Eleven years had passed since God told Abraham, "That one shall not be your heir; none but your very own issue shall be your heir" (Gen 15:4), and Sarai was still barren. There was a question of whether God's promises were still intact. Genesis 17 answers Abraham's question of an heir as the matriarch Sarah is designated as the mother of Isaac. The covenant in chapter 17 represents the reconfirmation of God's covenant and promises of chapter 15. Similar features are found in the "covenant between the pieces" and the "covenant in the flesh." The latter is presupposing and complements the former in several ways, which led scholars to characterize it as a confirmation of the initial covenant.[28] On the other hand, some scholars maintain that although the author of chapter 17 is aware of past events in Abraham's life, this does not support a literary dependence.[29] However, a close reading of chapters 15 and 17 shows a striking resemblance in themes and language. Both record divine theophany (15:1; 17:1–2), and the covenants are described by the word "$bərît$" (15:18; 17:2, 4, 7, 9–11; 13–14, 19). But in chapter 17, the covenant is defined as everlasting between God and Abraham and his offspring throughout the ages. Abraham is an active player in the covenants. In the first one, he took the animals as God ordered him to cut them in two, placing each half opposite the other; in the second one, he circumcised every male in his household. Both mentioned a promise of a son, but in chapter 17 it is Sarah who is elected as the mother of Abraham's son. A promise of many descendants (15:18; 17:8) and national territory (15:7, 18; 17:8) is mentioned, but in 17:8 the territory is an everlasting holding. Abraham's reaction is recorded as doubt, complaint (15:3, 8), the act of homage (17:3, 17), and laughter (17:17). This is not mere coincidence, and the connection between the two chapters was recognized by the biblical authors. In the book of Nehemiah, there is a prayer that combines elements from the two chapters: "You are the Lord God, who chose Abraham, who brought him out of Ur of the Chaldeans and changed his name to Abraham. Finding his heart true to You, You made a covenant with him to give the land of the Canaanite, the Hittite, and the Amorite, the Perizzite, the Jebusite, and Girgashite—to give it to his descendants (Neh 9:7–8).

Wenham pointed out that in Gen 12:1–3, God promised Abraham land, descendants, and a covenant relationship. These three elements are

---

28. Williamson, *Patriarchal Promise*, 315; Sarna, *Genesis*, 123.
29. Alexander, *Literary Analysis*, 170–82.

repeated in the following chapters, and their completion is fully displayed in chapter 17, which is the climax of these promises.[30] The land becomes "this land" in 12:7, "all the land which you can see" (13:15) "and from the river of Egypt to the great river, the Euphrates" (15:18). In chapter 17, the land is identified as the land of Canaan and it is for everlasting holding: "I assign the land you sojourn in to you and your offspring to come, all the land of Canaan, as an everlasting holding" (17:8).[31] Abraham was promised to become "a great nation" (12:2). In the following chapter he was promised that his descendants would be so numerous as the dust of the earth that cannot be counted (13:16). Chapter 15 states that Abraham would father a child, and his descendants would be as numerous as the stars (15:5). Fathering a child is recorded in chapter 16 with the birth of Ishmael. But in chapter 17, Abraham would become a father of a multitude of nations and kings shall come forth from him (17:6); a child was to be born to him through his elderly wife Sarah (17:16-17). The covenant in chapter 12 includes a promise of blessing and cursing—blessing on Abraham personally, a blessing on whom he interacts with, and a blessing on the entire human race and cursing on those who cursed him (17:2-3). Chapter 15 gives us a glimpse into the future—the Israelites would be enslaved and oppressed in Egypt and then would be delivered from bondage (15:13-14). Chapter 17 further hints at the future when it speaks about kings, which is a reference to the Davidic dynasty. The word "covenant" appears thirteen times in nine verses.[32] The chapter is the culmination of all the blessings and promises of an heir, many descendants, and the land. In chapter 17, God tells Abraham "to be God to you" (17:7-8), which is typical covenant language where God elects Israel to be his special people. This entails complete loyalty and commitment by the Israelites.

One of the marks of allegiance to God and his covenant is the requirement of circumcision. The other demand that is mentioned is "walk in My ways and be blameless" (17:1). Ramban links this command with Deut 18:13 wherein "you must be wholehearted with the Lord your God." Accordingly, humans should completely trust God who is the only one who has the power to do and to undo. They should be undivided in their loyalty to God, do whatever he commands, and rely on him as we read in Joshua: "Now, therefore, revere the Lord and serve Him with undivided loyalty;

---

30. Wenham, *Genesis 1–15*, 16–17.
31. Wenham, *Genesis 16–50*, 16–17.
32. Gen 17:2, 4, 7, 9, 10, 11, 13, 14, 19.

put away the gods that your forefathers served beyond the Euphrates and in Egypt, and serve the Lord" (24:14).

Notably, there is continuation to Gen 17 in Gen 18, which presupposes it. The verses that describe the announcement of a son to Sarah (18:9–15) appear to know chapter 17. The assumption of the etymology of Isaac and the usage of the names of Abraham and Sarah suggests that the author of chapter 18 was familiar with chapter 17. The promise of a son with the phrase "at the time next year" (18:10, 14) is based on the phrase "at this season next year" (17:21). This explains why Abraham does not show any surprise at the announcement of a birth of a son in chapter 18.[33] God's words in 18:19 "to keep the way of the Lord by doing what is just and right" are clearly modeled after "walks in My ways and be blameless" (17:1).

In conclusion, the "covenant in the flesh" continues the theme of many descendants and the promise of the land. It presupposes and complements the "covenant between the pieces"; it is a confirmation of the initial covenant. Abram and Sarai's names are changed, marking a change in their destiny. The patriarch would be a father of a multitude of nations and the matriarch the progenitrix of the future Israel. The rite of circumcision is tied to God's promise to give Abraham and his descendants everlasting possession of the land. It is not a reprojection from a later period, it is a rite that has its origin in antiquity. It is a symbol of dedication and commitment to live life according to the covenant, an external sign as the rainbow and the Sabbath. This is a constant reminder for the Israelites that they are God's people, and he is their God who chose them. In the next chapter, we will examine the story of Sodom and Gomorrah, their destruction, and Abraham's image in light of Gen 18.

---

33. Wenham, *Genesis 16–50*, 19.

Chapter 6

Will You Sweep Away the Innocent with the Guilty?

The story of the destruction of Sodom and Gomorrah is described in Gen 18–19. The unity of these chapters is exemplified by the appearance of the same characters in most of the scenes; the angels in 18:1–19:23, Lot in chapter 19 and by insinuation in 18:20–32, and Abraham throughout chapter 18 and 19:29.[1] In addition, many similar expressions are found in the two chapters. God decided to destroy these cities because of the grievous sins of its inhabitants. Abraham tried to persuade God to avert the calamity. Since not even ten righteous people were found in the cities, the judgment was executed. The story also contains a message of life. The three mysterious visitors who came to Abraham told the aged patriarch that his old wife Sarah would have a son. The story continues in chapter 19 where two of the three mysterious visitors went to Sodom. There the visitors were welcomed to Lot's house while the inhospitable people of Sodom came to molest them. There is a sharp contrast between Abraham's hospitality to the guests and how the Sodomites welcomed them. To protect Lot and his family, the visitors led them out of Sodom for safety. The cities of Sodom, Gomorrah, and two other cities in the plains beside Zoar were destroyed. The location of Sodom and Gomorrah is an open question, and several possibilities were offered by scholars. Therefore, the different possibilities will be assessed. The nature of the catastrophe is unclear: Was it a volcanic eruption that took place, or maybe

---

1. Wenham, *Genesis 16–50*, 40.

it is a description of one of the last earthquakes that formed the lower Jordan Valley? Considering chapter 18, how do we define Abraham's character? What did he do that made him such an important man in the history of mankind?

WELCOMING THREE STRANGERS

"The Lord appeared to him by the terebinth of Mamre" (18:1), is an editorial note like in the previous chapter: "The Lord appeared to Abram and said to him" (17:1). God disappeared from Abraham's sight following his instruction for the rite of circumcision (17:22). The Lord reappears to Abraham who was sitting at the entrance of his tent as the day grew hot. In the Talmud, we find that it was the third day after the circumcision, which was considered the most painful day (Gen 34:25).[2] Since there is no direct communication following this statement, the Talmud cites this verse as the reason for visiting the sick.[3] In contrast to previous theophanies, there is no mention of an act of worship or building an altar by Abraham. Thus, in the Talmud we read,

> Rav Yehuda said that Rav said on a related note: "Hospitality toward guests is greater than receiving the Divine Presence, as when Abraham invited his guests it is written: 'And he said: Lord, if now I have found favor in Your sight, please pass not from Your servant (Genesis 18:3).'"[4]

Maimonides, in *Guide for the Perplexed*, suggested that God appeared to Abraham in a prophetic vision. Genesis 18:2 describes the vision where Abraham saw three angels, and the whole exchange in the chapter took place in a vision.[5] Ramban refuted this assertion and said that if this was a vision then Sarah did not bake cake and she did not laugh, neither did Abraham prepare a bullock. He also points to Jacob's wrestling with the angel and wonders, if this was in a prophetic vision, then why did Jacob limp when he awoke. Ramban agrees with Maimonides and says that when the Scripture states an angel is being seen or heard, it refers to a vision since human senses cannot perceive an angel. According to him, this is still below the level of prophecy, and he points to several degrees

---

2. B. Meṣ. 86b.
3. Soṭah. 14a.
4. Šabb. 127a; Šebu. 35b.
5. Maimonides, *Guide for the Perplexed*, 3:43.

of prophecy. When the Torah describes angels appearing as humans as in our story, there is a special glory created in the angel that is known among students who are familiar with the mysteries of the Torah as a "garment." This allows humans to have visions even when they are awake. Ramban concluded that he could not explain any further.

Lifting his eyes Abraham saw three men who were standing near him. There was nothing superhuman about their appearance and Abraham perceived them to be human. Indeed, they bathed their feet and ate. Genesis 19, the next chapter, mentions "the two angels," which suggests that the one who was left with Abraham was different. This led to the belief that the three visitors were God and two of his angels. The two angels who accompanied God were messengers of death who came to destroy Sodom (19:13). This is like Hab 3:5 where "Dever and Reshef" ("Pestilence and Plague") escorted the Lord.[6] In the ancient Near East, the war god is often depicted as assisting in the battle by other gods.[7] Genesis 18 is the only place in the Hebrew Bible where three heavenly visitors appear. Greek mythology displays similar stories that describe the appearance of gods in different forms; in the *Odyssey* we read, "Aye, and the gods in the guise of strangers from afar put on all manner of shapes, and visit the cities, beholding the violence and righteousness of man."[8] This comparison with Greek mythology raises difficulties since it comes from a later period and a different culture.

Abraham ran towards the visitors greeting them and bowed to the ground as an expression of honor. It is not clear to whom Abraham was speaking—to the leader of the three ("My Lord") or all of them ("My Lords"). The verbs in verse 3 are in the singular, which suggests that he spoke only to their leader, but verses 4–5 are in the plural. Ramban pointed out that the *kametz* in the word "'*Adonāy*" implies that it refers to God—"My Lord." If it were secular, it would be vocalized "'*Adonê*" with a *patach*—"My Lords." Since it is written with *kametz* and Abraham was speaking with the angels, Ramban suggested that it was because he referred to them by the name of their master, and for this reason, he bowed to them. However, at this stage, Abraham was not aware of the identity of

---

6. The biblical description is close to the appearance of Haddad the storm god in the epic of Gilgamesh: "With the first glow of dawn, a black cloud rose up from the horizon. Inside it Adad thunders, while Shullat and Hanish go in front, moving as heralds over hill and plain." See Speiser, "Gilgamesh," 94.

7. Hiebert, *Victory*, 93; Miller, *Divine*, 8–63.

8. *Od.* 37:485–87.

his visitors, and it is unlikely that he would address any of them as God.[9] He probably addressed one of them who he identified as their leader.

Abraham is portrayed as a gracious host to ordinary human beings, total strangers. He offered water and invited his guests to bathe their feet and recline under the tree in its shade. He then offered them a morsel of bread, but instead prepared a lavish feast. According to the Talmud, "Rabbi Elazar said: 'From here we learn that the righteous say little and do much, whereas the wicked say much and do not do even a little.'"[10] He hastened to the tent and ordered Sarah to hurry to bake cakes, then ran to the herd, took a calf, and gave it to a servant boy to prepare it. Ramban pointed to Abraham's great desire to show kindness and hospitality. Abraham had many servants in his house, and he was old and weak following the circumcision. Still, he rushed to the tent, urged Sarah to make bread, and afterward ran to the herd and chose a calf to prepare for his guests. His actions show how eager he was to perform a good deed.

Abraham provided his guest with a calf, which was a sign of princely hospitality.[11] The main animals used for meat consumption were sheep, goats, and cattle. It was not prudent to slaughter animals that provided for cheese, curds, and milk. Meat was eaten only on special occasions, such as in our story. Abraham also provided his visitors with curds and milk. One of the by-products of milk is curd. It is believed that curds are the thick fatty part of milk, which is known today as yogurt. Milk was considered among the finest food. It was a symbol of abundance, as in a "land flowing with milk and honey" (Exod 3:8, 17; Num 13:27; Deut 6:3; Jer 11:5). In Isaiah, milk is counted among the basic foods, such as water, grain, and wine. A similar view appears in Sir 39:26, which mentions milk as one of the products necessary for human life. In the ancient world, milk was served to the gods. It was thought of as a source of vitality and possessing curative powers. Milk played a role in ancient Egypt, and it was served to the gods and the dead. The Greeks also served milk to their gods; they offered it with honey and water. In Israel, on the other hand, there are no milk offerings. This is because man gets milk without real labor, unlike that which is involved in products such as grain, oil, and wine, which subsequently are presented as offerings.[12]

9. Speiser, *Genesis*, 129.

10. B. Meṣ. 87a.

11. When Saul consulted the medium at Endor, she slaughters a stall-fed calf (1 Sam 28:24).

12. The only ritual regulation concerning milk is found later in Exodus and

That Abraham offered the visitors a young roasted kid with milk troubled the sages because of their dietary regulations, which prohibited mixing meat and dairy. Thus, it was suggested that the angels ate dairy and meat separately, or they did not eat at all.[13] According to the Talmud, they only gave the appearance of eating: "And they ate bread? Can it enter your mind that they actually ate food? Rather, say that they merely appeared as though they ate and drank."[14] The whole time Abraham waited on them as the king's servants stood and attended to the king's needs while he ate, so Abarvanel interpreted. Offering food to the gods in the ancient world was the norm. The Keret epic and the epic of Aqhat mention sacrifices that were made to the gods. Special attention is paid to the Keret epic where he lost his wife before she gave him an heir. Thus, he asked El to bring his wife back so he could have children. But these comparisons are not valid, since, as noted above, Abraham is not aware of the identity of his guests. More so, there is no suggestion in the biblical texts that Abraham's actions were motivated because of Sarah's bareness; his acts are a testimony to him being a gracious host.[15]

The angels asked Abraham, "Where is your wife, Sarah?" This was a rhetorical question that was intended to open their conversation with him like when God asked Adam, "Where are you?" (Gen 3:9). According to the Zohar, their questions were sincere because the angels did not know what was happening in this world except for what is necessary for their mission.[16] The promise of a son was revealed to Abraham, and the angel said that he would return next year. The phrase "next year" occurs only in our verse (18:10), in 2 Kgs 4:16, 17, and has its analogy in the Akkadian expression "*ana balaṭ*," or "next year."[17] The angel was speaking as God's messenger, suggesting that God would return.[18] As Ibn Ezra noted regarding 18:14, God himself said that he would return. God indeed returned. As we read in Gen 21:1, "The Lord took note of Sarah as He has promised, and the Lord did for Sarah as He had spoken." A similar story

---

Deuteronomy: "You shall not boil a kid in his mother's milk" (Deut 14:21).

13. *Gen. Rab.* 48:14.

14. *B. Meṣ.* 86b.

15. Hamilton, *Genesis*, 11.

16. Daniel, *Zohar*, 2:1:102a.

17. Lambert, *Babylonian*, 288. For a survey of the different interpretations, see Yaron, "*Kā'eth*," 500–501.

18. This is similar to the Hagar story where the angel spoke to Hagar (Gen 16:10) but was speaking as God's messenger.

appears in the writings of the Roman poet Ovid.[19] He wrote about an old childless man by the name of Hyrieus who was visited by three gods—Jupiter, Mercury, and Neptune—who dined with him. After the meal, they asked him to make a wish. Since he was childless, he asked for a son. In a miraculous way his wish was fulfilled, and he begot a son named Orion.[20]

During this exchange, Sarah was listening at the entrance of the tent. The narrator tells us that Abraham and Sarah were old, which came to explain why Sarah laughed in 18:12. Furthermore, we are told that her regular menstrual cycle had ceased. Sarah laughed at herself, literally within herself. Being withered, she was wondering whether she could have a child; her reaction shows disbelief. It was her reaction that caused God to be angry with her since this is not beyond God's powers. According to the Midrash, "[God said], 'I can create man from the beginning, yet [you would say] I cannot restore them to their youth!'"[21] But Sarah lied to God and said that she did not laugh, she was frightened. Her fear stems from realizing that God was reading her thoughts.

The messengers delivered their message about Sarah, and they continued their mission. They went to Sodom as it is written: "The two angels arrived in Sodom" (19:1), thus cementing the links between chapters 18 and 19. Before leaving, the angels gazed down looking toward Sodom. Each time that the word "gazing" is mentioned in the Torah it always appears with calamity, bringing evil. The only exception is Deut 26:15: "Look down from Your holy abode, from heaven, and bless Your people Israel." According to the Zohar, the compassion in Deuteronomy is like our verse: "They gazed—arousal of compassion to deliver Lot" [from Sodom]."[22]

Abraham went with the visitors "to see them off"; literally to send them. This indicates that Abraham was a gracious host, which is stressed in the Zohar:

> Rabbi Yeisa said, "If you say that Abraham knew they were angels, then why did he escort them?" Rabbi El'azar replied, "Because even though he knew, he regularly escorted all his guests. For a person must escort guests since all depends upon this."[23]

---

19. Ovid, *Fasti*, 5:494.
20. Delitzsch, *Genesis*, 44.
21. *Gen. Rab.* 48:19.
22. Daniel, *Zohar*, 2:1:104a.
23. Daniel, *Zohar*, 2:1:104a.

THE ANNOUNCEMENT ABOUT SODOM

One of the three visitors remained behind to speak with Abraham. Most of the commentators are of the opinion that it is God who is the speaker. He came to Abraham to visit him and was waiting while Abraham showed hospitality to the visitors. His appearance here comes to prepare the reader for what follows the announcement about Sodom. In Gen 18:17-21, the reader is informed that God was determined to pass judgment on Sodom and Gomorrah. As the prophet Amos noted, "Indeed my Lord God does nothing without having revealed His purpose to His servants the prophets" (Amos 3:7). God does not hide his intentions from the righteous; whatever he does or intends to do he does with the aid of the righteous. Their mission is to warn the wicked to turn back from sinning, so the wicked will not have any excuse about what he does.[24] According to the Midrash, "Even when the blessed Holy One grew angry over Sodom because of their wicked deeds and sought to overturn Sodom, He did not seal their decree of punishment before conferring with Abraham, as it is said: 'And YHVH said, 'Shall I hide from Abraham [what I am about to do]?'"[25] Like the prophets, Abraham is part of the divine council (Jer 23:18, 22) who hears the voice of God (Isa 6:8). God singled out Abraham because he knew that Abraham would instruct his children to keep the way of God by doing what is just and right, which is social justice. This is the only time in the patriarchal narrative where the moral religious mission of Israel is mentioned. Later, when the prophets described a future idyllic society, they mentioned David: "See, a time is coming—declares the Lord—when I will raise up a true branch of David's line. He shall reign as king and shall prosper and shall do what is just and right in the land" (Jer 23:5).[26]

Abraham would be made a great nation, and all nations would be blessed by him and his descendants would be a beacon of justice. God trusts that Abraham will transmit his heritage of righteousness and justice to his posterity.[27] It is ironic that God trusts Abraham to teach his children justice when Abraham himself raises the question of whether God will practice justice (Gen 18:25). The responsibility to teach the children and instruct them is repeated many times in the biblical law; it is the

---

24. Daniel, *Zohar*, 2:1:104b.
25. *Tanḥ. Gen.* Vayera, 6.
26. See also Isa 9:6; 16:5.
27. The Hebrew word "*sedekah*" can be explained as righteousness and charity. This already was noted in the "covenant between the pieces" in Isa 5:6.

duty of the parents to spread knowledge of God's laws (Exod 12:25–27; Deut 6:1–3, 6–7, 20–25). This teaching of morality *to walk the way of God* has guaranteed the posterity of Abraham's descendants.

In 13:13 there is a note that prepares the reader for the story of Sodom: "Now the inhabitance of Sodom were very wicked sinners against the Lord." It gives a reason for the destruction of the place. The upcoming destruction is already mentioned in verse 10. In the announcement about Sodom and Gomorrah to Abraham, "outrage" and "outcry" are the reasons for the upcoming calamity (18:20–21). The outcry is mentioned again in the next chapter in 19:13. The terms "outrage" and "outcry" indicate the anguished cries of the oppressed.[28] They connote pleas for help in cases of great injustices. According to the Ramban, the outcry is the cry of the oppressed begging for liberation. The prophet Jeremiah spoke about the prophets of Jerusalem; their behavior contributed to the breakdown of national morality and Jeremiah compared their acts to the inhabitants of Sodom and Gomorrah (Jer 23:14). These prophets were practicing adultery and false dealings. They encouraged evildoers without remorse. Speaking about Sodom, the prophet Ezekiel identified its crime with social injustice: "Only this was the sin of your sister Sodom: arrogance! She and her daughters had plenty of bread and untroubled tranquility, yet she did not support the poor and the needy" (16:49).

A different explanation is given in Gen 19. When the people of Sodom found out about the guests at Lot's house, they demanded to "know" them. The Hebrew stem *y.d.* includes a range of meanings, but in our verse it has a sexual connotation. As we read in Gen 4:1, "Now the man *knew* his wife Eve, and she conceived and bore Cain" (emphasis mine) This view appears in the Midrash that "we may know them for sexual purposes."[29] The description here refers to homosexuality, which was considered as one of the abhorrent behaviors of the Canaanites.[30] This view is expressed by Josephus, who said,

> About this time the Sodomites grew proud, on account of their riches and great wealth: they became unjust towards men, and impious towards God, insomuch that they did not call to mind

---

28. The two words "outrage" and "outcry" are interchangeable for the Israelites suffering oppression in Egypt (Exod 2:23; 3:7, 9) and the cry of the widow or orphan (Exod 22:21–22). Hamilton, *Genesis Chapters 18–50*, 20.

29. *Gen. Rab.* 50:5.

30. Lev 18:22, 24; 20:13, 23.

the advantages they received from him: they hated strangers and abused themselves with Sodomitical practices.[31]

The Talmud describes the horrific acts of the Sodomites. "They had beds on which they would lay their guests; when a guest was longer than the bed they would cut him, and when a guest was shorter than the bed, they would stretch him."[32] A similar description is found in Greek mythology where Procrustes also had a bed where he tried to fit his victim. In another description the Talmud mentioned a young girl by the name Riva; her name is a wordplay on the word "Rabbah" (great) "because the outcry of Sodom and Gomorrah has become great." According to the Talmud, the brutality towards the young girl sealed the fate of Sodom:

> There was a young woman who would take bread out to the poor people in a pitcher so the people of Sodom would not see it. The matter was revealed, and they smeared her with honey and positioned her on the wall of the city, and the hornets came and consumed her. And that is the meaning of that which is written: "And the Lord said: 'Because the cry of Sodom and Gomorrah is great [*rabba*]'" (Gen 18:20). And Rav Yehuda says that Rav says: "*Rabba* is an allusion to the matter of the young woman [*riva*] who was killed for her act of kindness. It is due to that sin that the fate of the people of Sodom was sealed."[33]

The intention to go down to investigate the cities by YHWH is clearly anthropomorphism. It is one of the ten instances when YHWH descended to the world.[34] God does not need to descend to the earth to see what is happening, more so, He already decided what to do with Sodom. The Torah uses this statement as an ethical lesson. A judge cannot pass a verdict in capital cases without investigating it personally. In *Perki Avot* we read, "Do not judge your fellow man until you have reached his place."[35] In other words, one should not pass judgment until he knows all the details. Radak suggested that the aim was to consider whether there were mitigating circumstances that would justify averting the punishment.

---

31. Josephus, *Ant.* 11:1.
32. *Sanh.* 109b.
33. *Sanh.* 109b.
34. *'Abot R. Nat.* 34.
35. *Pirkie Avot.* 2:4.

The two angels were sent to see how the Sodomites would treat them, which implies that the Sodomite's fate was not sealed, they were given a chance to repent. However, the concept of repentance is missing here. Abraham did not call his fellow humans to atone, he did not warn them about the imminent doom and neither did the angels. The motif of repentance appears only later in the Hebrew Bible. A classic example is the Jonah story where the prophet is sent to Nineveh to warn its inhabitants of the upcoming calamity so they can change and avert the disaster. One of the major duties of the prophets was to call upon the people to turn back to the way of the Lord, which ultimately would lead to forgiveness. The lack of the repentance concept in our story suggests that the story belongs to the earliest traditions of Israel.[36]

Beginning with fifty people, Abraham started to plead with God to save Sodom if there were fifty innocent people there, and he continued until the number ten. Abraham intercedes on behalf of total strangers. Before Abraham spoke with God for three times (Gen 15:2, 8; 17:7) and each time about his own well-being. Here, Abraham's virtue as a moral compassionate man who cares about other human beings is fully displayed. The Talmud points out that these qualities of Abraham were inherited by his descendants:

> Anyone who has compassion for God's creatures, it is known that he is of the descendants of Abraham, our father, and anyone who does not have compassion for God's creatures, is known that he is not of the descendants of Abraham, our father.[37]

Abraham is challenging God by asking if he will also sweep away the righteous with the wicked. He is concerned that the wickedness of some members of the community will bring destruction to the whole community. He believes that there are righteous people in the city, and they should not be destroyed with the sinners. In other words, "What determines God's judgment on Sodom, the wickedness of the many or the innocence of the few?" He raises the question of whether the merit of the righteous people will save the sinners and their lives spared. God agreed with Abraham that if even the number of righteous people is low, for their sake he would forgive the city. There are scholars who suggest that the question that is raised by Abraham reflects the important theme of

---

36. Sarna, *Genesis*, 133.
37. Beṣah. 32b.

the exilic period.[38] Discussing 18:20 von Rad says, "Actually, the section jumps over many generations and links up with the prophetic utterances about the Servant of God who works salvation 'for the many.'"[39] However, Abraham's questions are timeless, questions that are repeated over and over in the Hebrew Bible.

Abraham is wrestling with the question of individual vs. communal responsibility. He maintains that the existence of several righteous people should be a reason to save the entire community; he is asking for God's mercy. The question of individual vs. communal responsibility is controversial and is repeated in the Hebrew Bible.[40] It was believed that individual behavior influences the community. When God asked Cain, "Where is your brother Abel?" Cain answered that he did not know and "Am I my brother's keeper?" (Gen 4:9). His answer precisely shows that he is responsible for his brother. The people of Sodom were also responsible personally and collectively for the behavior of the entire city. What Abraham raised here was revolutionary—to spare the city on the merit of a few righteous people. Abraham's compassion and mercy for his fellow human beings are fully exhibited. He started at fifty and ended with ten and each time God gave the same answer. God agreed to forgive the whole place on the account of the righteous people. The Lord responded in the same way six times (18:26, 28, 29, 30, 31, 32) assuring Abraham that he will save the city. A small number of innocent men are more important, and He will show mercy and forgive the whole place. Later, in his words to the prophet Jeremiah, God said that even for one man He would exonerate the city: "Roam the street of Jerusalem, search its squares, look about and take note: you will not find a man, there is none who acts justly, who seeks integrity—That I should pardon her" (Jer 5:1). Abraham ended with ten people, which symbolized a community—in rabbinic Judaism, ten adults is the minimum for certain acts of public worship.[41] Community affairs could not be conducted with less than ten people (Ruth 4:2).

No extrabiblical sources refer to the story of Sodom and Gomorrah. The Greek and Latin authors who mention the catastrophe are from a later period and more than likely based their information on Jewish sources. Noth suggested that numerous local Palestinian traditions were

38. Van Seters, *Abraham*, 214.
39. Rad, *Old Testament Theology*, 395.
40. Exod 20:5; Deut 24:16; Jer 31:28; Ezek 18; 33:20.
41. *Meg.* 23b.

connected to the patriarchs, but originally those traditions were not associated with them. Those traditions included the entire story of Sodom, which is secondhand.[42] In other words, the biblical narrator adopted a popular saga and used it in accordance with his religious outlook. This might explain the attention to the moral lesson of the story and not to the description of the catastrophe itself.[43] Abraham, who received a call from God, appears here as a paradigm of the future prophets of Israel. In his acts, he foreshadows the later prophets who spoke against wickedness and injustice. He intercedes on behalf of total strangers—the wicked people of Sodom, gentiles who did not share with him the same values and beliefs. In his dialogue with God, he showed compassion towards other human beings. Abraham is the embodiment of the later prophets who spoke and demanded justice. His words and deeds are the fulfilment of following *the ways of the Lord*, which he transmitted to his descendants. Thus, the three major monotheistic religions—Judaism, Christianity, and Islam—perceive Abraham as their spiritual father.

THE ARRIVAL OF THE ANGELS AT SODOM

Chapter 18 provides the background and reasoning for the destruction of Sodom and Gomorrah. Chapter 19 continues the story and describes the destruction of the cities and its outcome. The two chapters, as noted before, appear as a cohesive unit and share similar elements. The angels who left Abraham's tent reappear in the opening scene. They appeared to Abraham as the day grew hot (18:1) and arrived in Sodom in the evening (19:1), which shows continuation. Abraham's hospitality to the angelic visitors (19:1–8) is matched by Lot's hospitality (19:1–3). The language in these two scenes is very similar. In addition, many expressions are found in the two chapters. Sarah's laugh (18:12, 13, 15) is paralleled by "his sons-in-law thought he was joking" (19:14). Other parallels include: "Will You sweep away" (18:23, 24) and "lest you be swept" (19:15, 17); Abraham's plea for Sodom (18:23–32) and Lot's pleas for Zoar (19:18–22); "to bring death" (18:25) and "I die" (19:19); "I will forgive" (18:26) and "I will grant" (19:21); "I will not destroy" (18: 28) and "For we are about to destroy. . . . sent us to destroy it (19:13)."[44]

---

42. Noth, *History of Israel*, 120.
43. Sarna, *Understanding*, 143.
44. Wenham, *Genesis 16–50*, 44; Rudin-O'Brasky, *Patriarchs*, 215–16.

Lot is a city dweller and he resides in a house. Following the feud between his herdsmen and Abraham's herdsmen, he chooses to separate himself from Abraham. The patriarch, despite his seniority, showed generosity toward Lot and gave his nephew the first choice of grazing land. Abraham wanted to avoid any confrontation with his nephew because as he said to him "for we are kinsmen" (Gen 13:8). Lot left the clan and moved next to Sodom; the fertility of the land attracted him. He examined the land but not its people; he was motivated by economic gains. He not only separated himself from Abraham but also separated himself from God. At first, he was living in the vicinity of the city (13:12). Later, he settled in the city (14:12), and his daughters were married to Sodomites (19:14). When the angels arrived at Sodom, he was sitting at the gate of the city, which served as a place for meetings, business transactions, and administration of justice. It was a place where the elders of the community (Deut 21:19; Josh 20:4) deliberated and publicized matters of public importance and prophets delivered their messages.[45] In Mesopotamia, royal inscriptions were displayed at the gate of the city.

The opening scene of Gen 19 is very similar to Gen 18. Like Abraham, Lot greeted the guests and bowed to them. He addressed them as my lords and himself as a servant. He invited the guests to his house to spend the night and bathed their feet. Then they could get up early and leave town. Before the visitors accepted Abraham's invitation, they refused Lot's invitation. Lot needed to urge them to come to his house; they wanted to spend the night in the square. Finally, they agreed and came to his house where he made a feast for them, which consisted of baked unleavened bread that was prepared quickly. Lot prepared a feast for them; the Hebrew word for "feast" indicates that wine was served. Later we read that Lot loved wine (19:32–35).[46]

The guests did not have a chance to lie down. All the people from every quarter of the city, young and old, surrounded Lot's house. They demanded he bring the guests out so they could be intimate with them. The mention of young and old suggests that the entire population of the city consisted of sinners. According to Ramban, the mistreatment of strangers was because the Sodomites tried to prevent strangers from

---

45. 2 Kgs 7:1, 18; Amos 5:10.

46. The word "feast" is mentioned with Abraham when the weaning of Isaac was celebrated (Gen 21:8). On that occasion, more than likely many people were invited and they probably loved to drink.

entering their fertile land; they refused to share their bounty with others.[47] Lot tried to be part of the community, but the local inhabitants rejected him. They referred to him as an alien, a person without any legal rights. They complained that he tried to act as a ruler. To protect the honor of his guests, Lot offered his two daughters "who have not known a man" (Gen 19:8). But later in 19:14 Lot was speaking to his sons-in-law. To solve this predicament the midrash states that Lot had four daughters: two betrothed and two married,[48] while the Vulgate translated "who were to marry," opting for a future tense.

THE DESTRUCTION OF SODOM AND GOMORRAH

Only two verses are devoted to the description of the destruction of the cities (19:24–25). Verse 24 describes the event itself, while verse 25 describes its consequences. This is because the Bible focuses on the moral significance of the events; the Bible has a didactic purpose that it tries to convey. The destruction is a punishment for the sinfulness of Sodom and Gomorrah. Twice the text stresses that it was the Lord who was responsible for the calamity, that it was not an accident but a punishment that was sent from heaven. According to the text, YHWH rains sulfurous fire. The description of the calamity might be a remanent of a catastrophe that took place. It is suggested by scholars that the disaster is described as an earthquake; cracks that are formed by seismic activity release gases of bitumen or asphalt and probably petroleum.[49] In some instances, lightning appears when the earthquakes generate electrical discharge. The fire that is described was caused by the ignition of gases and outflows of asphalt coming from the region, through lightning or the scattering of fires. This resulted in a frightful blaze, which explains what Abraham saw when he looked toward Sodom—"the smoke of the land rising like the smoke of a kiln" (Gen 19:28).

The location of Sodom and Gomorrah is an open question, and several possibilities were offered by scholars. It is suggested that the cities of the plain—Sodom, Gomorrah, Admah, and Zeboim—were in the southern part of the Dead Sea, which is covered now by water. The site of the

---

47. See also *Tosef. Soṭah* 3:11.

48. *Gen. Rab.* 50:9. According to the midrash, "sons-in-law" refers to those who are already married, while those who were taking his daughters are different ones.

49. Rad, *Genesis*, 220–21; Sarna, *Understanding*, 142; Driver, *Book of Genesis*, 202–3; Skinner, *Genesis*, 310–12. Vawter, *On Genesis*, 241.

Will You Sweep Away the Innocent with the Guilty? 99

fifth city, Zoar, is probably at the southeast corner of the Dead Sea. The five cities of the plain were flourishing in the twentieth century BCE, and in 1900 BCE some catastrophe brought an end to the cities of Sodom and Gomorrah and the other two cities. This area was known as the Valley of Siddim (Gen 14); it was flooded as the water level of the Dead Sea rose because of the earthquake. The water from the northern part of the Dead Sea discharges into the south of el-Lisan. However, there is no evidence from the biblical text that the cities were destroyed by flooding. On the contrary, the Bible describes the region as its soil was devastated by sulfur and salt beyond sowing and growing grass (Deut 29:22; Isa 13:19–22; Zeph 2:9).

A clue that might help to determine the location of the cities is the location of Zoar, which was not destroyed. The angels urged Lot to escape at dawn to Zoar (Gen 19:15–23). He arrived as the sun rose, which suggests that Sodom and Zoar were in close range. This is based on the Bible, Josephus,[50] the sixth-century mosaic map of Palestine from Medeba, and the medieval Arab geographer al-Dimashqi (1256–1327) who said that "Zugar lies in the district of aṣ-Ṣâfîyah in the Gawr (or el Ghôr, the Rift Valley)."[51] This suggests that Zoar was a site on the stream Seil el-Qurahi, around es-Safi. This stream flows into the south end of the east shore of the Dead Sea, which is a logical location for Zoar. Excavation of the surrounding area reveals remains of the Bronze Age, Nabatean, Roman Byzantine, and medieval Arab settlements, but not any remnants from biblical times of the city of Zoar.

In recent years, a place named Bab edh-Dhra—in the southeastern Dead Sea plain situated on the eastern edge of the Lisan peninsula—was suggested as the site of the city of Sodom.[52] The site is located not far away from other places such as Safi, Feifa, and Khanazir. A second place, Numeria, was believed to be the site of the city of Gomorrah.[53] It was suggested that it was a colony of Bab edh-Dhra. Pottery remnants indicate a commercial exchange between the two cities.[54] The absence of tombs in Numeira and ceramic evidence led scholars to believe that the inhabitants buried their dead outside Bab edh-Dhra. Lapp referred to the place

---

50. Josephus, *J.W.* 4 and 482.
51. Strange, *Palestine*, 213; Astour, "Zoar," 1107.
52. Udd, "Bâb edh-Dhrâ '."
53. Wood, "Discovery," 67–80.
54. Milevski, *Goods Exchange*, 32–61.

as the graveyard of the "cities of the plain."[55] These sites were occupied during the third millennium BCE and were destroyed around 2300 BCE; they were resettled two thousand years later in Roman times.

Rast and Schuab suggested that Bab edh-Dhra was abandoned by its populations and "suffered exposure to fire."[56] It is also possible that natural disasters such as earthquakes or external attacks led to the abandonment of Bab edh-Dhra and Numeira.[57] According to them, Bab edh-Dhra and Numeira were destroyed at the same time, 2350–2067 BCE. Now it is believed that Bab edh-Dhra was destroyed in 2350 BCE and Numeira in 2600 BCE. In other words, Numeira was destroyed two hundred years earlier than the assumed date for the destruction of the city of Sodom.[58] If we accept this chronology, this does not coincide with the time frame of Abraham; biblical scholars believe that the patriarchs lived in the Middle Bronze period from the late third millennium to the mid-second millennium BCE (2166–1805 BCE).[59] Also, the site could not be the biblical Sodom since the place was too small (ten acres). More so, as noted by Wood, the time for the destruction is essentially not reliable.[60] In spite of all the chronological difficulties, Rast and Shuab's suggestion for the location of Sodom and Gomorrah are the most likely.

In conclusion, the story of Sodom and Gomorrah is the embodiment of the wickedness, of evil-minded people. The cities were destroyed because their inhabitants neglected the virtue of hospitality. According to Jeremiah, the sins were adultery and immorality, while Ezekiel spoke about the neglect to support the poor and the needy. The accusations against Sodom lie in the moral realm, inappropriate behavior against strangers, their disregard of hospitality, and sexual perversion. Sexual crimes were considered atrocious, which might explain the devastation that the cities suffered. On the other hand, we read of Abraham who is the model of a God-fearing man. He shows hospitality to his guests and pleads with God to save the lives of total strangers, pagans whom he does not know. He tried to understand God and to persuade him to change his verdict. Abraham's voice is heard before the execution of judgment, which shows Abraham's worthiness in God's eyes. Abraham is God's confidant;

55. Lapp, "Bâb edh-Dhrâ '," 25.
56. Schaub and Rast, *Expedition*, 46.
57. Rast, "Bâb edh-Dhrâ '," 560.
58. Udd, "Bâb edh-Dhrâ '," 157.
59. Bimson, "Data," 53–89; Price, *Stones*, 92.
60. Wood, "Discovery," 66–88.

he is part of the divine council. He is a compassionate man who cares about the life of other human beings in contrast to Noah who "was silent saying nothing not pleading for mercy."[61] There is only a brief description of the destruction itself. It is suggested by scholars that the disaster that is described is a distant memory of the actual calamity. More than likely, it refers to one of the last earthquakes that formed this area, which is the result of tectonic plate activity. This takes place when Earth's crusts bump into one another as they slide on top of the layer. Several locations were offered by scholars for Sodom and Gomorrah. The most logical site was Bab edh-Dhra for Sodom and a second place Numeria was believed to be the site of the city of Gomorrah. However, the time of their destruction raises some chronological problems, which suggest that more study is required. In the next chapter, we will examine the fulfillment of the divine promise of heirs to Abraham—the birth of Isaac and Ishmael.

---

61. Daniel, Zohar, 2:1:106a: "You saved yourself, but you had no strength to deliver your generation." *Deut. Rabb.* 11:3.

Chapter 7

For It Is Through Isaac That Offspring Shall Be Continued

Isaac, the long-promised son, was born to Abraham when he was one hundred years old and Sarah was ninety-one. However, he is not the firstborn son of Abraham. Sarah was barren, so the matriarch resorted to the device of concubinage, giving her maidservant Hagar to Abraham. Examination of the social customs of the ancient Near East reveals that this was the norm and the respectable course of action. The union of Abraham and Hagar resulted in conception, and Ishmael was born. Abraham was eighty-six years old at that time. Eleven years had passed since his arrival in Canaan. Finally, after fourteen years of delay, Isaac, the promised son to Abraham and Sarah, was born (Gen 21:2). The book of Genesis describes the joyful and delightful events that led to the birth of Isaac. His name means "laughter," as explained in several episodes. Three times the Bible refers to the birth of Isaac (Gen 17:19; 18:12; 21:6), and all three occurrences connect his name with human laughter.

As Isaac grew and was weaned, Abraham held a great feast. During the celebration, Sarah saw Ishmael amusing himself, "playing" (*měṣaḥēq*), with Isaac. Sarah was seized with fear that the son of the concubine would inherit Abraham's heritage and not her son. Therefore, she demanded Hagar and her son be expelled. Abraham hesitated to comply with Sarah's request, and only after God ordered him did he send Hagar and Ishmael into the desert. The scene of Hagar and her son going into the desert is very similar to a previous episode where Hagar ran away from Sarah to the desert. The main characters in these two stories are the same: a jealous matriarch, a willing Abraham, and an Egyptian slave—Hagar. This raises questions about the similarities between the stories, in addition to why the biblical narrator went to such lengths to describe all the details that led to the birth and expulsion of Ishmael. The birth story of Isaac is inserted between the two episodes, which describe Hagar in the wilderness. There is a lengthy description leading to the birth of Isaac. This is in contrast to the birth of Abraham, where we were told in a single verse, "When Terah had lived seventy years, he begot Abram, Nahor and Haran" (Gen 11:26). Hence, Isaac's birth story will be analyzed and compared to Ishmael's birth story. How close or different are these stories? Did the author intentionally point out the theme of rivalry between the brothers—one that is so prevalent in the book of Genesis—or was it to show the differences between the brothers? Alternatively, the author had some other considerations, such as a theological one, which he wanted to convey through the comparison between the two brothers.

THE BIRTH OF ISHMAEL

When God elected Abraham, he promised, "I will make of you a great nation" (Gen 12:2). Still, years passed by, and the promise of descendants remained unfulfilled. Throughout all the years, Abraham maintained his silence. However, in his first dialogue with God, which appears in the "covenant between the pieces" (Gen 15), Abraham complained to God that God did not grant him offspring of his own and instead it was his servant who would be his heir. Abraham referred to a custom that was prevalent in the ancient world in which a childless couple could adopt a person who would become their heir. In exchange, that unrelated person had to take care of the physical needs of the elderly couple.

To remove Abraham's doubts, God, for the second time, promised Abraham many descendants (15:5). Despite God's promise of many descendants, we are told again that Abraham's wife Sarah had not borne him any children (17:1). The subject of Sarah's infertility was mentioned before when Terah took his family to go to Canaan (11:30). However, here we have a slight change—the narrator tells us that God kept Sarah from bearing (17:2), whereas before we were told that Sarah was barren. This change evidently stems from the narrator's knowledge of future events. The theme of barren women is a repeated motif in the Hebrew

Bible. Hence, we read of the matriarchs Rebekah and Rachel, and later Samson's mother and Samuel's mother, Hannah, who were all barren.

Since the matriarch Sarah was a barren woman and God's promises remained unfulfilled, Sarah gave Hagar to her husband Abraham so they would have a son through her. How Sarah acquired Hagar, we are not told. Therefore, it is possible that Hagar was probably among the servants that Abraham acquired during his stay in Egypt (Gen 12:16), or that she was part of Sarah's dowry.[1] Hagar was given to Abraham after he lived in Canaan for ten years. Therefore, according to the Talmud, if a man spent ten childless years with his wife, he could remarry, for he was not destined to have children by her.[2]

The purpose of marriage was procreation rather than companionship. Marriage contracts from the ancient Near East stipulate that a wife who failed to bear children had to provide her husband with a handmaid who would bear children for them. This practice of surrogate motherhood is attested from the third to the first millennium BCE. For Sarah to give Hagar to Abraham so she would have a son through her was not unusual. The Code of Hammurabi makes a provision for a barren wife to give a slave to her husband so he can have children.[3] However, in this case, it speaks about a priestess who was not permitted to have children. Documents from Nuzi attest to the practice of a barren woman giving her husband a secondary wife to bear a son who would become both the heir and the regarded son of the mother.[4] In Assyria, a marriage contract stipulates that the wife had to buy a slave for her husband if, after a period of two years, she could not give birth. When the slave girl had given birth, she was to be sold again.[5] In a document from Egypt, which dates to the first eighteen years of Ramses XI, we read about a couple without children who acquired a slave girl who then gave the husband three children, all of whom were adopted by the wife and therefore became legitimate.[6]

---

1. In the Aggadah, Hagar was the daughter of Pharaoh. After he witnessed the deeds performed on Sarah's behalf in his house, Pharaoh gave Hagar to Sarah, saying, "Better let my daughter be a handmaid in this house than a mistress in another's" (*Gen. Rab.* 45:1).
2. *Yebam.* 64a.
3. Meek, "Code of Hammurabi," 172.
4. Gordon, "Biblical Customs," 1–12.
5. Finkelstein, "Additional Documents," 543.
6. Gardiner, "Adoption," 23–29.

At first glance, it appears the author of Genesis approved of Sarah's actions; however, it is more likely there is criticism toward Sarah. The matriarch does not wait for God's help but takes it upon herself to resolve the problem. This is a reminder of Abraham's previous behavior when, in times of crisis, he did not rely on God but passed his wife off as his sister. The wording of Gen 16:2–3 suggests the narrator's disapproval, which clearly alludes to Gen 3.

In the ancient world, barrenness was regarded as a disgrace. Thus, when Hagar became pregnant, her mistress was lowered in her esteem. According to Rashi, Hagar was boasting to the ladies, "Since so many years have passed without Sarah having children, she cannot be as righteous as she seems. But I conceived immediately!" Similarly, we read in the midrash, "My mistress Sarah is not inwardly as she appears outwardly. She pretends to be a woman of piety, but she is not, as she has prevented conception in order to preserve her beauty."[7] According to Radak, since Hagar assured Abraham's posterity, she no longer felt subservient to Sarah.[8]

Hagar's attitude provoked Sarah's jealousy. Sarah appealed to God to judge between them. She refers to the wrong that was done to her as "ḥamas," a term used to describe the sins that prompted the flood (Gen 6:11, 13) and the vicious retaliation by Simeon and Levi (49:5; cf. 34:25). According to the midrash, she was blaming Abraham: "You heard me insulted and did not speak up on my behalf."[9] Sarah was probably also afraid that her servant might usurp her place in Abraham's heart. She allowed Hagar to be an instrument of procreation but not to be a recipient of Abraham's feelings and love. Therefore, she mistreated Hagar. The Hebrew verb *vat'anneha* implies that Sarah subjected Hagar to physical and psychological abuse. Ramban, in his commentary, says, "The matriarch sinned by such maltreatment and Abraham too by permitting it." Abarvanel, on the other hand, says that Sarah's intent was not malicious but to force Hagar to cease her insulting demeanor. Instead of acknowledging Sarah's superior status, Hagar fled.

Sarah treated Hagar harshly, so she fled into the wilderness of Shur, which is an area between Beersheba and Egypt. As she was passing a

---

7. *Gen. Rab.* 45:4.

8. The Laws of Ur-Nammu deal with a similar situation when a female slave-concubine claimed equality with her mistress because she bore children: "If a man's slave woman, comparing herself to her mistress, speaks insolently to her (or: him), her mouth shall be scoured with one quart of salt." Finkelstein, "Laws," 525.

9. *Gen. Rab.* 45:5.

water spring, an angel of the Lord appeared to her. This is the first reference to "the angel of the Lord" in the Hebrew Bible, where it occurs forty-eight times—six of which happened in Genesis, with four instances occurring in chapter 16 (16:7, 9, 10, 11) and two related to the binding of Isaac (22:11, 15). The angel told Hagar that she was to bear a son. His name would be Ishmael and through him would come a multitude of descendants. Indeed, later we read that Ishmael became a father of twelve tribes (25:12–18). The name Ishmael means "God hears" because God heard Hagar in her affliction.[10] At first, she probably did not realize to whom she was talking, but during the conversation she realized his identity. The "man" she met in the spring called her Hagar, a slave of Sarah. Strangely, he knows her name but asks (16:8), "Where have you come from, and where are you going?" This is evidently a rhetorical question. It reminds us of God asking Adam "Where are you?" (3:9), and also when God asked Cain "Where is Abel" (4:9)? In contrast to Adam and Cain, who evaded and stalled, Hagar answered that she was running away from her mistress Sarah. She does not respond to "Where are you going?" Therefore it is possible she tried to avoid stating the fact that Egypt was her destination.

The angel told Hagar to return to her mistress and to submit to her harsh treatment. It appears that this command is a device used by the narrator to prepare the reader for the story of 21:9–21. In addition, since Hagar is not in mortal danger, the purpose of the appearance of the angel is to have Hagar return to Sarah. Hagar does not contest even though she knows that she will suffer. The commandment to submit to Sarah's harsh treatment does not coincide with 16:11, where it says that God has taken note of her suffering. Still, God is aware of her maltreatment and will compensate her. Indeed, the divine command is followed by the announcement that God will increase her offspring, which is like the promises to the patriarchs (Gen 17:2; 22:17; 26:24). Only after that is the reader informed of the birth of a son: "Behold, you are with child and shall bear a son; you shall call him Ishmael" (16:11).

The future son of Hagar would be a wild ass of a man; in other words, he would be an undisciplined freeman, which is the opposite of his mother.[11] This metaphorical use points to the nomadic lifestyle of Ishmael and

---

10 For more on the name of Ishmael, see Dahood, "Yišmaʿēl," 87–88.

11 A wild ass is an onager; unlike most horses and donkeys, onagers have never been domesticated. They are very fast, and their place of habitat is in waste places (Job 39:5–8; Isa 32:14; Jer 14:6; Hos 8:9).

his descendants. This way of life is found in Gen 25:18, which describes the territorial boundaries of the Ishmaelites' confederation. According to Ibn Ezra, he would not submit to the rule of strangers and would take what he wanted by brutal force.

Hagar was so moved by her theophany experience, that she called the Lord who spoke to her "El Roi," which can be translated in various ways: "God of seeing" (Targum Onkelos); "God of my seeing" (Bekhor Shor, Joseph ben Isaac, twelfth century; and Radak); and "God who sees me" (LXX, Vulg.). According to Rashi, "The God of seeing" sees the humiliation of the humbled. Although an angel, and not God, spoke to her, she realized that it was God's emissary. Indeed, numerous emendations have been suggested to produce the sense or give it the meaning of "You are a God of (my) seeing"; that is to say, "Did I really see God and have yet remained alive?"[12]

Hagar names the place "Beer-lahai-roi." According to Sarna, the original meaning was "the well belonging to the clan of Roi." In Arabic, *hayy* means "a clan," and Roi could be a proper name.[13] This, however, does not explain her experience; therefore, it is more likely to mean "the well of the Living One who sees me."[14] Targum Onkelos translates it similarly: "The well where the living angel appeared." This new name of the place expresses her excitement and thanksgiving. Later, the well became a place of prayer (Gen 24:62). According to Gunkel, the Bible describes legends about God and the tribal ancestor who met in a specific place. Jacob, for example, slept in a certain place resting his head on a stone while seeing the heavenly ladder. Later, this stone became a sanctuary (Gen 28:10–22). Similarly, the well in Lahai-roi became a sanctuary for Ishmael because his mother met God at this well.[15] Another explanation might be that it is not Hagar who named the well. This is based on the fact that the verb *qr'*, "he called," is masculine singular. Therefore, the subject could not be Hagar. According to *Midrash Sechel Tov*, it is Abraham in agreement with Hagar who gave it its name.[16] It is also possible that the descendants of Ishmael gave the spring this name when later they dug a well in the same place to commemorate the miracle that happened to Hagar.

12. Tsevat, *Meaning*, 63.
13. Sarna, *Genesis*, 122.
14. Wenham, *Genesis 16–50*, 11.
15. Gunkel, *Legends*, 33.
16. *Midrash Sechel Tov*, 11.

Hagar accepted the words of the messenger, returned home, and bore a son to Abraham. The parenthood of the patriarch is mentioned three times (Gen 16:15–16). Furthermore, Abraham named the boy, and by doing so he recognized him as his legitimate son. Probably Hagar told him of her encounter with the angel, therefore he knew what to name his son.[17] Surprisingly, Sarah is not mentioned at all even though we would expect to find her in light of the prediction "Go back to your mistress" (16:9). Hence, it is possible that Abraham protected Hagar.

The story of the birth of Ishmael in Gen 16 is the opening event for the later story of the displacement of Ishmael.[18] As the reader recalls, we have already been told in 15:3–4 that a slave is not to be Abraham's heir. In that chapter, Abraham's complaint was about Eliezer Damascus, which, according to Thompson, prepares the reader for the greater story of the displacement of Ishmael.[19] The story of the birth of Ishmael is a delay in God's promise to Abraham for a son and heir. The son of a slave woman cannot be his true heir or his true son. This ultimately will be changed with the birth of Isaac. Similarly, Benno Jacob says that the story about Ishmael is a necessary part of Abraham's story. Abraham shall have a son and heir; however, his birth by Sarah is delayed so that it will be more appreciated.[20] The birth of Ishmael is a result of human interference as it was the outcome of Sarah giving Abraham her concubine Hagar. The matriarch does not wait for God's help but takes it upon herself to solve the problem. Isaac, on the other hand, as we shall see below, was born because of God's involvement.

THE BIRTH OF ISAAC

As mentioned before, three times the Bible refers to the birth of Isaac (17:19; 18:12; 21:6), and in these three occurrences the name relates to human laughter. It is suggested that the original name of Isaac is Isaac-el, "El laughs." The name consists of an imperfect verb and divine name, which is also found in names such as Ishmael and Israel. The subject of the verb *shq* is the deity, not the father or the child. Hence, Isaac-el would mean "El smiles" or "El is favorable." Support for this can be found in

---

17. Jacob, *Genesis*, 107.
18. Thompson, *Origin*, 90.
19. Thompson, *Origin*, 90.
20. Jacob, *Genesis*, 107.

Ugaritic texts where the god El is said to smile in expressing his favor or satisfaction.[21] However, we should point out that the form "Isaac-el," or any proper name with this stem, is not found in the Hebrew Bible.

Abraham's reaction to the announcement of the birth of Isaac is quite puzzling: "O that Ishmael might live by Your favor" (17:18). According to Rashi, Abraham's response has two parts: (1) I am unworthy of a great reward as to have a son now; and (2) it will suffice if only Ishmael lives righteously before you. Ramban has a different explanation. According to him, Abraham feared that the birth of Isaac as his true heir might signal Ishmael's death, so he prayed for his life. Furthermore, it appears that God's words excluded the boy from the covenant. Abraham loved his son Ishmael and did not want to lose him. Clines suggests that Abraham's reaction shows that he does not believe in this future son and that he is perfectly content with Ishmael.[22] For Abraham, Ishmael is the fulfillment of the promise of an heir, a son of his own loin who was circumcised according to the covenant. God promised Abraham that he would be a father of a multitude of nations (17:4–6). Abraham thought that Lot and Ishmael were the fulfillment of God's promise, but for God, it was Isaac who would carry the Abrahamic promises.

In Gen 15:4, God tells Abraham that his heir will be a natural-born son, while Gen 17:16–21 states that Sarah would be the mother of his child. Finally, a specific time is set: "I will return to you next year, and your wife Sarah shall have a son" (18:10)! This announcement by the angels of the birth of a son is like the previous announcement to Hagar by an angel. God's promise will materialize, as we are told: "The Lord took note of Sarah as he had promised, and the Lord did for Sarah as he had spoken" (21:1). The fulfillment of the promise is mentioned twice in the verse, stressing that God's promise came to fruition. The narrator uses the verb *pkd*, "took note," to describe God's visitation to Sarah. The same expression "took note" also appears in Samuel's birth story.[23] It is suggested that this phrase appears when the infant is a child of destiny. The verb *pkd* is mentioned in the Hebrew Bible when God is directly involved in human affairs. This verb appears as a recurring motif of divine promises of a national redemption from Egyptian slavery (Gen 50:24–25; Exod 4:31); to end famine (Ruth 1:6); and to bring the exiles home (Jer

---

21. Stamm, "Isaak," 35.
22. Clines, *Eve*, 75.
23. Sarna, *Genesis*, 145.

29:10).[24] Alternatively, *pkd* is used when a husband visits his wife for sexual purposes (Judg 15:1). In other words, our story is a myth about Isaac's divine paternity. In the ancient world, various myths about sexual relations between gods and daughters of men were prevalent. As a result of these unions, the children that were born were half gods or were raised to the status of deities. Thus, the story of the birth of Isaac may follow this pattern. However, we believe that our story is about divine mercy, how God delivers one from a hard situation like infertility.

Sarah conceived as promised and bore a son to Abraham. The Bible mentions Abraham's advanced age—he was a hundred years old, which stresses the late arrival of his heir. It is a late gift by God. This is a typical folk motif that describes the divine promise of a son to an elderly couple. Indeed, in the story about the Shunammite woman we read that her husband is old, like the words that described Abraham (2 Kgs 4:14). In the same way, in the New Testament, Elizabeth was barren, and she and her husband Zachariah were old (Luke 1:7). These stories share a basic structure: (1) a mention of infertility; (2) a prediction of childbirth at a set time; and (3) the fulfillment of the promise as foretold.

Did Sarah become pregnant after the incident in Gerar or before? Did a year pass from Gen 17:21 ("But my covenant I will establish with Isaac, whom Sarah shall bear to you at this season next year") until Isaac's birth in 21:2? Or did nine months pass from Gen 18:10 ("I will surely return to you next year") to the birth of Isaac in 21:2? Was Isaac born after the story in Gen 20 about Abimelech? In that story, Abraham referred to his pregnant wife as his sister.[25] Clines suggests that at the beginning of chapter 20, Abraham still does not believe in YHWH's promise of Isaac. If he really believed in God, he would know that the child to be born is in danger, just like his mother. Another question that needs to be asked: is, What was Abraham doing at Gerar since there is no mention of famine? He puts his family in unnecessary danger.[26]

To remove any suspicion that Abraham is not the father of Isaac because Abimelech took Sarah to his harem, the author repeats twice that Abraham is the father of Isaac: "This is the story of Isaac, son of Abraham. Abraham begot Isaac" (Gen 25:19). This kind of usage is not recorded. However, later the chronicler used the same pattern to record that the sons

---

24. Wenham, *Genesis 16–50*, 80.
25. Clines, *Eve*, 75–76.
26. For more on these subjects, see chapter 7.

of Abraham were Isaac and Ishmael (1 Chr 1:28), and then again said that "Abraham begot Isaac" (1:34). Evidently, what the author wanted to emphasize was that Abraham is the father of Isaac, who is the sole successor to the Abrahamic covenant. Rashi, in his commentary on verse 19, says that there was a need to repeat twice that Abraham was the father. Scorners of that generation were saying "From Abimelech did Sarah conceive since for many years she tarried with Abraham and did not conceive from him." What did the Holy One, Blessed be He, do? He formed the features of Isaac's face similar to Abraham and there attested everyone, "Abraham begot Isaac." And that is why it is written here, "Isaac was the son of Abraham," for there is testimony that "Abraham begot Isaac."[27]

When Isaac was born, Abraham named his son as he was told to do by God (Gen 17:19). Because his name is fixed by God, Isaac is the only patriarch whose name was not changed. God revealed his name before he was born. Abraham circumcised him on the eighth day as set out in 17:12. Isaac is the first person who was circumcised on the eighth day, in contrast to Ishmael who was circumcised when he was thirteen. This detail comes to emphasize that Isaac is the true heir to the Abrahamic covenant. Surprisingly, we do not find any emotional reaction by Abraham at the birth of his son. On the other hand, the matriarch's reaction is recorded. Sarah breaks into laughter; this is joyous laughter in contrast to her earlier laughter of disbelief. She utters a short song: a poetic cry of joy that contains three lines with three Hebrew words in each:

> Who would have said to Abraham. That Sarah would suckle children! Yet I have borne a son in his old age. (Gen 21:7)

According to Sarna, the forms of the verbs and the stem *mll* seem to indicate that Sarah uttered an ancient poem.[28] It is suggested that "it is an ancient traditional form of informing the father: Sarah suckles a child!"[29] The second part of the announcement mentioned the cry of joy: I have born my husband a son in his old age! The last sentence (21:6b) refers to the surprise of others: everyone who hears will laugh with me.[30] It is suggested this call to celebrate the birth of the rightful heir was meant to insult Hagar and her son.[31]

27. See also *B. Meṣ.* 87a.
28. Sarna, *Genesis*, 146.
29. Westermann, *Genesis 12–36*, 334.
30. Westermann, *Genesis 12–36*, 334.
31. Mathews, *Genesis*, 268.

Abraham held a great feast on the day Isaac was weaned. This normally occurred at the age of two or three (1 Sam 1:22–24; Hos 1:8). In Egypt and Assyria, breastfeeding frequently lasted three years; this was also a prevalent practice in Israel during the Second Temple times.[32] One statement in the Talmud limits the practice to twenty-four months, while another refers to a period of four or five years.[33] It was a family feast that celebrated an important event that the child passed the first stage of his life.

The celebration was interrupted when Sarah saw Ishmael playing. The meaning of the word "playing" (*metsaḥek*) is not clear so it was given a different interpretation.[34] The LXX and Vulgate added "with her son Isaac" after playing. Thus, the question arises: Was Ishmael playing innocently with Isaac or abusing him? Paul, in his writings, suggests that Ishmael was "persecuting" (*edíōken*) Isaac (Gal 4:29). This can mean verbal or physical, as in sexual abuse. In the book of Jubilees, we find a different interpretation: "Sarah saw Ishmael playing and dancing, and Abraham rejoicing with great joy, and she became jealous of Ishmael" (Jub. 17:4). Ralbag pointed out that Ishmael mocked the great feast since he was also Abraham's son, but there was no feast when he was weaned. According to Benno Jacob, Ishmael boasted of his earlier birth just like his mother did (Gen 16:4).[35]

THE BANISHMENT OF ISHMAEL

The scene of Ishmael playing with Isaac was too much for Sarah. Therefore, she demanded that Abraham drive out Hagar and Ishmael. The narrator uses the verb "*gāraš*," which is the same verb that describes the banishment of Adam, Eve, and Cain from the garden of Eden (Gen 3:24; 4:14). This verb is also used in the Bible as a term for divorce (Lev 21:7, 14; 22:13), which is evidently implied here too. When Abraham later sent Hagar away, the Bible uses the verb "*shillaḥ*," which is used for divorce as well as the release of slaves (Deut 22:19, 29; 24:1, 3; Jer 34:9, 16; Mal 2:16). Sarah's forcefulness and determination are revealed in the expulsion of Hagar and her son. Ishmael was a legitimate son of Abraham and was entitled to the rights of inheritance. However, Sarah wanted the line of

---

32. 2 Macc 7:27.
33. *Ketub.* 60a; *Git* 75b.
34. Pinker, "Expulsion," 3–6.
35. Jacob, *Genesis*, 137.

Abraham to continue only through her son Isaac. Thus, she demanded that Abraham cast out the slave wife and her son. Though Ishmael is the main character in the story, he is not mentioned by name throughout the whole account. By not mentioning Hagar's and Ishmael's names, Sarah was belittling them. The matriarch did not have any relationship with Hagar, and she did not have any interest in Hagar's son. Sarah did not want Isaac and Ishmael to share Abraham's inheritance. Children who were born to a slave wife could inherit along with the children of the primary wife.[36] The laws of Lipit-Ishtar indicate that the father may grant freedom to the slave woman and her children, and by doing so they would forfeit their share of the paternal property.[37] Sarah was not afraid of the division of the inheritance; what she feared was Ishmael. She was afraid that his physical powers and seniority would drive Isaac away, and Ishmael would seize the entire inheritance for himself.

Sarah's demand was very painful for Abraham who became distressed. Abraham considered Ishmael his son. The fact that he rejected his son in this fashion does not bode well with Abraham as a moral man. It was only after God confronted him that he complied with Sarah's request. The line of Abraham would continue through Isaac. God referred here to Ishmael as "the youth" rather than "your son." Later, in Gen 21:14, when Abraham fulfills God's order to expel Ishmael and Hagar, he refers to Ishmael as "the boy" rather than "my son."

God told Abraham to listen to Sarah. In many biblical texts, important decisions about family, children, and succession were determined by the women. This is evident here with Sarah and later with Rebekah. God told Abraham to heed Sarah and trust her judgment because, as a woman, she had a deeper insight into the character than he did. It was Sarah's vision and foresight that determined the continuity of the family. Here, Abraham is subordinate to Sarah. The sages pointed out that the patriarchs were dependent on the superior powers of the matriarchs. They said that Sarah possessed prophetic powers and was one of the seven prophetesses, and her prophetic gifts were even superior to Abraham's.[38] Since Abraham loved his son, Ishmael, God reassured Abraham that no harm would befall Hagar and Ishmael in the wilderness. Ishmael was a descendant of Abraham with a great future awaiting him, and he would be rewarded with greatness and would also become a nation (Gen

---

36. Fensham, "Son of a Handmaid," 312–21; Thompson, *Historicity*, 263–67.
37. Kramer, "Lipit-Ishtar," 160.
38. *Exod. Rab.* 1:1.

21:13). This blessing is a repetition of the former blessing that God promised Abraham about Ishmael: "And I will make him a great nation" (Gen 17:20). These promises are like promises that were given to the patriarchs.

Early in the morning, Abraham took bread and the water container, giving them to Hagar. He did it early in the morning since he probably wanted to do it privately. He was reluctant to send Hagar with his son and did not want to show any emotion in the presence of his wife Sarah. He supplied Hagar with basic provisions, which is quite puzzling. Calvin is baffled by Abraham's behavior:

> But with how slender a provision (*tenui . . . viatico*) does he endow his wife and son? He places a flagon of water and bread on the shoulder. Why does he not load an ass, at least, with a moderate supply of food? Why does he not add one of his servants, of which his house contained plenty, as a companion?[39]

Was it Abraham's secret intention to make sure Hagar could not go too far? The fact that Hagar was able to carry the boy, bread, and water sack shows that Abraham indeed gave her very little. According to Calvin, Abraham's treatment of Hagar and Ishmael is the result of pride and ingratitude:

> God willed that the banishment of Ishmael should be so harsh and sorrowful (*tam dura et tristis*), so that his example might strike terror into the proud, who . . . trample under the foot the very grace to which they are indebted for all things. Therefore, he led them both to a miserable end.[40]

Cohen, on the other hand, sees in Abraham's behavior an expression of his total faith in God: "Convinced that God had great, though awesome, plans for Ishmael, Abraham was in no way callous in sending the young Ishmael off into the desert with only his mother to protect him. As far as Abraham was concerned, his son had a far greater Protector than his mother to secure his safety."[41] Nikaido, meanwhile, suggests that "the meager supply of provisions (contrast Gen 25:6) given to Hagar and her infant son for a grueling trek through the desert (cf. Exod 15:22f) conveys a clear message: Ishmael is not the heir—not anyone's heir."[42]

---

39. Calvin, *Commentaries*, 548; Thompson, "Hagar," 223.
40. Thompson, "Hagar," 223.
41. Cohen, "Abraham," 181.
42. Nikaido, "Hagar and Ishmael," 224.

Hagar probably went toward her native Egypt, but she lost her way in the wilderness of Beersheba. When the water supply was gone, Hagar left her son under one of the bushes so at least he would be protected from the sun. She was anticipating his death as she could not prevent it. To avoid seeing his death and hearing his cries, she sat at a distance. The distance is described as a bowshot away, which alludes to Ishmael's later profession as a bowman (Gen 21:20). Hagar was crying and so was Ishmael. God heard Ishmael's cries in light of his promises to Abraham. It is God who hears the cries of the boy, but it is the angel of God who called Hagar. The mention that "God heard" further explains the name "Ishmael," which was given in chapter 16. As noted previously, this chapter never mentions—not even once—the name Ishmael, instead he is described as a "son," "lad," or a "child." As Wenham points out, the cryptic reference to Ishmael's name is meant to recall his origin: "You shall name him Ishmael, for the Lord has noticed your oppression" (16:11).[43] The promise given to Abraham in 21:13, that Ishmael would become a great nation, is repeated here (21:18) because in verse 13 it was only Abraham who heard it. Now it must be repeated to Hagar since she now takes the place of his father Abraham.

The two stories about Hagar in 16:1–4 and 21:8–21 contain many similar details. The main characters are the same: a jealous matriarch, a willing Abraham, and the Egyptian slave Hagar. The jealousy of Sarah is mentioned in both stories and Abraham's reaction is similar, namely, he accommodated Sarah's request. In both stories, Hagar leaves and goes into the wilderness. In the wilderness, God reveals himself at the well and delivers a message of encouragement and posterity. It is because both accounts contained common features that it has been suggested that they were alternate accounts of the same incident.[44] Despite the common motifs in 16:1–16 and 21:1–21, there are still some differences between the two stories. In the first story, Hagar runs away from Sarah; in the second story, she is banished. In chapter 16, there is rivalry between the barren Sarah and her pregnant maidservant; but in chapter 21, the main issue is a conflict over the inheritance. In chapter 16, Hagar knows her way; in chapter 21, she loses her way. In the first story God hears of the mistreatment of Hagar; in the second he hears the crying of the boy. In the first story, the unborn child receives his name and so the well also gets

---

43. Wenham, *Genesis 16–50*, 85.

44. Skinner, *Genesis*, 285; Speiser, *Genesis*, 156; Rad, *Genesis*, 191; Gunkel, *Genesis*, 158.

a name; in the second story, there is no mention of the boy's name or that of the well. In the first story, Hagar sees the well; in the second the angel has to open her eyes in order to see the well. In the second story, Hagar is in great distress; while in the first one, she takes the initiative and runs away.[45]

To solve the literary and chronological difficulties in the texts of Gen 16:1–14 and 21:1–21, modern scholars who adhere to the documentary hypothesis assign the first tradition about Hagar (16:1–14) as predominantly J, with P inserting verses 1a, 3, 15–16; the second story (21:1–21) is entirely E. It was also suggested that 16:9 was a late redaction whose purpose was to give sequence to the narrative. However, the attempt to assign these narratives to different sources proves to be unconvincing. As Speiser notes, "The various emendations that have been proposed merely substitute one set of problems for another. An acceptable solution has yet to be discovered."[46] More than likely the stories have an etiological purpose, which is to explain the name Ishmael. Therefore, the root *šmʿ* is repeated in the two chapters. The verb *šmʿ* is part of the name Ishmael. Abraham heeds (*šmʿ*) Sarah's request when she offers him her maid (16:2). The angel tells Hagar that she will call her son Ishmael because "the Lord has paid heed (*šmʿ*) to your suffering" (16:11). When Sarah requests Abraham to expel Hagar, God tells Abraham, "Whatever Sarah tells you, do as she says (*šmʿ*)" (21:12). When Hagar loses her way in the desert the text says: "God *heard* the cry of the boy.... God *heeded* (*šmʿ*) the cry of the boy" (21:17). The stories serve as an etiology of the Ishmaelite-Hagarite tribes and to explain Ishmael's presence in the wilderness. These stories were linked to the theme of Isaac. However, this combination created chronological problems that did not exist when these traditions were independent.

According to Gen 16:16, Abraham was eighty-six years old at the birth of Ishmael and one hundred when Isaac was born (21:5). This would make Ishmael more than fourteen years old when he was expelled (21:10–19). Ishmael is repeatedly referred to as a child (21:14, 15, 16), and boy (21:17, 18, 19, 20). It is inconceivable that Hagar carried her son who was fourteen on her back. Speiser pointed out that the Hebrew text is obscure, and the translation of the LXX and Syr. "would not guarantee its authenticity"; he translates verse 14 as follows: "Early next morning

---

45 For the differences between the texts, see Alexander, "Hagar," 132–33; Emerton, "Abraham," 53–56; Neff, "Annunciation," 51–60.

46. Speiser, *Genesis*, 155.

Abraham got some bread and a skin of water to give to Hagar. He placed them on her back and sent her away with the child."[47]

What emerges from our study is that chapters 16 and 21 are different and are not variant accounts of the same event. There were two stories of the banishment of Hagar—one before her pregnancy and a second one after the birth of Isaac. The story in chapter 21 anticipates that the reader is familiar with the events narrated in chapter 16.[48] The banishment account of Hagar and her younger son was combined with the story of the birth of Isaac in Abraham's old age by a later redactor.

ISHMAEL VERSUS ISAAC

The stories of the birth of Ishmael and Isaac come to show the differences between the two brothers. Ishmael is a hunter, while Isaac, as the reader will discover later, is quite a peaceful tent dweller. Ishmael's story explains etiologically how Ishmael received his name and became a Bedouin. It describes the nature of the Ishmaelites as a wild nomadic people who roamed the desert between Israel and Egypt; as it says, "He shall be a wild ass of a man; his hand against everyone. And everyone's hand against him; he shall dwell alongside all his kinsmen" (Gen 16:12). Hunting is not mentioned much in the Hebrew Bible. The only hunters who are mentioned are Nimrod ("a mighty hunter," Gen 10:9); Ishmael ("a bowman," Gen 21:20); and Esau, who is described as going to the field with a quiver and bow (Gen 27:2). The Bible held hunting in low esteem and has a negative attitude toward hunting as a way of life. Much of Near Eastern art portrays kings as engaged in hunting, but not so the Israelites or Judean kings. The animals that the Israelites used for sacrifice were restricted to domesticated animals.[49] By describing Ishmael as a hunter, the biblical narrator shows his contempt toward Ishmael. In other words, he is not worthy of being Abraham's heir, so it is the second son who would become the next patriarch. It is notable that in the Hebrew Bible, we have many examples of the younger brother replacing the older brother. The first example is Isaac and Ishmael, but later there are Jacob and Esau, Zerah and Perz, Ephraim and Manasseh, David and his older brothers, as well as Solomon and Adonijah.

47. Speiser, *Genesis*, 154–55.
48. Alexander, *Abraham in the Negev*, 69.
49. Sarna, *Understanding Genesis*, 181.

The insertion of the Hagar-Ishmael stories has one purpose: to show that Isaac is the true heir to Abraham. It comes to stress the supremacy of the Israelites over the Ishmaelites who also trace their lineage through Abraham. Isaac is the son of the chief wife/matriarch and Ishmael is the son of an Egyptian maidservant. The banishment of Ishmael in Gen 21 serves three functions.[50] First, it allows Isaac to replace Ishmael as the true heir of Abraham as promised in the stories in Gen 15 and 16. Second, it prepares the reader for Gen 21, which knows nothing about Abraham's son Ishmael and sees only Isaac as the only *begotten son*. Finally, it also brings the story of Ishmael to a close in light of Gen 17:4–6; in those verses, Abraham is understood to be the father of many nations, not just Israel and Ishmael. Like Isaac, Ishmael is to be made into a nation; a great future awaits him. Ishmael is to become the father of twelve tribes (16:10). He is circumcised according to the covenant with YHWH (17:7, 23). However, there is a major difference between the brothers, which is that "in Isaac shall your descendants be called" (21:12).

In conclusion, Abraham was promised to have many descendants, but without any details or explanation as to how it would materialize. The births of his two sons, Ishmael and Isaac, are the fulfillment of God's promises. However, the birth of Ishmael is the result of human interference; it was the outcome of Sarah giving Abraham her concubine Hagar. Isaac, on the other hand, was born because of God's involvement. The stories come to explain the origin of the Ishmaelites and Israelites. It explains the nature of the Ishmaelites as a wild nomadic people who roamed the desert between Israel and Egypt. The story of the banishment of Ishmael comes to legitimize Isaac as the true heir to the Abrahamic covenant. Through Isaac, the line of Abraham would continue.

Abraham waited many years for the birth of Isaac, and then the next time that Isaac was mentioned Abraham was told by God to sacrifice him. Hence, in the next chapter, we will examine the story of the binding of Isaac and try to understand the purpose of this story. In addition, we will examine the character of Abraham in light of this ordeal that results from God's request.

---

50. Thompson, *Tradition of Ancient Israel*, 96.

Chapter 8

Take Your Son, Your Favored One, Isaac

The story of the binding of Isaac is the climax of Abraham's religious odyssey and the ultimate trial of his faith. God asked Abraham to sacrifice his son Isaac, a son he had waited so many years for. Compliance with God's request means an end to his future dreams and nullification of the promises of Abraham's posterity. However, a question needs to be raised here: Why does God need to test Abraham? God knows everything. Different interpretations are given to the nature of this test. It is believed that the story is an etiological legend that came to explain why the custom of the sacrifice of a child at a certain place was substituted by a ram. In other words, the story is a transition from human sacrifice to animal sacrifice. Others suggest that originally the story must have dealt with another figure and not with Isaac. What can we learn about Abraham's conduct before and after this horrific story? Before Abraham interceded on behalf of total strangers, the people of Sodom, but here he did not question God and complied. He did not try to save his son's life, uttering only a single word: "Here I am." (*hinneni*) Additionally, how was the persona of Isaac perceived in later writings? Was Isaac a willing victim, or did he resist his father? To answer these and other questions we will analyze the story through a close reading of the biblical text and explore the postbiblical texts that are relevant to our study.

TESTING ABRAHAM

The story starts with the introduction that God tested Abraham. Testing is found in other instances in the Hebrew Bible. For example, God tested the Israelites in the wilderness (Exod 15:25; 16:4; Deut 8:2, 16). He tested Job. Job's devotion to God was called into question by Satan (Job 1:9). This resulted in suffering that included the loss of his children. Abraham and Job both survived the test and were found to be "God-fearing" men (Gen 22:12; Job 1:9). They complained about divine justice, with Abraham saying, "Shall not the judge of all earth deal justly?" (Gen 18:25), and Job saying, "Will the Almighty prevent justice?" (Job 8:3).

The fact that Abraham is given a test is revealed at the outset of the story to the reader, but not to Abraham. It comes to remove any impression that God requires human sacrifice. The reader knows that his son will not be slaughtered. Thus, the question that is left to the reader is, Will Abraham comply with God's request or will his love for his son prevent him from submitting to God's command?

Before receiving God's command, Abraham uttered one word—*hinneni*, "Here I am"—which expresses attentiveness. This is the only word that Abraham says to God in the whole story. Earlier in the story of Sodom and Gomorrah, Abraham intercedes on behalf of total strangers to save their lives. Here, when he received the command from God to sacrifice his own son, he did not plead for his son's life, neither did he try to save him. The Hebrew single word for "Here I am" appears again in the text when Isaac turns to his father with a question and Abraham replies, "Here I am" (Gen 22:7). Similarly, when the angel of the Lord called Abraham from heaven, the patriarch answered, "Here I am" (22:11). Three times the name of the patriarch "Abraham (my father)" is mentioned (22:1, 7, 11) before being followed by the response, "Here I am." Each points to a new development in the narrative.[1]

When God told Abraham "Take your son," the Hebrew adds the participle (*na'*), which is translated as "please" or "I beg you."[2] Rashi says *na'* is primarily an expression of entreaty,[3] although in other instances Rashi explains *na'* as "now" (12:11; 19:2); here he says the meaning is "please" in order to avoid the idea that God caused Abraham to panic. In other words, by adding the word *na'*, God has given Abraham complete

---

1. Wenham, *Genesis 16–50*, 104.
2. Hamilton, *Genesis, Chapters 18–50*, 101.
3. *Sanh.* 89b; *Gen. Rab.* 55:7.

freedom of choice. Abarvanel, however, says that the word may be interpreted in two ways: "please take" or "take now." The meaning of "now" is the appropriate time to perform the task of taking his son and offering him as a sacrifice.

The identity of the sacrifice is described in ascending order to stress the severity of the sacrifice: "Your son, your favored one, Isaac, whom you love" (22:2). This description from the general to the specific is like the first command Abraham received from God: "Go forth from your native land, and from your father's house to the land that I will show you" (12:1). In both instances, the phrase "go forth" is used. The ascending order and similarity between the two calls were noted in the midrash:

> And He said: "Take, I pray Thee, Thy Son, etc. (22:2)." Said He to him: "Take, I Pray Thee—I beg thee—Thy Son." "Which son?" he asked. "Thine Only Son," replied He. "But each is the only one of his mother?"—"Whom Thou Lovest."—"Is there a limit to the affection?" "Even Isaac," said He. And why did he not reveal it to him without delay? To make him [Isaac] even more beloved in his eyes and reward him for every word spoken. This agrees with the dictum of R. Joḥanan, who said: "*Get thee out of thy country*" (Gen 12:1) means from thy province; "*And from thy kindred*" (ibid.) from the place where thou art settled; "*And from thy father's house*"—literally thy father's house. "*Unto the land that I will show thee*" (ibid). Why did He not reveal it to him there and then? In order to make it more beloved in his eyes and to reward him for every step.[4]

Abraham is told to take Isaac to the land of Moriah. The only other time that this place is mentioned is in 2 Chr 3:1, which says, "Solomon began to build the House of the Lord in Jerusalem on Mount Moriah." This association was the source of the belief that Mt. Moriah was in Jerusalem.[5] In the book of Jubilees, we read, "And Abraham called that place 'The Lord hath seen,' so that it is said in the mount the Lord hath seen: that is Mount Zion" (18:13). Zion is referred to as "the mountain of the Lord" in some biblical passages.[6] Ramban points to the interpretation that equates Moriah with the Temple Mount in Jerusalem, although there was no temple during Abraham's time. This suggests that the usage of the name Moriah, in those days, was prophetically given. Among modern

---

4. *Gen. Rab.* 55:7.
5. *Gen. Rab.* 55:7; Kalimi, "Land of Moriah," 345–62.
6. Isa 2:3; 30:29; Mic 4:2; Zech 8:3; Ps 24:3.

scholars, Noth dismisses the identification because "the original tradition of Abraham, which like that of Isaac, was native to the Negeb, did not extend further to the north at all,"[7] while according to Levenson, if Gen 22:1–19 is a later tradition than most of Abraham and Isaac's tradition, then it is more likely that the story refers to a Judean cult site that became important in Israelite tradition only with the Davidic monarchy.[8]

There is no Mount Moriah in Gen 22. Genesis mentions the land of Moriah "on one of the mountains" (22:2). In the ancient world it was believed that the gods lived on mountaintops. Hence, the Canaanites worshiped "on the high mountains" (Deut 12:2). God revealed himself to his people on Mount Sinai (Exod 19). It appears that a mountain was an appropriate place for meeting God, as mentioned in verse 14: "And Abraham names the site the Lord will see, whence the present saying, 'On the mount of the Lord there is vision.'"[9]

As for the name Moriah, different interpretations were offered by our sages, who explained why it is called Moriah:

> One said: "To the place whence instruction (*hora'ah*) went forth to the world." While the other explained it: "To the place whence religious awe (*yirah*) went forth to the world." (Similarly, the word *aron* (the Ark). R. Ḥiyya and R. Jannai—one said: "The place whence *Torah* (light) goes forth to the world. . . . To the place where incense would be offered, as you read, 'I will get me to the mountain of myrrh—Mor.'"[10]

Rashi pointed out that God did not say to slaughter Isaac because it was never his intention that he should be slaughtered. Instead, it says that God told him "Bring him up to the mountain and prepare him as a burnt offering." Since Abraham complied with the test and brought Isaac up, God told him to bring his son back down (22:12). According to Rashi, "The Holy One Blessed Be He causes the righteous to wonder, and afterward He reveals to them. All this (is done) in order to increase their reward." Although this is a very interesting interpretation, we should point out that the verb "to bring up" is used in connection with sacrificial offerings (Lev 14:20; 17:8; Josh 22:23; Judg 6:26; 11:31; 1 Sam 13:9;

---

7. Noth, *History of Israel*, 125.
8. Levenson, *Death and Resurrection*, 121.
9. Wenham, *Genesis 16–50*, 106.
10. *Gen. Rab.* 55:7.

Jer 14:12; Ezek 43:24). More importantly, Abraham understood it as an actual slaughter, otherwise it would not be a test.

Following God's command, Abraham rose early in the morning. The Bible does not say a word about Abraham's emotional state or his feelings. This is quite surprising, as the previous chapter—the story of the expulsion of Ishmael—says, "The matter distressed Abraham greatly" (22:11). The rabbis say that even though it was hard on him, Abraham did not delay. He woke up early in the morning and saddled the donkey instead of having the servants do it. All of this shows that he was zealously hastening to perform his religious duty, which is why it is customary to perform the circumcision early in the morning.[11] They also point out that the love of God causes one to ignore normal rules of personal conduct.[12]

We believe that Abraham wrestled with his own thoughts, thinking about God's command. His activities in the morning point to his psychological state. He saddled his ass, took the two servants and his son Isaac, and split the wood. It is strange that he cut the wood last, as it makes more sense to do it first. This illogical order shows that he was preoccupied; he was not thinking straight. He was trying to conceal the true purpose of the journey. He did conceal it from Isaac. Furthermore, his wife Sarah is not mentioned at all in this chapter.

According to Josephus, Abraham concealed it from his wife Sarah and everyone in his household out of fear that she might hinder him from doing God's service.[13] Strangely, Abraham had to saddle the ass and cut the wood; these were the servants' tasks. Abraham was a wealthy man with high social status; all of this normally had to be carried out by the servants. The servants do nothing in the whole story; they are simply there. This is not a coincidence; Abraham tries to occupy himself to divert his thoughts from God's command.[14] We can sense that Abraham struggles within himself; he is preoccupied and cannot concentrate. The impression is that Abraham tries to delay the binding by procrastinating. In 22:6 we read, "And Abraham took the wood for burnt offerings and put it on his son Isaac. He himself took the firestone and the knife." The order of his acts is highly significant. Abraham taking the knife is suspended until the last moment, as if to say he was delaying and hoping for a miracle.

11. *Pesaḥ.* 4a.
12. *Sanh.* 105b.
13. Josephus, *Ant.* 1.12.2.
14. Mazor, "Genesis," 22, 87.

Early in the morning, Abraham saddled his donkey. He took his two young men, his son Isaac, and the chopped wood for offering. It is not clear why he carried the wood for three days. It is possible that he thought that he would not find wood in the place he was ordered to go, or he took good quality wood from his house for fear that he would not find the right wood for altar offerings. This is in accordance with the writing of the Talmud: "And any piece of wood in which a worm was found was disqualified from being used upon the Altar."[15] In addition, he took his two young men with him. According to Abarvanel, he did it without explaining the purpose of the journey to avoid any questions. Also, Rashi says that a man of importance is not permitted to embark on a journey without two men accompanying him.

On the third day, Abraham saw the place from afar. In the Hebrew Bible, three days signifies a period of time. Hence, on the third day, Laban was told that Jacob escaped (Gen 31:22); Moses was instructed by God to go to the pharaoh and ask him to let the Israelites go for three days into the wilderness to make a sacrifice (Exod 3:18). The Israelites traveled in the wilderness of Shur for three days (15:22). By mentioning three days, the Bible stresses the fact that a period passed by. It comes to show us that Abraham had the time to think and reconsider his actions. If Abraham complied with God's request and acted at once we could say that he was in a state of shock, that he was too emotional. The three days gave Abraham the time to make a clearheaded decision without hastiness. Indeed, Rabbi Akiba says in the midrash that "He tested him unequivocally, that people might not say that He confused and perplexed him so that he did not know what to do."[16]

When Abraham saw the place from afar, he told his servants to stay with the ass. Therefore, the question becomes, What did Abraham see? Furthermore, God said that he would show Abraham the place for offering. However, the text does not say that God did this. Nevertheless, Sforno (Obadiah ben Jacob, ca. 1470–ca. 1550) maintains that divine providence directed his gaze to that spot, and he perceived it as the place. According to the midrash, "He saw a cloud enveloping the mountain and said: 'It appears that is the place where the Holy One, blessed be He, told me to sacrifice my son.'"[17] The midrash explains the word *makom*, "place," as a reference to God; thus, Abraham saw the glory of Shekhinaha as a

---

15 *Mid.* 2:5.
16. *Gen. Rab.* 55:6.
17. *Gen. Rab.* 56:1.

manifestation of God's presence.¹⁸ According to the literal interpretation, he saw the land of Moriah from afar, which was well known to him.

Abraham told the servants that he and the lad would go up there to worship and that they would return. By using the plural form, he concealed the purpose of the journey from Isaac. Commentators tried to explain the patriarch's behavior of utterly lying. Benno Jacob says that, unknowingly, Abraham did speak the truth.¹⁹ Dillmann says that it was an expression of "quiet hope that God may yet determine otherwise,"²⁰ while in *Genesis Rabbah* we read, "He thus informed him that he [Isaac] would return safely from Mount Moriah."²¹ In other words, God informed Abraham, by making him unintentionally prophesize, *that we would come back*. Hebrews 11:17-19 portrays Abraham's words as an example of the patriarch's faith that God was able to raise Isaac. No indication is given as to why Abraham wanted the servant out of his way. Several suggestions have been given, such as that God told him to leave them or Abraham did not want them to see the sacrifice, but more likely he was afraid that they might interfere. It is noteworthy that Abraham refers here to his son Isaac as "the lad" rather than "my son." Thus, we can say that he has already given Isaac to God and, in a sense, Isaac is no longer Abraham's son.²²

Abraham took the wood and put it on Isaac. It is Isaac who carries the instrument of his own destruction. As the midrash says, "like one who carries his stake on his shoulder."²³ The one to be executed carries his own stake, whereas Abraham carries the fire and the knife. The fire probably refers to firestone since it is unlikely that he carried fire for three days. As for the knife, the Bible uses the rare Hebrew *"ma'akhelet."* This word is found in Judg 19:29 where it has the meaning of cutting up a human body, and in Prov 30:14 where it refers to a sword.²⁴ What we have in the Genesis text is a wordplay of the word "knife," *ma'akhelet*, and the word *"mal'akh,"* "angel," the angel who saved Isaac from the knife of death. Abraham laid the wood of the burnt offering on Isaac, which is

---

18. *Pirqe R. El.* 31.
19. Jacob, *First Book*, 144.
20. Dillman, *Genesis*, 2:144.
21. *Gen. Rab.* 56:2.
22. Wenham, *Genesis 16–50*, 107.
23. *Gen. Rab.* 56:3.
24. Sarna, *Genesis*, 152.

reminiscent of Abraham placing the bread and water on Hagar's shoulders. In both cases, the patriarch is going to cut himself off from his own family.

According to the Bible "the two walked together" (22:6), which implies complete harmony; Abraham knew what he was going to do—that is, to slay his son—and Isaac knew nothing. One was to slaughter and the other to be slaughtered. Still, they went together in the same spirit. Until now, Isaac did not know the purpose of the trip. The silence is broken when Isaac addresses his father and asks, "Where is the lamb for offering?" He noticed the fire and the wood, but the crucial element for the sacrifice was missing. In response, Abraham said that God will seek out for himself the lamb for the offering. In other words, we are preparing for the offering, but God will choose the lamb. The phrase "and the two of them walked together" is repeated in verse 8. It is mentioned after Abraham said that God himself will provide the sacrifice. This repetition was suspicious in the eyes of the interpreters. It was suggested that at that moment Isaac understood that he would be the lamb for the burnt offering. Indeed, the midrash says, "God will provide Himself the lamb, O my son; and if not, Thou art for a burnt-offering, my son."[25] According to Rashi, even though Isaac understood that he was going to be slaughtered, they still walked forward with a common purpose.

Upon arriving at the place, Abraham built the altar. Previously, Abraham built altars because of God's promises (12:7, 8; 13:18); now he built an altar as a response to God's order, which threatened those promises. It was not an ordinary altar, but "the altar." The usage of the definite "the altar" may indicate an existing altar that was rebuilt by Abraham. This view is found in the midrashim. In *Pirqe Rabbi Eliezer*, this is the altar where Adam sacrificed, where Cain and Abel sacrificed, and where Noah and his sons sacrificed.[26] However, we should point out that the place was unknown to Abraham. The usage of the definite article came to stress and commemorate this place as "the altar" of the binding of Isaac.

The Bible describes the stoic regularity with which Abraham proceeded. First, he built the altar, then he arranged the wood, and then he tied his son. According to Abarvanel, this shows that Abraham acted with a clear mind—he was aware of what he was doing, and he did not act impulsively. He bound Isaac and laid him on the altar. The Hebrew

---

25. *Gen. Rab.* 56:4.
26. *Pirqe R. El.* 31.

word "'*kad*," bound, is not found anywhere else in the Hebrew Bible. According to the Talmud, it means the tying of hands and feet.[27] Isaac's hands and feet were tied together behind him, and his neck was stretched backward. The Jewish tradition named Gen 22 the *Akedah* after the verb. Abraham's act of tying Isaac to the altar atop the wood is unusual. The explanation for this abnormality may lie in the fact that this is the only account of the procedure for human sacrifice.[28] When Abraham stretched his hand and took the knife to slaughter his son, the angel of the Lord called from heaven. Angels need to travel between heaven and earth, but here, because it was an urgent moment, the angel called from heaven. This call from heaven is reminiscent of the call the angel made to Hagar in 21:17. In other words, Abraham's two sons were saved by the call of an angel from heaven. The angel called Abraham's name in rapid succession—"Abraham, Abraham"—which expressed the urgency of the moment. According to Pesikta Rabbati,

> Abraham was hastening to cut Isaac's throat, and like a man crying out in sharp distress, the angel burst out at him: "What are thou at?" Abraham turned his face toward the angel. When the angel burst out: "What art thou at? Lay not thy hand upon the lad."[29]

The angel told Abraham not to harm his son. Ramban explains that Abraham's fear of God was still concealed; it had not yet emerged into actuality using a great deed. But now, with the attempted performance of this deed, it became known indeed and his merit became complete. The words "For now I know that you are a God-fearing man" troubled commentators. How could it say that he knew only now that Abraham feared him? Furthermore, there is a contradiction between "now" and "knew," which is in the past tense. Rashi resolved the difficulties by saying, "I have something with which to answer Satan and the non-Jewish nations who wonder what is the cause of My love for you. I have a justification that they see 'that you are God-fearing.'"

The text does not record a verbal response by Abraham to the angel's call nor Isaac's reaction to his release from the altar. What the text describes is how Abraham saw a ram caught in the thicket by its horn. The appearance of the ram was a total surprise to Abraham as the Hebrew

---

27. *Šabb.* 54a.
28. Levenson, *Death and Resurrection*, 135.
29. *Pesiq. Rab.* 40.

word "*vhinneh*," literally "and lo," suggests. Before, Isaac asked, "Where is the sheep?" (22:7). Abraham answered, "God will see to the sheep for His burnt offering." Here God provided an animal, but a different one from what Abraham expected. According to Radak, he looked about to see if there was another ritually clean animal that he could offer instead of his son. Abraham was ordered to sacrifice his son; since this command was nullified, he needed to make a substitute.

Abraham named the place "The Lord will see." Naming a place was important in the ancient world. The place of theophany became a holy place and future generations venerated it. It turned into a cultic center where people would make sacrifices and pray to God. The name of the place reflects Abraham's reaction to his personal experience and is linked to Gen 22:8. As Gunkle noticed, "Abraham gratefully remembers the words he spoke in extreme duress to his son (v. 8): 'God will see it.'"[30] Similarly, Radak understood the name as an allusion to Abraham's prophetic assurance to Isaac: "God will seek out for himself the lamb for burnt offering." Von Rad believed that the narrative concluded with verse 14, comprised of God's appearance, the offering of the sacrifice, and the naming of the place. The second call by the angel in verse 15 is an addition to an ancient cult legend. It was added to link the narrative with the motif of "promise," which unites all of Abraham's narratives.[31] However, it is possible that the second call came because the angel's first address was interrupted by the sacrifice of the ram. After Abraham proved his obedience to God's will, all the previous promises needed to be reaffirmed. For the first time, the promises are introduced by a solemn oath, with God swearing by his own being.[32] As Radak comments, it is an irrevocable oath: "Just as I am eternal, so is My oath eternal." The midrash raises the question, What was the need for this oath?

> He had begged Him: "Swear to me not to try me again henceforth, nor my son Isaac." R. Levi in the name of R. Ḥama b. R. Ḥanina gave another reason for this oath: He had begged: "Swear to me not to test me again henceforth."[33]

---

30. Gunkel, *Genesis*, 236.
31. Rad, *Genesis*, 242.
32. Sarna, *Genesis*, 154.
33. *Gen. Rab.* 56:11.

ISAAC IN LIGHT OF THE AKEDAH

The climax of the Isaac narrative is the story of his binding. In this story, he plays a secondary role to his father Abraham who is the main character. As a child, he was submissive, which is evident from his silence at his sacrifice. He carries the wood that was supposed to be used for his own sacrifice and walks in silence at his father's side on the way to Mount Moriah. The only time that he speaks is when he asks about the sheep for the burnt offering. Abraham uttered an ambiguous response and still Isaac maintained his silence. Isaac accepted his father's response; he trusted his father. Alternatively, he may have sensed that he was the intended sacrificial lamb. If this was the case, it shows his total obedience to his father.[34] Abraham appears as the dominant father and Isaac as the archetypical submissive son. Abraham overshadows his timid son, who displays no personality apart from his father. It appears that Isaac was a willing victim. There is no indication in the text that Isaac resisted his father or tried to flee. Abraham was an old man, and Isaac was probably thirty-seven years old; he could have easily escaped.[35] Thus, Josephus in his writings observed,

> [Abraham tells Isaac that he is to be the sacrifice.] Isaac, however, since he was descended from such a father, could be no less noble of spirit [than Abraham], and received these words with delight. He said that he never would have been worthy of being born in the first place, were he not now to carry out the decision of God and his father and submit himself to the will of both.[36]

A similar view is found in the writings of 1 Clement:

> Why was our father Abraham blessed? Was it not because he acted righteously and truthfully through faith? Isaac knowing full well what was to happen was willingly led forth to be scarified.[37]

This shift from the passive Isaac to a willing victim is also found in the rabbinic writings. In *Genesis Rabbah*, we read of a debate between Isaac and Ishmael:

---

34. Wenham, *Genesis 16–50*, 108.
35. According to *Gen. Rab.* 56:8, Isaac was twenty-six years old while, in a pre-rabbinic Jewish tradition, he was fifteen (Jub. 17:15–16).
36. Josephus, *Ant.* 1:232.
37. 1 Clem. 31:2–4.

> Isaac and Ishmael were engaged in controversy: the latter argued, "I am more beloved than thou because I was circumcised at the age of thirteen"; while the other retorted, "I am more beloved than thou because I was circumcised at the eight days." Said Ishmael to him: "I am more beloved because I could have protested yet did not." At that moment Isaac exclaimed: "O that God would appear to me and bid me cut off one of my limbs! then I would not refuse." Said God: "Even if I bid thee sacrifice thyself, thou wilt not refuse."[38]

A later midrash, *Sifre Deut.* 32, from the end of the fourth century CE, portrays Isaac as binding himself:

> R. Meir says: "Scripture says, '*Thou shalt love the Lord, thy God, with all thy heart.*' Love Him with all your heart, as did your father Abraham, of whom it is said, '*But thou Israel, My servant, Jacob, whom I have chosen, the seed of Abraham My friend*' (Isa 41:8). '*And with all thy soul,*' as did Isaac, who bound himself upon the altar, as it said, '*And Abraham stretched forth his hand and took the knife to slay his son*'" (Gen 22:10).

Similarly, we find in *Leviticus Rabbah*: "Isaac fulfilled that which is written in the Torah, in that he cast himself before his father as a lamb that is to be sacrificed."[39] On the other hand, in *Genesis Rabbah*, we find that Isaac must be tied so he will not fall into temptation:

> R. Isaac said: "When Abraham wished to sacrifice his son, Isaac, he said to him: 'Father I am a young man and am afraid that my body may tremble through fear of the knife and I will grieve thee, whereby the slaughter may be rendered unfit and this will not count as a real sacrifice; therefore bind me ever firmly.'"[40]

In another text, the *Biblical Antiquities* (of Pseudo-Philo, first century CE), we read that since Isaac was a willing victim, he was announcing that his sacrifice would be more effective than the other sacrifices for future generations:[41]

> And as he [Abraham] was setting out, he said to his son, "Behold now, my son, I am offering you as a burnt offering and I am returning you into the hand of Him who gave you to me."

---

38. *Gen. Rab.* 55:4.
39. *Lev Rab.* 2:10.
40. *Gen. Rab.* 56:8.
41. *L.A.B.* 32:2–4.

> But the son said to the father, "Hear me, father. If [ordinarily] a lamb of the flocks is accepted as a sacrifice to the Lord with sweet savor, and if such flocks have been set aside for slaughter [in order to atone] for human iniquity, while man, on the contrary, has been designated to inherit this world—why should you be saying to me now, 'Come and inherit eternal life and time without measure?' Why if not that I was indeed born in this world *in order* to be offered as a sacrifice to Him who made me? Indeed, this [sacrifice] will be [the mark of] my blessedness over other men—for no such thing will ever be [again]—and in me, the generation will be proclaimed and through me, nations will understand how God made human soul worthy for sacrifice."

Christians saw in the binding of Isaac the foreshadowing of the crucifixion. In the epistle of Barnabas (ca. 70–132 CE), it was said,

> "Whoever does not keep the fast shall surely die" was written, the Lord commanded it because he himself was planning to offer the vessel of his spirit as a sacrifice for our sins, in order that the type established by Isaac, who was offered upon the altar, might be fulfilled.[42]

The book of Romans says, "If God is for us, then who is against us? He who did not spare his own son but gave him up for us all, will he not also give us all things along with him?"[43] Irenaeus (ca. 120–ca. 203 CE), Bishop of Lugdunum, said that "Abraham, according to his faith, followed the commandment of the Word of God, and with a ready mind Abraham delivered up, as a sacrifice to God, his only-begotten and beloved son, in order that God also might be pleased to offer up for all his seed his own beloved and only-begotten Son, as a sacrifice for our redemption."[44] According to the Christian theologian Augustine (354–430 CE),

> For this reason, even as the Lord carried his own cross, so Isaac himself also carried to the place of sacrifice the wood on which he too was to have been placed. Finally, since it was not fitting that Isaac should be slain, now after his father had been forbidden to strike him, who was that ram whose immolation completed the sacrifice by the blood that was fraught with meaning? Note that when Abraham saw the ram it was caught in a thicket

---

42. Barn. 7:3.
43. Rom 8:31–32.
44. Irenaeus, *Heresies*, 4:5:4.

by its horns. Who then was symbolized by the ram but Jesus, crowned with Jewish thorns before he was sacrificed?[45]

After the binding, the text says that Abraham returned from Moriah, but there is no mention of Isaac. "Abraham then returned to his servant, and they departed together for Beer-Sheba, and Abraham stayed in Beer-Sheba" (Gen 22:19). It is possible that Isaac did not return with his father. The trauma of a near-death experience broke the bond between father and son; there was no longer trust between them. They never spoke again—each of them went his own way. Indeed, the rabbis asked: "And where was Isaac? R. Baḥya ben Asher (thirteenth century) said in the name of the Rabbis of the other place: 'He sent him to Shem to study Torah.'"[46] Similarly, in Targum Pseudo-Jonathan, we read that the angels took Isaac to the schoolhouse of Shem and he was there for three years. This explains the fact that he was thirty-seven years old at the time of the Aqedah and forty when he returned from the school of Shem and married Rebekah.

THE PURPOSE OF THE STORY

It is not clear why God had to put Abraham through such an ordeal. God knows everything, so why is he asking Abraham to do such a cruel thing? According to Maimonides, "The sole object of all the trials mentioned in Scripture is to teach man what he ought to do or believe; so that the event which forms the actual trial is not the end desired; it is but an example for our instruction and guidance."[47] Maimonides says that God tested Abraham because he knew that he would pass the test. Abraham's faith would shine like a beacon and be a sign to the nations. The emphasis is not on Abraham's suffering but on his strength. According to Speiser, the object of the test "was to discover how firm the patriarch's faith was in the ultimate divine purpose."[48] The fact that this was a test was divulged to the reader at the beginning. This was done to remove any misunderstanding that God demands human sacrifice. Since the reader knows that God does not require a human sacrifice, the focus is on Abraham. What is left for the reader to see is whether Abraham will comply with God's request

---

45. Augustine, *City of God*, 16.32.
46. *Gen. Rab.* 56:11.
47. Maimonides, *Guide for the Perplexed*, 3:24.
48. Speiser, *Genesis*, 166.

Take Your Son, Your Favored One, Isaac

or not. God knew how Abraham would respond but wanted Abraham to discover his strength of faith. Abraham's passing the test serves as an example to the next generation of Israel. Abraham is the father of the faith who passed the test and trusted God, so likewise should all devotees of YHWH do. The story stands in contrast to Abraham's lack of faith portrayed in stories such as Gen 12:10–20 and Gen 16.

In the Rabbinic literature, this was the last of the ten trials to which Abraham was subjected.[49] According to Abarvanel, this is the only one of Abraham's ten trials that the Torah calls a test. In the other incidents, Abraham completed the trials. He indeed left his homeland, sent away Ishmael, and so on. Here, in our story, it remained nothing more than a test since God did not allow Abraham to slaughter his son. This was also the last theophany Abraham received from God.

Modern scholars maintain that the story was an etiological legend, and that its purpose was to explain why the custom of sacrificing a child at a certain place was substituted by the sacrifice of a ram.[50] It is a transitional story between human sacrifice and animal sacrifice. However, this understanding of the story cannot be supported considering the biblical tradition. Sacrifice is already mentioned in the story of Cain and Abel where animals and products of the soil constitute an offering (Gen 4:3). Noah, when he came out of the ark, sacrificed animals and birds (8:20). The substitution of a ram for Isaac was Abraham's own idea and was not ordained by God. Animal sacrifice was a custom that was practiced regularly in the ancient world since it was believed that the gods needed animal sacrifices to exist.

Human sacrifice, and especially child sacrifice, was widespread among the Canaanites, Phoenicians, Egyptians, and among the Moabites and Ammonites. The Bible condemns this practice: "Do not allow any of your offspring to be offered up to Molech" (Lev 18:21; 20:2; Deut 12:31). Molech is a deity that was worshiped by some of Israel's neighbors. According to 2 Kgs 23:10, it was King Josiah who destroyed a cultic site in

---

49. 'Abot 5:3. There are several versions of what the test was. What follows is the list of tests given by Maimonides: (1) Abraham exiled from his family and homeland; (2) the hunger in Canaan after God had assured him that he would become a great nation there; (3) the corruption in Egypt that resulted in the abduction of Sarah; (4) the war with the four kings; (5) Abraham's marriage to Hagar after having despaired that Sarah would never give birth; (6) the commandment of circumcision; (7) Abimelech's abduction of Sarah; (8) driving Hagar away after she had given birth; (9) the very distasteful command to drive away Ishmael; and (10) the binding of Isaac on the altar.

50. Gunkel, *Genesis*, 239–40; Skinner, *Genesis*, 332.

the vicinity of Jerusalem where children had been sacrificed to Molech. This form of sacrifice was prevalent during the reign of Manasseh, king of Judah. In 2 Kgs 16:3, we read that King Ahaz of Judah burned his own son in a fire. The Moabite king Mesha sacrificed his son on the battlefield to achieve victory (2 Kgs 3:27). Jephthah sacrificed his daughter in fulfillment of a vow to get a military victory (Judg 11). Later we read of the denunciation of human sacrifice by the prophets Jeremiah and Ezekiel. The fact that the kings of Israel practiced human sacrifice and the prophets denounced it shows that human sacrifices continued. Therefore, the story of the binding of Isaac was not a transitional story from human sacrifice to animal sacrifice. Nevertheless, one of its goals was to denounce human sacrifice.[51] In other words, human sacrifice is not the right way to worship God; thus, we read of the prohibition of it and its denunciation. Indeed, the prophet Micah mentioned the futility of child sacrifice: "With what shall I approach the Lord. . . . Shall I approach him with burnt offerings. . . . Shall I give my firstborn for my transgression, the fruit of my body for my sins?" (6:6-7).

Gunkel pointed to expressions such as "*Adonai yireh*" (22:14b), "*Elohim yireh*" (22:8), and "*vyirah vhineh 'ayil*" (22:13), and from this he concluded that the original name of the sanctuary was "*Jeruel.*" He identified the site with Jeriel that is mentioned in 2 Chr 20:16, which is near Tekoa. The substitution of Moriah for Jeruel/Jeriel was because of the close similarity of the name of the cult site to Ariel, one of the names of Jerusalem (Isa 29:1-8). Thus, according to him, Gen 22 was originally a legend of child sacrifice at Jeruel. It tells the reader that the deity wanted the firstborn son as a sacrifice but explained how the deity accepted a goat as a substitute for the boy.[52] In other words, the basis of Gen 22 was a local cult legend of this place. However, this is no more than philological speculation. This place is mentioned once in all of Scripture and there is no evidence that it ever served as a cultic site. The story had to be more than an explanation of the name of a place or a protest of human sacrifice. The story as it appears has a deeper meaning.

Noth says that the story is a folk narrative that was passed orally. It was originally about a child that was symbolically offered on the altar but at the last moment was substituted by a ram.[53] Reading the story in Genesis shows that there are so many obscure details that the story cannot

---

51. Skinner, *Genesis*, 331-32.
52. Gunkel, *Genesis*, 238-39.
53. Noth, *History of Pentateuchal Traditions*, 114-15.

be analyzed historically with any certainty. Because Isaac plays such a passive role, the identification of the "son" with Isaac is a late tradition, historically. Originally the story must have dealt with another figure. The merging of the southern wilderness Isaac tradition with the Abraham tradition occurred most likely in the context of the six-tribe confederacy of Hebron. In this manner, the Isaac tradition was absorbed into the dominant Abraham tradition and consequently made Isaac the son of Abraham, their ancestral patron.[54] However, there is no support for his suggestion in the biblical text, so this is purely guesswork.

In conclusion, the story of the binding of Isaac is not a transitional story between human sacrifice and animal sacrifice. Sacrificing animals was already mentioned before Abraham's time and human sacrifice lasted long after Abraham's time. What the story conveys is that human sacrifice is not the right way to worship. God knew that Abraham would pass the test. By Abraham passing the test, it shows his obedience and love of God; it is a sign of strength for his faith. Abraham's love and trust in God serve as a model to other nations. Abraham was tested because, from his first call in Haran, he was only rewarded, receiving promises of land and many descendants. Abraham is designated as the father of a new nation, and as such, he must prove his worthiness to God. Therefore, throughout the whole episode, the focus is on Abraham. Not surprisingly, Isaac is overshadowed by his father Abraham and is passive. In the midrashim, he is portrayed as a willing victim who does not resist his father. Christians saw the binding of Isaac as the foreshadowing of the crucifixion.

On two occasions Abraham passed his wife Sarah as his sister (Gen 12:10–20; 20) and Isaac passed his wife Rebecca as his sister (26:1–11). In the next chapter, we will examine these stories to see how similar or different they are, and to see what we can learn about Abraham's persona in light of his deceitful act.

---

54. Noth, *History of Pentateuchal Traditions*, 115.

Chapter 9

Please Say That You Are My Sister

Twice Abraham passed his wife Sarah off as his sister (Gen 12:10–20; 20); a similar story is repeated for a third time when Isaac passes off his wife Rebecca as his sister (26:1–11). These stories were believed to be three alternatives of a folktale; however, there is no consensus among scholars as to which of the three represents the oldest form of the story. Gunkel, for example, claimed that the account in 12:10–20 was the oldest.[1] Accordingly, some folkloristic features that are noticeable in this account are weaker in others. Genesis 20 is a "legend"; it glorifies God and his help, there are no profane ideas, and there is no mention of Abraham's cleverness or Sarah's beauty. As for Gen 26, he pointed out that there are neither "profane adventures," nor interventions by God, only implying that God protected Rebekah. In addition, he proposed that the story did not originate with the patriarch, but was a popular story transferred to him. According to Gunkel, the sequence of the stories is Gen 12, Gen 20, and then Gen 26.

Some scholars maintain that 26:1–13 is the earliest of the wife-sister narrative.[2] Noth suggested the account in 26 is the oldest; he believed that the tradition about Beersheba and the south originated with Isaac and only afterward was transferred to Abraham.[3] This story about Isaac is distinct from the two Abraham stories. It appears here in completely "profane"

---

1. Gunkel, *Genesis*, 223–25; Skinner, *Genesis*, 365.
2. Kuenen, *Historical-Critical*, 234–35; Holzinger, *Genesis*, 176; Maly, "Genesis," 260–61; Speiser, *Genesis*, 203; Rendtorff, *Problem*, 46.
3. Noth, *History of Pentateuchal Traditions*, 102–9.

form.⁴ There is no divine intervention that makes it closer to a folktale. Genesis 26 omits many details found in Gen 12. The story is simpler and condensed, and specifics are left to the reader's imagination. Therefore he believed Gen 26 was the oldest, containing the most original tradition, after which came Gen 12:10–20 and lastly Gen 20:2–18. Scholars who adhere to the documentary hypothesis suggested the existence of parallel documents in Genesis. Chapter 20 version B was assigned to E and the accounts in Gen 12 version A and 26 version C were believed to originate from J.⁵ Furthermore, it was suggested that narratives A and C indicate that J is composed of two separate sources.⁶ Based on form criticism, it was suggested that the three episodes developed as oral alternatives to one original story.⁷ In recent years scholars advocated that accounts B (Gen 20) and C (Gen 26) were literary arrangements based on A (Gen 12).⁸ In the current chapter, we examine the three variant stories separately to see how they relate to each other. Was the narrator familiar with an earlier account and expanded it? Also, which of the three stories is the original one? In addition, how can we explain Abraham's behavior, which appears to be dishonest and immoral?

A. ABRAHAM IN EGYPT (GENESIS 12)

There was a famine, and as a result, Abraham was forced to go down to Egypt. Before entering Egypt, Abraham told his wife Sarah to say that she was his sister. Sarah was a beautiful woman, and being his wife could conceivably endanger his life. Abraham and Sarah acted here as a brother and sister. This means that Abraham acted as her guardian so that he would be treated well on her account. The plan was put into motion, and it succeeded. When Abraham entered Egypt, the Egyptians saw how beautiful Sarah was and took her to Pharaoh's palace. Because of Sarah, Abraham received sheep, oxen, asses, male and female slaves, she-asses, and camels. Meanwhile, God intervened, inflicting Pharaoh and his household with mighty plagues because of Sarah. Pharaoh summoned Abraham to his palace and complained to him: "What is this you have

---

4. Noth, *History of Pentateuchal Traditions*, 105.
5. Skinner, *Genesis*, 242–3, 315, 363; Speiser, *Genesis*, 91; Rad, *Genesis*, 226, 270.
6. Skinner, *Genesis*, 251, 363.
7. Koch, *Growth*, 111–32.
8. Van Seters, *Abraham*, 167–91; Westermann, *Genesis*, 161–62; 318–20.

done to me! Why did you not tell me that she was your wife? Why did you say, 'She is my sister,' so that I took her as my wife?" (Gen 12:19). Pharaoh ordered Abraham to take his wife and leave. He expelled him and his wife and all that he possessed.

From a structural point of view, the story is a self-contained unit.[9] The problem that the patriarch faced is mentioned in verse 10. A plan was put into motion in verses 11–13, and its subsequent implementation and resulting complications are found in verses 14–16. The divine intervention and the outcome are mentioned in verses 17–20. This unit of this story has no link to the previous story or the story that follows it. Lot, Abraham's nephew who appeared in verses 4–5, does not appear in our story, but would appear later in chapter 13. As for this story unit, Gunkel pointed to a mixture of worldly and religious motifs that existed at that time. According to him, the legend celebrates the cleverness of the patriarch, the beautiful matriarch, and the ever-faithful God.[10] In addition, it contains pleasure due to the misfortune of Pharaoh.

Some questions need to be asked. Did Pharaoh have a sexual relationship with Sarah? Why is the king punished, even though he did not know that Sarah was Abraham's wife? How did Pharaoh realize the plague was because he abducted Sarah? Was Abraham a liar when he claimed that Sarah was his sister? Was it moral for Abraham to accept gifts from Pharaoh when Sarah was abducted? As we shall see below, all these questions are answered indirectly in chapter 20 where the narrative displays moral and theological issues.[11] Furthermore, the brevity of detail in Gen 20:2 regarding Abraham's plan and the abduction of Sarah shows that the reader was familiar with 12:11–15.[12]

B. ABRAHAM IN GERAR (GENESIS 20)

Now this story takes place in Gerar. There is no mention of famine in the land so why did Abraham have to leave his place of habitat? No reason is given for Abraham's travels from the oasis of Kadesh and Shur to Gerar. In addition, the text does not suggest that Abraham was facing danger. Without any background or preparation, there is a statement that

---

9. Van Seters, *Abraham*, 169.
10. Gunkel, *Genesis*, 224.
11. Alexander, *Abraham*, 43.
12. Alexander, "Wife/Sister Incidents," 147.

Abraham said of his wife Sarah, "She is my sister" (20:2). This declaration by Abraham is explained later in verse 11. Meanwhile, we are told that Abimelech, the king of Gerar, took Sarah to his harem. There is no motive given for why he took her. At that time, the matriarch was nearly ninety years old. Van Seters pointed out that the current account is double in length than version A. Hence, the minimal details in verse 2 can be explained because version A was known already. Therefore, there was no need to recount the whole story again.[13] Indeed in verse 13 Abraham said, "So when God made me wander from my father's house, I said to her, 'Let this be the kindness that you shall do me: whatever place we come to, say there of me: He is my brother.'" This really shows that it was not a one-time incident, but a general practice. Furthermore, the mention of God taking him from his birthplace brings us back to chapter 12.

The questions that we raised in version A—Why did God punish Pharaoh when he did not know that Sarah was Abraham's wife? And how did the king know that God was angry with him?—find their answers in version B (20:3–7). God appeared to Abimelech in a dream at night. According to Petersen, the dream has two functions within the narrative: it comes to prevent adultery, and secondly, it introduces the theme of guilty innocence.[14] In the dream, God warned Abimelech and told him, "You are to die because of the woman that you have taken, for she is a married woman" (20:3). Abimelech defended himself; he did not have sexual relations with Sarah, and he did not approach her. This is significant because the punishment for a person who has lain with someone's wife was the death penalty (Deut 22:22). Abraham deceived him when he said "she is my sister" and Sarah said that Abraham was her brother. These alleged words by Sarah were not recorded earlier. Abimelech ends his response to God by saying that he had no evil intentions, but that he acted with sincerity and innocence. In his response, God agrees with Abimelech: "I knew that you did this with a blameless heart" (20: 6), and he further told him that he prevented the violation of Sarah. Adultery is viewed as a sin against God. How God prevented Abimelech from approaching Sarah is not stated. God ordered Abimelech to return Sarah to Abraham. Interestingly, Abraham is not mentioned by name, but only as the husband of the woman who was taken by Abimelech. He is also referred to as "the man" and a "prophet," perhaps to indicate the distance between Abraham and Abimelech.

13. Van Seters, *Abraham*, 171.
14. Petersen, "Thrice-Told Tale," 38–39.

God's warning is concise and unambiguous. It is phrased in the present tense, as was noted by Sforno, who paraphrased it as "You are going to succumb to a disease that will begin with you because the Lord has closed fast." Indeed, the chapter concludes with the report that the Lord healed Abimelech and his wife and his slave girls (20:17). On the surface, the text seems to be speaking of infertility, but Shadal (S. D. Luzzatto, 1800–1865 CE) believed that the reference was about some sort of venereal disease that prevented the king from having sexual relations with his wife and concubines. After Abraham prayed on their behalf, the king and his wives were cured and the latter could give birth.

The need for Abraham to intercede is somewhat strange because Abimelech himself conducts a dialogue with the Lord. Why, then, did Abraham have to pray for the king? We can only note the tradition ascribed to various prophets—Moses (Num 12:13), Elijah (1 Kgs 17:20–22), and Elisha (2 Kgs 4:33–35)—and their ability to make supplication and heal others. That Abraham intercedes on behalf of the king is a reminder of his intercession on behalf of the people of Sodom and Gomorra. His role as a prophet appears in the phrase "the word of YHWH came to Abraham" (Gen 15:1). It is suggested that the depiction of Abraham as a prophet and the interest in the problem of guilt reflects a later era.[15] Nevertheless, the chapter does not resolve some moral questions that were raised in chapters 12:10–13:1.[16] Abraham received gifts from Abimelech as he received from Pharaoh. He also said that Sarah is not only his wife but his sister. According to the biblical law, one may not marry a half-sister (Lev 18:9, 11; 20:17; Deut 27:22).[17] The Leviticus text introduced incestuous rules that were unknown in the patriarchal era. This suggests that Abraham marrying his half-sister reflects an ancient tradition.[18]

God's appearance to Abimelech resembles a judicial proceeding. There are several stages in the process: the indictment (20:3), the accused's presentation of his defense (20:4–5), acceptance of his argument, and reversal of the original verdict (20:6–7). Although the sin Abimelech was to be punished for was adultery, even before he answered God the text emphasizes the euphemism "approached"; that Abimelech had not

---

15. Westermann, *Genesis 12–36*, 328–29.

16. Alexander, *Abraham in the Negev*, 46.

17. Brother-sister marriages were practiced in Egypt and Phoenicia, mostly among royalty. See Tigay, *Deuteronomy*, 256; Černý, "Consanguineous Marriages," 23–29.

18. Wenham, *Genesis 1–15*, 273.

yet had sexual relations with Sarah.[19] Answering God as if he is conversing with his own deity, he asks, "O Lord, will You slay people even though innocent?" (Gen 20:4). Interestingly, this question about the nature of divine justice echoes Abraham's regarding the impending doom of the Sodomites (Gen 18:23). Then shifting the blame to Abraham, who misled him—"She is my sister"—and Sarah, who corroborated this statement—"He is my brother"—Abimelech goes on to argue that he had not known that Sarah was a married woman. The Lord accepts Abimelech's defense and tells him that he had in fact been aware of his innocence.

The exchange between God and Abimelech is in the form of a dream. Such a dream, dealing with past events, is rare since dreams are usually future-oriented. But the Lord's warning to Abimelech is in fact meant to keep him from sinning. He instructs Abimelech as to what he must do to clear his name—return Sarah to Abraham. Then God repeats his earlier warning ("You are about to die," 20:3); here, however, the Lord says to him, "You will surely die." The duplication "*môt tāmût*" emphasizes the gravity of God's warning. It applies not only to Abimelech but also to everything that belongs to him. "Know that you shall die, you and all that are yours" (Gen 20:7).[20] Thus, the dream is based upon two warnings, supplemented by instructions as to how the admonished one can purge himself of guilt.

In response to God's appearance in his dream, Abimelech acts promptly and without hesitation to do precisely as he is instructed. First thing in the morning, he summons all his servants, who are "greatly frightened" (Gen 20:8) when he tells them about the dream. The Lord has punished Abimelech because of his "great sin," namely adultery. The same idiom is found in Egyptian documents, as well as in Akkadian documents from Ugarit: "That woman has sinned a great sin against you," which evidently alludes to adultery.[21]

Abimelech acts at once to compensate Abraham for the damage to Sarah's reputation, giving him sheep, cattle, and slaves. The paired verbs "took" and "gave" constitute a hendiadys, expressing the actions of donating. This idiom is common in Hittite and Ugaritic gifting documents.[22]

---

19. The root "*krb*" frequently has a sexual connotation in the Bible. See Lev 18:6; 14:19; Deut 22:14; and Isa 8:3.

20. In a similar vein, the entire people are punished for David's sin (2 Sam 24:15).

21. PRU IV, 139–40; Rabinowitz, "'Great Sin,'" 73; Moran, "Scandal," 280–81; Milgrom, *Cult*, 132–33.

22. Labuschagne "*Našû-nadānu* Formula," 176–80.

Sarah also receives financial compensation for the slight to her reputation. As Rashbam states, it is so that "the people will not look at you disparagingly and say, 'Abimelech treated this woman wantonly,' because everyone knew that he took her in an honorable way and returned her against his will." The financial compensation to Sarah is referred to as "a covering of the eyes," that is, a ransom payment to cover guilt.[23] In the Middle Assyrian Laws (Tablet A, section 22), we find that if a man takes a married woman on a business trip and does not know that she is married he must take an oath to this effect and give two ingots of tin to her husband.[24]

C. ISAAC IN GERAR (GENESIS 26)

Later, like his father Abraham, Isaac experiences famine and thus sets out for Egypt. Along the way he makes a stop, visiting Abimelech, the king of the Philistines, at Gerar. This opening statement indicates that the narrator is familiar with accounts A and B and combines elements from both stories. The mention of the famine recalls Abraham's migration to Egypt in version A. Going to Abimelech and staying in Gerar reminds us of version B. At Gerar, God appeared to him and barred him from migrating to Egypt, and instead ordered him to stay at Gerar. In addition, God reaffirms to Isaac the covenant he had made with his father Abraham. He promised him "all these lands" and numerous descendants. The usage of the plural form in the Hebrew word "lands" is unusual and it evidently refers to neighboring groups in the territories of Sidon, Tyre, Byblos, Hermon, Lebanon, and the land of the Philistines.[25]

While staying in Gerar, the men of the place inquire about Rebekah. There was no threat to the matriarch, but Isaac felt threatened. Isaac was afraid to say that Rebekah was his wife because the Gerarites would kill him due to Rebekah's beauty. Indeed, in Gen 24:16 she is described as very beautiful. Isaac is afraid to lose his wife and perhaps his own life.

---

23. The literal sense of "*kesût 'ênayim*" is "mask that covers the eyes." It should be compared to two similar expressions: the "*sātar pānîm*" (facemask) worn by an adulterer to conceal his identity (Job 24:15) and the "*mash*" (veil) that Moses places over his face to block the light radiating from it (Exod 34:34). In the present verse, however, "*kesût 'ênayim*" should not be understood literally, but as an idiom. See also Levine, *Presence of the Lord*, 60.

24. Driver and Miles, *Assyrian*, 105–11; Cardascia, *Lois Assyriennes*, 138–41.

25. Sarna, *Genesis*, 183.

Thus, he resorts to deception and says she is his sister. He assures his own safety, but not hers. He emulates his father Abraham who also used deception when he stayed in Gerar. Verse 7, which describes the events that took place in Gerar, is a reminder of story B: "When the men of the place asked him about his wife, he said, 'She is my sister,' for he was afraid to say, 'my wife' thinking, 'The men of the place might kill me on account of Rebekah, for she is beautiful.'" Isaac's words "She is my sister" are the same words that his father Abraham used (20:2). The element of fear because of Rebekah's beauty has its parallel in 20:11: "Surely there is no fear of god in this place, and they will kill me because of my wife."

Isaac stayed in Gerar a long time, which shows that he and his wife Rebekah did not face any danger and that his fears were unfounded. One day, by chance, Abimelech discovered the true nature of Isaac and Rebekah's relationship. Looking through his palace window, he saw Isaac fondling his wife Rebekah (26:8). The king immediately sent for Isaac and rebuked him; he wanted to know the motive for Isaac's action: "So she is your wife! Why then did you say: 'She is my sister'" (26:9)? Abimelech repeated here the same words of Isaac from verse 7. In his response, Isaac also, with some modification, repeated his previous thoughts: "Because I thought I might lose my life on account of her" (26:9). Abimelech continued and accused Isaac: "What have you done to us!" (26:10) As noted above, the king uses the same words that appeared in story B: "What have you done to us?" (20:9). He was afraid that one of his people might have lain with Isaac's wife, and thus harm could be done to the whole city. Abimelech shows that he is a God-fearing man. He issues a royal decree stating that any man who touches Isaac and his wife will be put to death. Gunkel raises the question, Why did Abimelech use such a forceful statement since no one considered harming Isaac? Therefore, according to him, "The narrator had other recessions in view where such harm has, indeed, taken place."[26]

In chapter 25, we read of the birth of Jacob and Esau. Here, on the other hand, there is no mention of the children at all. Isaac and Rebekah appear not to have any children, which contradicts both the previous chapter and the following one. If they already had children, no one in Gerar would have believed that they were brother and sister.[27] Hence,

---

26. Gunkel, *Genesis*, 223.
27. Koch, *Growth*, 118.

it appears that we have an independent narrative inserted in the wrong spot. The stories do not follow a chronological order.

COMPARISON OF STORY A AND B

Story A starts with famine, which was the main reason for the patriarch to go down to Egypt. In story B, there is no explanation for why Abraham went to Gerar. In A, Abraham passes his wife off as his sister because Sarah is a beautiful woman, and he is afraid that the Egyptians will kill him and let her live. If she would say that she is his sister, both would stay alive. In story B, on the other hand, there is no explanation for why Abraham ordered his wife Sarah to say that she is his sister, and there is not a single word about her beauty. It is only later in verse 11 that Abraham explains why he passed his wife off as his sister: "Surely there is no fear of God in this place, and they will kill me because of my wife." In story A, as Abraham predicted, Pharaoh's courtier sees how beautiful Sarah is and takes her into the king's palace. Because of Sarah, the king gives Abraham presents when he takes Sarah. In story B, Sarah is taken to Abimelech and there is no mention of gifts. The gifts are lavished on Abraham when Abimelech sends Sarah back to him and are meant as compensation. In addition, Abraham is not expelled from Gerar; rather, the king gives him permission to stay in his territory: "Here, my land is before you; settle wherever you please" (20:15). The fact that Abraham received gifts and the permission to stay in the land shows that the king accepted the patriarch's explanations. It appears that the king is the guilty party and not Abraham. In story A, on the other hand, after Pharaoh finds out that Abraham deceived him, he sends him away from his territory; he expels him. Here, Abraham is the guilty party and not Pharaoh. According to Van Seters, the relationship between Abraham and King Abimelech is reversed from story A "in order to give moral stature to the patriarch."[28]

In story A, Abraham does not respond to the king's accusation. He does not make any attempt to clear himself, which can be interpreted as an admission of guilt. In story B, he defends himself by saying that he did not expect to find "the fear of God in this place." In other words, he did not believe that a high code of ethical behavior was part of the fabric of the city. However, according to verse 8, King Abimelech and his people were greatly frightened. Abraham further explains that he does

---

28. Van Seters, *Abraham*, 175.

not see any wrong in his behavior since Sarah indeed is his sister. She is his father's daughter but not of the same mother; she is a half-sister. As noted before, marriage within the family—endogamy—was commonly practiced among the patriarchs. It was only later that marriage to a half-sister was forbidden, which points to the antiquity of our story.

The comparison between stories A and B shows that story B has several features that indicate the author of B had previous knowledge of version A. Therefore, in version B there is no rationale for Abraham going to Gerar, neither is there any explanation for Abraham's plan. We are simply told that Abraham said that Sarah is his sister. It is not clear why Abimelech sent for Sarah to be brought to his palace. However, in version A we were told already that Sarah was a beautiful woman, which explains the monarch's action. Indeed, some of the laconic description in version B shows that the author was expecting the reader to be familiar with the events narrated in version A (12:11–15). Indeed, version B (20:2) cannot be understood without 12:11–15.[29] Furthermore, Abraham's statement in 20:13—"Whatever place we come to, say there of me: 'He is my brother'"—suggests that he refers to the previous events of 12:10–13.

STORY C IN COMPARISON TO A AND B

According to Van Seters, when we examine version C, it is not an independent folk tale, but rather a "further version of both stories A and B."[30] It is a story that comes to show the parallels between the lives of Isaac and Abraham, "an artificial literary tradition about Isaac based directly on the traditions of Abraham."[31] In addition to the wife-sister motif, the chapter includes other parallels between the life of Abraham and Isaac. Like his father Abraham, Isaac signed a treaty with Abimelech (26:26–31; cf. 21:22–34) and named a well Beersheba (26:33; cf. 21:31).

Traveling

According to version A, Abraham travels to Egypt to the land of Pharaoh. In version B, Abraham travels to Gerar, and in version C it is Isaac who travels to Gerar. Abimelech and Pharaoh are the counter-heroes.

---

29. Alexander, "Wife/Sister Incidents," 147.
30. Van Seters, *Abraham*, 177.
31. Van Seters, *Abraham*, 183.

Abimelech and Gerar are mentioned twice, while Pharaoh only once. Hence, it is more logical to transfer a story about a less important king and a small country than a well-known king and country such as Egypt, rather than the other way around.[32]

Reasoning for the Deception

In version A, we are told that Sarah is a beautiful woman. Thus, to save his life, Abraham asks her to lie and say that she is his sister. In version B, it is only after Abimelech finds out the truth in a dream and rebukes Abraham that the patriarch explains his behavior. Accordingly, there is no fear of God in the place, and he is afraid he will be killed because of his wife. Furthermore, Abraham answers by explaining that she is indeed his sister from his father's side. In other words, she is a half-sister. It appears version B is very sensitive to the plausibility of the relationship between Abimelech and Sarah where a sin might be committed in addition to the lie that Abraham uttered. Version C is very similar to A; we read that Rebekah is very beautiful. Thus, Isaac fears for his life so he passes his wife Rebekah off as his sister. This explanation is repeated after Abimelech rebukes Isaac: "Because I thought I might lose my life on account of her" (26:9).

Discovery of the Deception

In version A, there is no explanation of how Pharaoh discovers that Sarah is Abraham's wife. Also, the text does not say that he approaches her. In version B, God tells Abimelech in a dream that Sarah is a married woman. God warns him not to touch Sarah, and he indeed does not come close to her. In version C, the discovery that Rebekah is Isaac's wife is by chance. It is noteworthy that the language used by the monarch upon discovering the truth is similar:

- "What is this you have done to me?" (Gen 12:18)
- "What have you done to us?" (Gen 20:9)
- "What is this you have done to us?" (Gen 26:10)

---

32. Koch, *Growth*, 125.

Punishment

In version A, the Lord afflicted Pharaoh and his household with mighty plagues. In version B, some sort of venereal disease, and there is a threat of death. In version C, there are no plagues, no disease, and no threats since the king discovered that Rebekah was Isaac's wife.

Adultery

In version A, Pharaoh takes Sarah into his court. What happens between them is not explicitly stated, but one can imagine. In version B, we read several times that nothing offensive takes place because God prevents it. In version C, the narrator removes any possibility of something taking place, but suggests that someone could have desired the matriarch. Since version A contains *offensive things*, it is the most *morally offensive*, which is not the case with versions B and C.

Acceptance of Guilt

In version A, Pharaoh complains that Abraham misled him, but there is not a single word about the sin that was committed or about to be committed. In version B, Abimelech complains about the great sin that Abraham has caused him and his kingdom. He asks him to explain the purpose of misleading him. In response, Abraham apologizes, saying he thought there was no fear of God in this place. In version C, there is a development regarding sin. The king could commit a sin and the whole community would have been subjected to punishment.

Presents and Wealth

According to version A, Pharaoh gives Abraham presents when he takes Sarah to his house, which makes it appear as though he purchases Sarah. The story starts with Abraham having little or no wealth and ends with Abraham being a wealthy man. In version B, Abraham is already a rich man; as is stated in Gen 13:2, "Now Abraham was very rich in cattle, in silver, and in gold." The presents he receives are to compensate Abraham for the fact that Sarah is taken to Abimelech's house; the presents are a form of reparation. In version C, there is no harm done to Rebekah, thus there is no reason for gifts. Nevertheless, after the event, Isaac receives blessings from God, not men: "The Lord blessed him, and the man grew richer and richer until he was very wealthy: he acquired flocks and herds, and a large household" (Gen 26:12–13).

Protection

In version A, God inflicts Pharaoh with plagues, preventing him from touching Sarah. In version B, God warns Abimelech in a dream not to touch Sarah. In version C, it is Abimelech himself who threatens his people with the death penalty if Sarah is touched. God's protection is missing here; it only appears in the background (Gen 26:3). Since no evil occurs, there is no need for God's involvement. The more detailed versions (A and B) contain an explanation for divine revelation. Version C is a simple story where the king perceives the truth by himself. There is no need for divine intervention, which suggests it was the original story.[33] It is the most primitive version and when the tradition developed the element of divine intervention was inserted.[34]

Expulsion

In version A, Pharaoh provides guards to accompany the patriarch's departure from his country. In version B, Abraham can stay in Gerar. In version C, Isaac can stay, but later the king asks him to leave: "Go away from us, for you have become far too big for us" (26:16). Isaac is sent away because of jealousy; he has become too rich.

ABRAHAM'S IMAGE

Speaking about Abraham, Gunkel believed that the story in Gen 12:10–20 had a "*novellistischen*" origin. As mentioned before, the story came to celebrate the cleverness of the patriarch, the beauty of his wife Sarah and her submission, and God's help.[35] But a close reading of this story shows otherwise. Abraham is portrayed negatively; he appears to be an immoral

---

33. Lutz, "Isaac," 141.
34. Kuenen, *Historical-Critical*, 105; Koch, *Growth*, 125.
35. Gunkel, *Genesis*, 173.

person. This evidently bothered the rabbis who believed that it was impossible to think that Abraham would have told a lie. They wonder, *Was she then his sister?* She was really his niece (Gen 11:29). Although the two had different mothers, they shared the same father (20:12)! Lineage was traced through the mother, therefore marriages between children of the same father but not the same mother were permissible. This is called metronymic and is found in the Hebrew Bible (2 Sam 13:13). We also must consider the usage of the word "sister," which at this time had additional meanings. The sages said that a man often referred to his female relatives as his sisters. Interestingly, in Egyptian "sister" was used both for sweetheart and wife. Scholars pointed out that in a Hurrian society, a man could adopt his wife as his sister, thus giving her a special status.[36] It is possible that Abraham instructed Sarah to mention her privilege as a "sister" so they would be treated with reverence. Hoffmeier also explains Abraham's behavior considering social customs, namely diplomatic marriage. In the ancient world, kings cemented their relationships by giving their daughters in marriage. Since Abraham did not have a daughter, he deceived Pharaoh and Abimelech by maintaining that Sarah was his sister so he could ratify a treaty with them.[37] But if this was the case why didn't Abraham present one of his concubines as his sister? So far, no adequate answer has been given by scholars for this ruse.

Another negative feature was Abraham's conduct. The patriarch put his wife in an immoral situation because Sarah was taken to the pharaoh's harem. In exchange, he was compensated because of her. Abraham acquired sheep, oxen, and asses, as well as male and female slaves. Was it greed and financial gains that motivated Abraham to pass his wife off as his sister? According to medieval commentators, fear was behind Abraham's actions. Ramban, in his commentary, says, "Know that our father Abraham inadvertently committed a great sin by placing his virtuous wife in a compromising situation because of his fear of being killed. He should have trusted God to save him, his wife, and all he had, for God has the power to help and to save." Radak, on the other hand, expressed a different view. According to him, Abraham was faced with a real danger and had to choose between two evils. If he would tell the truth, he would be killed, and his wife would be living a life of shame and abuse. Abraham is forced to choose between human life and human dignity.

---

36. Speiser, *Genesis*, 92; Speiser, "Wife-Sister Motif," 15–28. For rejection of this proposal, see Greengus, "Sisterhood Adoption," 5–31.

37. Hoffmeier, "Wives," 81–99.

Since Abraham's conduct was shameful, ancient writers tried to rehabilitate his character by adding some new details to the story. They felt that Sarah was taken by force to Pharaoh's palace. It is written in the book of Jubilees:

> So Abraham went to Egypt [and] lived in Egypt five years before his wife was taken from him by force. . . . When Pharaoh took Abraham's wife Sarai by force for himself, the Lord punished Pharaoh and his household very severely because of Abraham's wife Sarai.[38]

In the Dead Sea Scrolls, there is an attempt to rationalize Abraham's behavior. According to this account,

> I, Abram, dreamt a dream on the night that I entered the land of Egypt, and I saw in my dream a cedar tree and a beautiful, tall palm tree. Then some people came and sought to cut down and uproot the cedar and leave the palm tree alone. But the palm tree protested, "Do not cut down the cedar, for both of us are from the same root." So, the cedar was spared for the palm tree's sake, and it was not cut down. That night I awoke from my sleep and said to my wife Sarah, "I dreamt a dream and I am frightened by this dream." And she said, "Tell me your dream so that I may know." And I began to tell her the dream, and I made known to her the meaning of the dream. (1QapGen ar 19:14–19)

In the dream, the cedar is Abraham and the palm tree is Sarah. Thus, Abraham's life is in danger; he can only be saved if Sarah says the right thing. If indeed he had a dream, it would be a divine commandment since God delivered messages through dreams. So, Abraham's behavior was not an act of cowardice, but obedience to God.

STORY REPETITION

As noted before by Ramban, "Whatever happened to the patriarchs is a portent for the children." In the Torah, we read at length about the patriarchs' journeys and digging of wells because they serve as lessons for the future. Repetition is a well-known technique that was used by the biblical narrator and is found in the literature of the ancient world. By repeating stories and adding or subtracting details, the narrator could stress a point. The patriarchs were fallible human beings. There is no attempt to

---

38. Jub. 13:11–13.

idealize them. They are described with all their faults and weaknesses, with stories portraying simple people who are living their daily lives. The audience was familiar already with the stories and their outcome and enjoyed hearing the stories repeatedly. When the author wanted to stress a point, he would repeat the story. Therefore, when Pharaoh had a dream about the seven cows, it was followed by a second dream of seven ears of grain. Joseph, while interpreting Pharaoh's dream, said, "Pharaoh's dreams are one and the same: God has told Pharaoh what He is about to do" (Gen 41:25). In other words, every time the author wanted to emphasize a point, he would repeat the story. He would alter and change some of the story motifs but preserved its core by using similar words and expressions.

Deception was a way of life in the ancient world, and in this respect, the Hebrews were no different from other people. In the Jacob cycle, for example, trickery and deceptions are one of the main motifs. All protagonists take part and play a role in deception. Similarly, in Greek literature, humans and gods deceive each other. Athena dressed herself up as an old man. Penelope lied about Laertes's magically-shrinking shroud. Odysseus was the king of liars. As for the gods, they, too, deceived all the time. These deceptions aimed to gain the advantage of being in control, to have the upper hand. However, as we read in the Ten Commandments (Exod 20:7), the Hebrew Bible, with its high moral standard, did not approve of this kind of trickery. Surprisingly, Abraham and Isaac are not punished for their deception. In fact, God protects them. God—who chose Abraham, made promises to him, watched over him and his wife, and rescued them from danger—does the same with Isaac.

As Ramban pointed out, the stories foreshadowed future events. Hence, the story about Abraham and Sarah's migration to Egypt is very similar to the story of the Israelites' descent to Egypt and the Exodus.[39] This is not limited to subject matter but also to the usage of language. Abraham went to Egypt because of the famine (Gen 12:10); later, the famine was again the reason Israelites went down to Egypt (43:1). In both incidents, the famine is described as severe. The fear that Abraham expressed—"they will kill me and let you live" (12:12)—is a reminder of "if it is a boy, kill him; if it is a girl, let her live" (Exod 1:16). Taking Sarah to Pharaoh's harem is parallel to the taking of the Israelites into slavery. The presents that Abraham received in Egypt (Gen 12:16), and the mention

---

39. Cassuto, *"Quaestio" of Genesis*, 258.

of it when he left Egypt ("cattle, silver, and gold," 13:2), are like the silver and gold the Israelites received from the Egyptians when they left Egypt (Exod 3:21–22; 11:2–3; 12:35–36). God interceded in both stories and inflicted plagues on the Egyptians (Gen 12:17; Exod 11:1). These parallels are not coincidence, but further proof of the author's desire to show the similarities between the stories.[40]

The stories about Abraham and Sarah in Egypt and Gerar serve as background for story about Isaac and Rebekah in Gerar. The author created a story here, which encompasses elements from the previous stories in Genesis. Despite all the troubles with the Egyptians and the Philistines, God protected Abraham and Isaac. Similarly, he would later protect his descendants as we read in the stories of the Exodus and the return of the ark (1 Sam 6). The way that God helped the patriarchs in the past was a testimony for the future—God would guide and protect the Israelites. It is a message of faith that the author conveyed so the Israelites could be sure God would come to their aid in times of need.[41] What we witnessed here is one story about a patriarch who faced danger in a foreign land and in order to avert the danger passed his wife off as his sister. Repetitions and parallel stories are a pattern that exists in the patriarchal narrative. This is not a patchwork of different sources; rather, by repeating the stories and making changes, the author tried to display the similarities and differences between the patriarchs.[42]

In conclusion, the danger that the matriarchs faced in foreign territory is described in the book of Genesis three times. Version A is Sarah in the house of Pharaoh (chapter 12); version B is Sarah in the house of Abimelech (chapter 20); and version C is Rebekah and Abimelech (chapter 26). An examination of these stories shows that there are progressive developments originating from an early story A. Story B has several features that indicate the author of B had previous knowledge of version A. Furthermore, in version B we find answers to some of the questions that were left open in version A. In version C, we find elements from both stories A and B. During its inclusion within the book of Genesis, story C was altered to show the parallels between the lives of Abraham and Isaac. However, it is missing the moral and theological questions regarding the wife-sister deception. It is clearly an artificial literary tradition about Isaac based directly on the traditions of Abraham. Probably

---

40. Cassuto, *"Quaestio" of Genesis*, 258–59.
41. Cassuto, *"Quaestio" of Genesis*, 261.
42. Cassuto, *"Quaestio" of Genesis*, 262–64.

during the process of their incorporation into the book of Genesis, the three accounts were modified considering each other. Examination of the three versions shows that they are organized chronologically. Version A is the most ancient one. Version B appeared later and is based on version A. Version C is the most recent based on the previous two. The story about Abraham foreshadows future events that happened to him and is repeated with his son Isaac and later with the Israelites in Egypt. These stories serve as a prophetic indicator of what is to take place in future generations: "The deeds of the fathers are signs to the sons." Abraham's depiction in the stories is negative; he appears as a dishonest person. He should have relied on God and not used deception.

The next chapter will examine if there is any reference to religious customs in the Abrahamic stories.

Chapter 10

And He Circumcised the Flesh of Their Foreskins

The law of circumcision is the first and only deed in the Torah that was given to Abraham and his descendants; no other laws are mentioned with Abraham. God gave only promises of nationhood and posterity to the patriarch. Not surprisingly, as mentioned earlier, some scholars claim there is no such thing as a patriarchal period or patriarchal religion.[1] Scholars maintain that the stories in Genesis are late retrojections composed during the monarchial period. The rabbis were also aware of the lack of moral responsibility and lack of law. However, they solved this difficulty by claiming the existence of a divine covenant with the whole human race. According to them, God made a covenant with Adam and Noah. This came to be known as the Noachian commandments. To reconstruct the religious customs of the patriarchs and assign a precise date to the stories, scholars used extrabiblical sources. Despite using similar data, they arrived at contrasting conclusions. Evidently, this kind of methodology had some flaws and did not offer an adequate solution.[2] One of the main problems is the fact that some of the religious practices and social customs in the book of Genesis remained unchanged

---

1. Wellhausen, *Prolegomena*, 318–19; Hoftijzer, *Verheissunge*, 6–30; Van Seters, *Abraham*, 220–33.

2. Talmon, "Comparative Method," 320–56; Warner, "Patriarchs," 50–61; Millard, "Methods of Studying," 35–51; Luke, "Abraham," 35–47; Miller, "Patriarchs," 62–66.

And He Circumcised the Flesh of Their Foreskins

for centuries.[3] This, in turn, led scholars to reevaluate their thinking and methodology. Examination of the book of Genesis shows that there are already some clues to religious customs that relate to Abraham, such as building altars, offering sacrifices, setting up pillars, planting sacred trees, praying, blessing, and circumcision. This makes one wonder about the purpose of these customs and their inclusion in the Abrahamic stories. Answering it will help us to see if indeed the religious customs of the patriarch Abraham were authentic presentations of his faith during his time, or a representation of the later monarchial period.

ALTARS

Genesis mentions the building of altars quite often. The patriarchs built new altars, and afterward, they reused the ones they built. Following God's theophany at the terebinth of Moreh, Abraham built an altar as a way of showing gratitude for the promise of the land (Gen 12:7). Abraham built a second altar between Beth El and Ai where he invoked the Lord by name (12:8). Returning from Egypt, he stopped at the same altar and invoked the name of God (13:4). A third altar is mentioned in Gen 13:18, where Abraham, who lived by the terebinths of Mamre in Hebron, built an altar there unto the Lord. There is still another instance of Abraham building an altar in the story of the binding of Isaac. However, this altar was a different one; here he built an altar because of God's request to sacrifice Isaac. This fact is more significant because this is the only time that the patriarch made a sacrifice. Abraham built altars before, but there was no mention of sacrifice. It has been suggested that Abraham's altars were already sacred places.[4] This assumption was based on the use of the phrases "the place," "the Oak of Moreh," and "the Oaks of Mamre." In other words, this is a testimony to a primitive religion, animistic in its nature. However, we should point out that "the place" does not always refer to a holy site.

The building of the altars was spontaneous; there are only two occasions where God instructed Abraham and later Jacob to build an altar (Gen 22:2; 35:1). The altars were a place to commune with God, therefore the patriarchs invoked God's name. The altars were built on the occasion of the epiphanies, not for sacrifice but as enduring signs. They served

---

3. Freedman, "Chronology," 205; Selman, "Comparative Customs," 125–26.
4. Skinner, *Genesis*, 246; Westermann, *Genesis*, 153–54.

as a sign of gratitude for God's promises. Segal explained the building of altars as the attachment of spiritual context to the place. Accordingly, the patriarchs built altars where they prayed to God, but they removed the pagan element, which was symbolized by the sacrifice.[5] The custom of the naming of altars or invoking God's name continued with Moses (Exod 17:15) and Gideon (Judg 6:24), but was not mentioned afterward. Only in one instance, the binding of Isaac, did Abraham make a sacrifice on an altar that he built (Gen 22:13). Not surprisingly, the patriarchs did not have priests. Priests would appear in Israel only after the exodus, with the dedication of Aaron and his sons by Moses (Exod 28–29; Lev 8–10). Before the existence of the priesthood, it was the head of the family who brought sacrifices and blessed the members of his family (Gen 28:1–4; 48:9–20; 49:3–28). In the book of Exodus, the firstborn leads the community (Exod 22:28). In Exod 24:5, they are referred to as the "young men of the people of Israel." However, they lost their important role after the story of the golden calf (Exod 34:26; Num 8:2–26). In Num 8:18, this change is echoed: "Now I take the Levites instead of every firstborn of the Israelite."

SACRIFICE

The first mention of offering a sacrifice appears in the story of the binding of Isaac. Abraham took the ram and offered it up as a burnt offering in place of his son. As mentioned before, some suggest that the story of the binding of Isaac is a polemic against human sacrifice. The binding of Isaac is a transitional story from human sacrifice to animal sacrifice. However, an examination of the biblical narrative does not support this view. Human sacrifice did not end with the binding of Isaac. On the contrary, we still read about it in the Hebrew Bible. The story had a didactic purpose to show Abraham's love and devotion to God. The sacrifice, which is described in the binding of Isaac, is typical of the patriarchal narrative. Neither a priest nor an established cult is involved. This matter is between the patriarch and God. It is different from later periods where organized sacrifice was offered during festivals and public occasions. The sacrifices functioned as a removal of sin and healing, neither of which are mentioned here.

---

5. Segal, "Religion of Israel," 220–21.

PRAYERS

Prayers are mentioned several times in Genesis. The first time that prayer is mentioned is in Abimelech's dream. God told Abimelech that Abraham would intercede on his behalf and pray for him (Gen 20:7). In verse 17, Abraham prays to God and God heals Abimelech, his wife, and his slave girls. The prayer is mentioned here, but the content of the prayer is not recorded. It was not uncommon for people to pray for one another. Later, Moses prayed for his sister Miriam (Num 12:13). Job prayed to God for his three friends (Job 42:8). This was also common in the ancient Near East where kings prayed for the healing of people and to avert divine judgment. A good example is Mursilis, who prayed to remove the plague that had affected his kingdom since the days of his father Suppiluliumas I.[6]

In Gen 24:12–14, when Abraham's servant was sent to Mesopotamia to bring a wife for Isaac, he prayed for guidance. This is the first occurrence of a prayer for guidance. The servant starts his prayer with an appeal to God to "keep faith with my master Abraham." Then he requests a sign from God when he says, "Grant me good fortune this day" (24:12). He wants a sign on the same day. This is the first passage in the Hebrew Bible where God answers a prayer on the same day that it was prayed.[7] Recognizing that his prayer was answered, the servant bowed to the Lord, thanking God in prayer (24:26–27). The action and the prayer in verses 26–27 are parallel to the prayer at the arrival at the well. The prayer itself is simple and starts with praise to God—"Blessed be the Lord"—and is expanded to "The God of my master Abraham, who has not withheld his steadfast faithfulness from my master." According to Towner, it is a spontaneous, non-cultic blessing of YHWH.[8] He believes that the usage of the formula "Blessed be YHWH" was used in conversation between people, and it was uttered for the benefit of the listener.[9] Therefore, the servant was praying in the presence of the girl, and in the following verse may even be addressing her: "For I have been guided on my errand by the Lord, to the house of my master's kinsmen" (24:27). No intermediaries are involved in the servant's prayer; it is a direct call for God's help. It was followed by a "thanks prayer" to God. The prayers were natural, spontaneous expressions of God's close relationship with his people.

6. Goetze, "Plague," 394–96.
7. Hamilton, *Genesis*, 145.
8. Towner, "'Blessed Be YHWH,'" 388–89.
9. Towner, "'Blessed Be YHWH,'" 389.

When Abraham worshiped, he invoked the name of God (Gen 12:8; 13:4; 21:33). The same act is mentioned later with Isaac: "So he built an altar there and invoked the Lord by name" (26:25). The calling of the name is an act of worship. This invocation relates to the ancient Near Eastern notion of a connection between a person and their name. But the connection is not just lexical; it is symphonic since the way a name is pronounced has mystical implications on the meaning of that name. Medieval commentators such as Ibn Ezra and Radak understood the calling of the name YHWH as a proclamation of God's unity and a call to all men to worship him. The midrash says, "And called upon the name of the Lord: with prayer. Another interpretation of this is: that he began to make converts."[10] Ramban, in his commentary, maintains that Abraham loudly proclaimed the name of YHWH before the altar, teaching the people to know God and his divine essence. In Ur of the Chaldeans, he already did it, but people refused to listen to him. Now, after his arrival to the land of Canaan where he had been promised "I will bless them that bless thee," he built an altar and made his duty to teach and to proclaim the deity. Returning from his journey to Egypt, Abraham went to the altar that he erected before and he invoked the Lord by name (Gen 13:4). In other words, he reestablishes his spiritual connection with the place. Most medieval commentators say that Abraham invokes the Lord by name to indicate the continuation of his mission. In the book of Genesis, there is no suggestion that this form of invoking the name of the Lord received a response. However, the form "call upon the name of YHWH" is found outside the Pentateuch only when an answer from the deity was expected (1 Kgs 18:24; 2 Kgs 5:11; Ps 116:14; Isa 64:6; Lam 3:55; Joel 3:5; Zech 13:9), or it is used doxologically (Ps 80:19; 105:1; 116:13, 17; Isa 12:4; Zeph 3:9).[11] We can see that prayers in the book of Genesis were a spontaneous outpouring of the heart. They were individual and tailored for the specific occasion. They were not connected to a specific site or a cult.

TAMARISK

In Gen 21:33 Abraham invokes the name of the Lord, the everlasting God. This invocation followed Abraham's planting of a tamarisk. According to Maimonides, the usage of El Olam alludes to God as the first

---

10. *Gen. Rab.* 39:16.
11. Hamilton, *Genesis Chapters 18–50*, 378.

cause who is eternal and existed before the creation.[12] We are not told why Abraham planted the tree. According to Gunkel, Abraham is a cult founder, but we should ask if one can plant a holy tree.[13] Beno Jacob interpreted differently; he suggested that the planting of the tree was so that "the tree shall be a permanent memorial of the event."[14] Abraham planted the tree as a marker for the place where he called on his God. Planting a tree is like an building an altar and marks the foundation of the great shrine of Beersheba. While according to Radak, Abraham planted the tree next to the well as a testimony that the well belonged to him, it was a public demonstration of his undisputed ownership of the well. We have to remember that trees were often used to mark the boundary between fields belonging to different owners. By planting the tree, Abraham was claiming the territory as rightfully his, and for which he had agreed with Abimelech. Specification of trees in the sale of the land was common in ancient contracts in all periods. Indeed, a Babylonian bill of sale listed trees along the property. From the Second Temple period, we read that a person who purchased a field with trees in it had a claim for the ground around it.[15]

It is interesting to note that Abraham's first stop in the promise land was by a tree (Gen 12:6). In 13:18 he built an altar by the tree of Mamre. He lived near trees (14:13), and in 18:1 he entertained YHWH under the trees. Finally, here he plants a tree. A review of the book of Genesis shows that there is no trace of the patriarch Abraham engaging in any religious rites at these trees. It is only in later periods that we read about the Israelites who had worshiped YHWH on mountains, in the hills, or under any spreading trees (Deut 12:2; 1 Kgs 14:23; Jer 2:20). It was this late Bible reading and later traditions that associated Abraham and sacred trees. Not surprisingly, as mentioned before, the Aramaic translators avoided translating the word "tree." Instead, they gave it a different meaning using the word "plain," which is a flat land found at the bottom of a valley, to avoid any association between Abraham and paganism.[16]

---

12. Maimonides, *Guide for the Perplexed*, 2:13; 3:29.
13. Gunkel, *Genesis*, 253.
14. Benno Jacob, *Genesis*, 141.
15. *B. Bat.* 82b.
16. For further study about trees, see Bar, "Abraham's Trees," 2–20.

SWEARING

Swearing is another religious act mentioned in Genesis. In Abraham's pact with Abimelech, the king asked Abraham to swear to him. In addition, Abimelech asked Abraham not to deal falsely with him or with his posterity (Gen 21:23). Ibn Ezra pointed out that the Hebrew verb "deal falsely" appears only in our verse in the *kal* conjugation. This verb is also found in the eighth-century-BCE Sefire treaty, meaning "to be guilty of a breach of contractual commitment."[17] The usage of the verb *šbʿ* in the text is the first allusion to the name Beersheba. In his request to Abraham, Abimelech is concerned about the future of his offspring and the land in which Abraham dwells. To Abimelech's request, Abraham responded, "I swear it" (21:24), which again is play on the name Beersheba. This exchange between Abraham and Abimelech led to a covenant between the two parties. While accepting Abimelech's request, Abraham reapproached the king for the well of water that the servant of Abimelech seized. In the midrash we find the view "reproof leads to love, as it says, 'Reprove a wise man, and he will love thee (Prov 9:8).'"[18] Abimelech, on his part, maintained that "I do not know who did this" (Gen 21:26). He also complained that Abraham did not tell him about it until today. In other words, it is Abraham's fault that he was left ignorant. This is a reminder of the previous episode where Abimelech was unaware that Sarah was a married woman until God told him that in a dream (20:3–7). Following Abimelech's grievousness, Abraham took sheep and cattle and gave them to Abimelech, and the two of them made a treaty. It is Abraham who gave the gifts, which suggests that he is the weaker party and the side that is the beneficiary of the treaty. It is possible that Abraham gave the gifts as a payback for the gifts that he received from Abimelech (20:14), so now he enters as equal to the king. But he did not give him male and female slaves as the king did because Abraham does not give people as a gift. It was pointed out that later laws prohibit making treaty covenants with the inhabitants of Canaan (Exod 23:33; Duet 7:2). Abraham's acts suggest that he was not aware of later legal norms and point to the antiquity of this episode.[19]

In addition to the gift of sheep and cattle, which was mentioned in Gen 21:27, we read of seven lambs that Abraham set separately (21:28)

---

17. Fitzmeyer, *Aramaic Inscription of Sefire*, 107.
18. *Gen. Rabb.* 54:3.
19. Wenham, *Genesis 16–50*, 93.

and gave them to Abimelech. By accepting them as a gift, the king acknowledges Abraham's ownership of the wells. What Abraham wanted here was guarantees for the usage of the well that he had dug. The lambs are to be a witness to the agreement between the two parties. For a second time, Abraham and Abimelech swore, and because of it, the name of the place is called Beersheba. The name can be explained as "well of oath" or "well of seven." Again, we are told that both parties, the patriarch and the king, made a covenant (21:32). This was already mentioned in verse 27, therefore this may be a summary of the whole episode. The act of swearing gave the treaty its authoritative stamp.[20]

In his encounter with the king of Sodom, Abraham swears to "the Lord, God Most High, Creator of heaven and earth" (14:22). In the text we read that Abraham said to the king of Sodom, "I lift up my hand," which implies an oath and is like Deut 32:40—"I raise my hand to heaven." Raising the hand towards heaven included invoking God in an oath (Exod 6:8; Num 14:30; Ezek 20:5; Dan 12:7). By his act, Abraham indicated his reliance on God. Raising the hand is a motion that is a part of oath-taking. Even today, this tradition can be seen in customs such as raising one hand, while the other rests on the Bible, before testifying in a judicial court.[21] Abraham's servant, before he was sent on his mission to bring Isaac a wife, swears to Abraham by the Lord, the God of heaven and earth (24:3). It has been suggested that this expression is a Hebrew adaptation of an oath formula in which the gods of heaven and earth are summoned to witness an oath.[22] It also might be that since the mission involves travel to a distant land, the servant invokes God's universal sovereignty. In addition, the servant puts his hands under Abraham's thigh, which is a euphemism for touching the genitalia. According to Vawter, we have here an ancient ceremony that "reverenced the organ of the generation as the seat of life and symbol of sacredness: the same mentality that found expression in phallic worship and fertility ritual."[23] The touching of the circumcised membrane is a reminder of the covenant with God, and by that act it calls upon God as the guarantor of the covenant.

---

20. Similarly, Isaac and Abimelech made a pact (26:31). Abimelech, his councilor Ahuzzah, and Phicol, chief of his troops, initiated the pact; they asked Isaac for a sworn treaty. A curse was attached to the treaty that was sealed by an oath.

21. Exod 6:8; Num 14:30; Deut 32:40; Ezek 20:23.

22. Andrews, "YHWH," 45–47.

23. Vawter, *On Genesis*, 267.

BLESSING

The most common Hebrew word for "blessing" is *berakah*. It was believed that there is power in spoken words. Two major types of blessing are found in the Hebrew Bible: the pronouncement of the blessing and requests of blessings. When God does the blessing, it is a decree, and when man does the blessing the source of power is the deity. The first occurrence of a blessing is found in Gen 1:22 when God blessed the sea creatures and birds to be fruitful and multiply in the seas and the earth. Similarly, God blessed Adam and Eve and told them to be fertile and increase and to have dominion over creation (1:28). When God told Abraham to go to the land of Canaan, he blessed him and promised to make his name great. In addition, Abraham would be a blessing to those who blessed him, so they, too, would enjoy God's blessing. Following the binding of Isaac, God again blessed Abraham as a reward for his devotion and obedience. God blessed him with posterity and victory over his foe.

God is not the only one who makes the blessing. Rebekah, before her departure to the land of Canaan, received a blessing from her family:

> O sister!
> May you grow
> Into thousands of myriads;
> May your offspring seize
> The gates of their foes. (Gen 24:60)

The blessing contains posterity and security. What is interesting is that she received the same blessing that God gave Abraham following the binding of Isaac: "I will greatly increase your offspring" (22:17). In other words, her marriage is preordained, and the divine promises are to come through her. In addition, her family wished that her offspring would always be victorious in battle. The blessing that Rebekah received is used today at the veiling of the bride, which takes place before the Jewish wedding ceremony.

The Bible does not mention that Abraham blessed his son Isaac. Targum Pseudo-Jonathan adds that Abraham refused to bless Isaac for fear that Ishmael might hate Isaac, as happens later with Esau and Jacob. In the Midrash, on the other hand, we read: "If I bless Isaac the children of Ishmael and Keturah are included; while if I do not bless the children of Ishmael and of Keturah, how can I bless Isaac?"[24] So instead of

---

24. *Gen. Rab.* 61:6.

Abraham's blessing, the Bible tells us that it was God who blessed Isaac (Gen 25:11). By mentioning it, the narrator confirms the transition of the divine blessing from Abraham to Isaac in fulfillment of the promise of 17:21—"But my covenant I will maintain with Isaac, whom Sarah shall bear to you at this season next year."

Blessing is mentioned in the meeting between Melchizedek, king of Salem, and Abraham. Melchizedek is referred to as a priest of God Most High. The book of Psalms speaks of him as an ideal priest (110:4), and in Christianity he becomes a prototype of the Messiah (Heb 7:1). This is the only priestly blessing in the book of Genesis. Later it was the priests who blessed the Israelites (Num 6:24–26; Deut 10:8), and sometimes it was a national leader such as Moses and David (Exod 39:43; 2 Sam 6:18) or a family member (Gen 24:60; Ruth 2:19–20; 2 Sam 6:20). The king-priest blessed Abraham for his victory over his enemies. He acknowledges that the victory was the act of God Most High.[25] He says that God is the creator of heaven and earth and recognizes Abraham's God as the universal creator and self-governing over all the people. It appears that the formula "Creator of heaven and earth" is universalistic and fits the meeting between two different people. The language that was used by Melchizedek is used by Abraham when he meets the king of Sodom: "God Most High, Creator of heaven and earth" (Gen 14:22). Since Melchizedek and Abraham used the same epithet for God, did Melchizedek worship the same God as Abraham? And how did he know the Lord? These are open questions that led to many speculations about his identity, his name, and his city name.[26]

The sages pointed out that the Melchizedek first blessed Abraham and only afterward blessed God:

> Abraham said to him: "And does one place the blessing of the servant before the blessing of his master? You should have blessed God first." Immediately the Holy One, Blessed be He, gave the priesthood to Abraham, as it is stated: "The Lord says to my lord: Sit at My right hand, until I make your enemies your footstool" (Ps 110:1), and afterward it is written: "The Lord has sworn, and will not repent: You shall be a priest forever, because you are a king of righteousness [*al divrati malki tzedek*]" (Ps 110:4), which is why explained homiletically to mean: Due to

---

25. For the epithet "El-Elyon God Most High," see Hundley, *YHWH*, 209–10.
26. Kugel, *Bible*, 151–62; McNamara, "Melchizedek," 1–31.

the improper words [*divrati*] of Melchizedek, the offspring of Abraham shall be priests of God forever.[27]

CIRCUMCISION

An important institution in the Jewish religion is the practice of circumcision.[28] As we discussed earlier, this custom is first mentioned in Gen 17:9–14. It serves as a sign of an eternal covenant between God and his people, like the rainbow and the Sabbath. In Exod 4:24–26, circumcision comes to protect the person from the anger of God. The usage of a flint-blade knife for circumcision points to the antiquity of this custom (Exod 4:25; Josh. 5:2), since this type of knife is from the Bronze Age. Abraham did not start the practice of circumcision because he knew what to do. Not surprisingly, the rabbinic legend suggests that it was known before.[29]

In the book of Genesis, all the descendants of Abraham are circumcised—Isaac, Ishmael, and the sons of Keturah. Abraham was ninety-nine years old when he circumcised the flesh of his foreskin, and his son Ishmael was thirteen years old. Abraham also circumcised all his household males; this included two groups of slaves. In contrast, Isaac was the first person circumcised when he was eight days old by the command in 17:12—"eight days old." This underscored his role as the true heir to the Abrahamic covenant. Abarvanel suggests that the phrase "at the age of eight days" speaks of not only the time of circumcision but also the time that Abraham named his son. Ramban, on the other hand, suggests that Abraham named Isaac on the day he was born because the name had been commanded by God (17:19). The sages derive from the word "him" that only the father is obligated to perform the rite of circumcision and not the mother.[30]

The antiquity of circumcision is attested in extrabiblical sources. According to Herodotus, Egyptians practiced circumcision "for the sake of cleanliness, considering it better to be clean than comely."[31] A stela from Naga ed-Der in Middle Egypt from the first intermediate period 23 BCE

---

27. *Ned.* 32b.

28. For a general study on circumcision, see Morgenson, "Bloody," 35–70; Morgenson, *Rites*, 1025–31.

29. *Gen. Rab.* 42:8.

30. *Kid.* 29a.

31. Herodotus, *Histories*, 2:37.

gives us a report of a mass circumcision of 120 men. A tomb relief from Saqqara from 2350 BCE depicts an operation on a boy. However, it is not clear if this practice of circumcision was widespread or restricted to a certain class. It is also unknown if it was obligatory or voluntary. Circumcision among the Canaanites is found in the writings of Philo of Byblos: "At the occurrence of a fatal plague, Kronos immolated his only son to his father Ouranos, and circumcised himself, forcing the allies who were with him to do the same."[32] The Hebrews probably adopted the practice of circumcision as they moved into Canaan (Gen 17; Josh 5:2–9). It was believed that circumcision originated in Egypt and from there spread to east and west around the Mediterranean to Phoenicia. A different view is suggested by Sasson who pointed out portrayals of circumcision among Syrian warriors in Syria that date to the early third millennium. He believes that the practice began among NW Semites communities and spread south where the Egyptians adopted it.[33]

Irrespective of whether the custom came from north or south, the meaning and significance of the customs varied among the different cultures and originated in an early period. The Hebrew Bible gave the custom a different meaning than the pagan world did. Instead of a social custom or continuation of tribal tradition in the Bible, it was transformed into a law, divinely ordained. It had to be kept throughout the ages as an everlasting pact. The rite was changed from puberty to eight days of birth.[34] And as noted before, it became the "sign of the covenant" and the covenant itself. The rite became the norm among the Hebrews. When Hamor wanted to marry Dinah, Jacob's sons insisted that he undergo circumcision (Gen 34:14). According to the book of Exodus, only circumcised males could celebrate the paschal offering (12:44, 48). Before the Israelites entered the land of Canaan they were circumcised by Joshua (Josh 5:2).

The Hebrew Bible uses a negative tone when speaking of uncircumcised people. During the wars with the Philistines, the word "uncircumcised" became a term for the enemy (1 Sam 14:6; 17:26, 36; 31:4).[35] In the books of Isaiah and Ezekiel, the lack of circumcision is identified with cultic impurity (Ezek 44:7, 9; Isa 52:1; Exod 12:48). The prophets used the term "uncircumcised" allegorically to refer to the rebellious heart or to

---

32. Philo of Byblos, *Phoenician*, 1:33–34.
33. Sasson, "Circumcision," 473–76.
34. Saran, *Understanding Genesis*, 132.
35. For the term "uncircumcised," see Mayer, "עָרֵל 'āral," 359–61.

the obdurate ear (Ezek 44:9; Jer 6:10). Jeremiah stated that all the nations were uncircumcised in the flesh, but the whole house of Israel was of the uncircumcised heart (Jer 9:25). Impeded speech was referred to as uncircumcised lips (Exod 6:12; 30). The prophet Ezekiel threatens the Phoenicians (Ezek 28:10) and Egyptians (31:18; 32:17–32) with lying among the uncircumcised in their death as well as those slain by the sword, obtaining a special place in the underworld. Israel's neighbors who practiced circumcision stopped during the Second Temple period because of Persian and Greek cultural influences. From that period onward, circumcision became a sign of recognition for Jews and converts to Judaism.

In conclusion, an examination of the Abrahamic narrative shows no regular patterns of worship. It lacked a liturgical calendar and specific places for worship. The religion developed as a reaction to a developing situation. There were no temples and no priests. Abraham built altars to God as a form of worship and invoked his name. No sacrifices are mentioned on the altars except in the story of the binding of Isaac. Prayers and swearing are a simple, spontaneous outpouring of the heart and are not connected to a site or a cult. They were individual and tailored for a specific purpose. Blessings are pronounced by God, but also by individuals. The source of the power of a blessing is God. The custom of circumcision was an ancient one and was also practiced by the Egyptians. In the Bible, it is the sign of the covenant and the covenant itself. In Genesis, all of Abraham's descendants are circumcised. Later, the Hebrew Bible uses a negative tone while describing the uncircumcised. Reading the book of Genesis reveals that there is no religious antagonism. There is no mention of conflict with idolatry. The difference in beliefs between the Israelites and their neighbors will become more apparent only after the covenant at Sinai. From that point on, Israelites inhabit one side of the world, with Gentiles on the other side. The religious customs that appear in Genesis point to a distant early stage of the Israelite religion, which has similar elements to Israel's neighbors.[36] In Genesis, we have the first steps toward monotheism that developed fully only after Israel received its laws and commandments.

Now that we have dealt with the religious customs of the patriarch Abraham, the next stage of our study is to consider whom Abraham worshiped. The different names for God and the form of God's appearance will be examined.

---

36. For a different view, see Van Seters, "Religion of the Patriarchs," 220–33.

Chapter 11

I Am YHWH; I Appeared to Abraham, Isaac, and Jacob as El Shaddai

The first time the name YHWH is mentioned in Gen 2:4 is when the first man invoked the Lord (YHWH) by name. In other words, monotheism was the first original religion of humans. Later, according to Gen 12:1; YHWH called Abraham to leave his native land. YHWH was also known to the other patriarchs who built altars to him and invoked his name. However, this tradition differs from the book of Exodus, which says the initial revelation of the name YHWH took place during the time of Moses: "I am YHWH; I appeared to Abraham, Isaac, and Jacob as El Shaddai, but by my name YHWH I did not make myself known to them" (Exod 6:2–3). Although it was YHWH who appeared to the patriarchs, they did not know him by that name. Proper names mentioned in the Torah before the time of Moses are not constructed with the divine element based on this name. Thus, names with the prefix *yeho/yo* or the suffix *yahu/yah* started to appear only after the birth of Moses.[1] On the other hand, the patriarchs were familiar with personal and place names with the divine epithet El (e.g., Ishmael, Israel, Bethel). From the time of Wellhausen, the consensus is that J is the oldest of the Pentateuchal sources. Thus, if J is earlier than E and P, Why do these sources suggest that the

---

1. The Hebrew name of Moses' mother, "Yokheved," is the first of these types of names.

patriarchs did not know the name YHWH? In addition to YHWH, Abraham worshipped El Shaddai, El Olam, Elohim, and El Roi, which is mentioned with Hagar. Later the "God of my father" with the name Abraham is mentioned. It was suggested that the usage of different names for God is because Genesis is composed of different sources, which is the main argument by scholars for source division. However, according to Westermann, "None of the attempts to explain the variation in the name of God in another way have so far led to any convincing result."[2] This raises more questions about whether Abraham was a true monotheist or whether he worshiped many gods. In addition to God's names, the forms of God's theophany need attention; did God appear directly to Abraham or speak to him through the medium of vision? More so, was it God or an angel who revealed himself to Abraham?

THE WORSHIP OF ELIM

All accounts agree that the patriarchs worshiped different Elim. "El" is common to all Semitic languages as a general term for God. The etymology of "El" is uncertain and perhaps derives from a Semitic root, "to be strong." The patriarchs worshiped God under the name El, thus "El Elyon" (Gen 14:18–22), "El Olam" (21:33), "El Roi" (16:13), "El-elohei Israel" (33:20), "El Bethel" (31:13; 35:7), and "El Shaddai" (17:1; 28:3; 35:11; 43:13; 48:3; 49:25). Examination of these titles shows they are connected to certain locales: El Bethel to Beth El; El Olam to Beersheba; El Roi to a sanctuary farther south near Kadesh; and El-elohei Israel to the vicinity of Shechem. On the other hand, El Elyon and El Shaddai do not correspond to a place. According to the book of Genesis, Abraham worshiped "El Elyon," "El Olam," and "El Shaddai."

El-Elyon—"God Most High"—is mentioned for the first time when Abraham met King Melchizedek of Salem, who is referred to as a priest of God Most High (Gen 14:19–20). El-Elyon is identified with YHWH when Abraham met with the king of Sodom—"I swear to the Lord, God Most High, Creator of heaven and earth" (14:22). The epithet "El-Elyon" encompasses God's characteristic and describes him as the creator of heaven and earth. Elyon is a common title of God in the Bible, mainly in poetry. Genesis 14 and Ps 78:35 are the only places in the Hebrew Bible where El and Elyon are linked together. In other instances, El and

---

2 Westermann, *Genesis 1–11*, 578.

Elyon are mentioned in parallelism: "How could God [El] know? Is there knowledge with the Most High?" (Ps 73:11); "Because they defied the word of God [El], spurned the counsel of the Most High" (107:11). The epithet "God Most High" is not exclusive to the Hebrew Bible and is used also by non-Israelites. Its usage in the Bible comes to emphasize God's supremacy over the other deities. Outside of the Bible, El and Elyon appear separately but they are associated deities. In a late Greek account of Phoenician mythology, we read of "Eliuom who is referred to as the Most High father of heaven and earth and grandfather of El."[3] Another source, an Aramaic treaty from Sfire from the eighth century BCE, mentions the names of divine witnesses to the treaty. The names of the different gods are mentioned first and are followed by "El and Elyon, before Heaven [and Earth, before Abyss] and Sources, and before Day and Night."[4] El was known as the supreme Canaanite god and is described as the creator of the earth. Therefore, more than likely it was the Canaanite influence that led to its assimilation into Israelite traditions. Cross surmises that El and Elyon of Genesis represent an early form referring to a single deity that later split into a pair of gods.[5] What is clear is that El and Elyon were deities other than YHWH and the Hebrew Bible linked them to YHWH. Elyon is used in the Bible in poetic texts, which points to its antiquity since poetic texts preserve archaic words and phrases. By mentioning YHWH before El-Elyon, Abraham makes the latter an epithet.[6] What we have here is an archaic divine title that was replaced and instead is used to describe the different attributes of God.

EL OLAM—THE EVERLASTING GOD

Following a treaty with Abimelech, Abraham plants a tamarisk tree in Beersheba and calls on the name of YHWH, El-Olam (Gen 21:33). El-Olam is equated here with YHWH and the patriarch commemorated the event by planting a tree. The author included "Everlasting God" since the treaty was with the Philistines and the epithet "Olam" (ancient eternal) was used for Canaanite El. El, as noted above, was the head of the Canaanite pantheon. The title *'el ḏu 'olam*, "El the eternal one," was found in an

---

3. Attridge and Oden, *Philo of Byblos*, 47.
4. Rosenthal, "Treaty," 659.
5. Cross, *Canaanite*, 52.
6. Hundley, *YHWH*, 210.

inscription at Serbit el-Khādem from the fifteenth century BCE, and "the goddess, the everlasting." *'lt 'olam*, appears as late as the seventh century BCE in the Phoenician incantation text from Arslan Tash.[7] It should be noted that this can also means the "everlasting oath."[8] It appears that the epithet "the Everlasting God" existed in antiquity and was not unique to the Bible. As Jenni pointed out, "One may conclude from the brief notice in Gen 21:33 that there existed a pre-Israelite cult of *el ʿōlām* which the Israelites transferred to YHWH."[9]

Sarna pointed out that the Hebrew does not allow a proper name in a construct state joined to a noun: "Hence El in the phrase El Olam can no longer be the proper name of a god but means simply 'God.'"[10] The antiquity of this term in the Hebrew Bible can be supported by Deut 33:27—"The ancient God is a refuge, A support are the arms everlasting." Therefore, the ancient God *ʾelohei* is synonymous with El Olam[11] The reference to YHWH as eternal suits the biblical narrative, which describes God as outside of time; he has no beginning and no end and he is everlasting. Maimonides, in *Guide for the Perplexed*, says that El Olam alludes to God as the first cause, who is eternal and existed before the creation of time.[12] On the other hand, the world that God created is not eternal and was created with limitations of time.

EL SHADDAI

According to Exodus, the patriarchs knew God mainly as El Shaddai (6:3). In other words, the patriarchs worshiped El Shaddai, they did not know he was YHWH until it was revealed at the time of Moses. El Shaddai is the most common name constructed with the initial prefix "El." The epithet "Shaddai" appears alone or in combination with "El." The full name "El Shaddai" appears only in Genesis with connection to Abraham (17:1), Isaac (28:3), and Jacob (35:11; 43:14; 48:3). The word "Shaddai" appears alone as God's name in the oracles of Balaam (Num 24:4, 6), in poetic passages (Isa 13:6; Ezek 1:24; Joel 1:15; Ps 68:15; 91:1

---

7. *KAI* 27:9–10; Cross, "YHWH and the God," 236–41.
8. See Pury, "EL-OLAM," 290.
9. Jenni, "'ōlām" (1952), 197–248 and "'ōlām" (1953), 1–35.
10. Sarna, *Genesis*, 150.
11. Hab 1:12; Ps 74:12; Isa 51:9; Prov 8:23.
12. Maimonides, *Guide for the Perplexed*, 2:13; 3:29.

and thirty-one times in Job); and archaic prose (Ruth 1:20–21). The distribution of "El Shaddai" and "Shaddai" points mostly to poetic texts, which testify to their antiquity since Hebrew poetry tends to preserve the earliest forms of language.[13] The divine name "El Shaddai" was from the pre-Mosaic age and lost its significance in Israel. Indeed, there are only two names in the Hebrew Bible constructed with the element "Shaddai": Zurishaddai and Ammishaddai, and both were born in Egypt.[14] The etymology of the epithet "Shaddai" is obscure. The Greek translation of the epithet is "He that is sufficient," which is found in Aquila, Symmachus, and Theodotian versions and is like what we find in the Midrash.[15] Modern scholars connect "Shaddai" with Akkadian *šadu*, "a mountain," used as a divine epithet. In other words, it has meant "The one of the Mountain," referring to the divine epithet "The Rock." No Canaanite text mentions El as Shaddai, which led Frank Moore Cross to suggest that *šadday* might be of Amorite origin and the patriarch brought it from Mesopotamia.[16] Koch maintains that the etymology does not help us to understand the meaning of Shaddai.[17] The usage of Shaddai in the book of Job suggests that it was a separate name for God and points to his nearness and protectiveness. In Genesis, Shaddai appears with the promise of many descendants and blessings as God told Abraham: "I will make you exceedingly fertile and make nations of you, and kings shall come forth from you" (Gen 17:6). The character of Shaddai is like the God of the fathers; hence Koch suggests the two deities were identified in the pre-monarchy period. In a later period, Shaddai was identified with El creating the double name "El Shaddai." However, this interpretation needs to consider that El is paired with Shaddai in early poems (Gen 49:25; Num 24:4, 16). In his work on the religion of the patriarchs, Haran pointed out that the patriarchs did not worship at the existing Canaanite shrines. They built their own shrines when God appeared to them. Their worship of El Shaddai was common with the other sons of Eber, which included Arameans, Ammonites, Moabites, Midianites, and the Ishmaelite tribes.

---

13. Sarna, *Exploring Exodus*, 51.

14. "Zurishaddai" means "My Rock is Shaddai," and "Ammishaddai" means "My Kinsman is Shaddai." Both names belong to two Israelites who were born in Egypt. Interestingly, the second name was discovered in a hieroglyphic inscription in Egypt from the fourteenth century BCE. See Cross, *Canaanite*, 53.

15. *Gen. Rab.* 46:3.

16. Cross, *Canaanite*, 57; Bailey, "Israelite," 434–38; Ouellette, "More," 470–71.

17. Koch "Šaddaj," 299–332.

In other words, El Shaddai was not borrowed from the Canaanites but was common to many peoples.[18]

In Targum Pseudo-Jonathan and commentaries of the medieval period, there is an attempt to solve the predicament that the patriarchs worshiped El Shaddai but did not know that they worshiped YHWH. According to Pseudo-Jonathan, "I revealed myself to Abraham, Isaac, and Jacob as El Shaddai and my name YHWH but in the character of my Shekinah, I did not make myself known to them." This implies that the patriarchs knew the name YHWH but did not experience the glory of Shekinah that is associated with the name. Medieval commentators explain that his name in Exod 6:3 refers to some aspects of his character. The patriarchs knew the name YHWH but did not understand the characters of this name. Rashi, for example, says that the divine characteristic of YHWH was the promises that were made by YHWH to the patriarchs, but these promises were not fulfilled. Maimonides pointed to the differences between God as El Shaddai and God as YHWH. According to him, the difference is between the power of God and his actual miracle-working power.[19] In other words, the patriarchs experienced God's protection in natural ways while Moses experienced miraculous intervention by God.[20] Similarly, Cassuto says that the name El Shaddai describes God as a giver of fertility, which is mentioned in Genesis in the promises of being fruitful and multiplying, while YHWH means "He is the One who carries out His promises."[21]

The mention of the different *elim* in Genesis points to an earlier phase of worshiping God. When the first Hebrews moved into Canaan, they found altars and sanctuaries where El was worshiped. Since El had many traits in common with their own clan deity, they identified him with their own God.[22] The Canaanite El was assimilated into the biblical concept

---

18. Haran, "Religion," 30–55.
19. Maimonides, *Guide for the Perplexed*, 1:63.
20. Leibowitz, *Studies in Shemot*, 132–35.
21. Cassuto, *Exodus*, 79.

22. Genesis shows that the characteristics of the biblical El are very similar to those of El in the Canaanite epics from Ugarit. In these, El is the king of gods. His description resembles the god El that the patriarchs worshiped. El is the creator of the universe, the creator of the human race, and the father of gods and humans. His attributes as kind and compassionate are the same as the biblical El. He lives on a mountain from which all the freshwater comes into the world. He also lives in a tent and not a temple. In the epics of Kirta and Aqhat, he is the one who provides offspring to the childless couple. See Pitard, "Before Israel," 73–74.

of God at an early stage in the patriarchal narrative. Thus, when Abraham meets Melchizedek, the king of Salem, he uses one of El's lofty titles, "El Elyon," the "God Most High," for his own God YHWH (Gen 14:22). Hagar identifies El Roi, the "God of Seeing," with YHWH (16:13). Abraham, after he planted a tree at Beersheba, uses the epithet "El Olam," or "the Everlasting God," for YHWH. Jacob named his resting place in Beth El, the "House of El" (28:12–19). The fusion between El and YHWH took place at an early stage; this is probably the reason why there is nothing negative about El, even though he was worshiped by the Canaanites. Conversely, Baal, the Canaanite god of storm and fertility, is condemned time after time in the Hebrew Bible. Baal is the chief rival of YHWH, who led the Israelites astray from their covenant with God. The absence of Baal in the book of Genesis is evidence of the antiquity of the Genesis tradition. This was noted already by Mettinger, who said, "It is thus astonishing to note to what degree the patriarchal stories keep silent about Baal. If these texts were really explicated as literary products of the period of the monarchy, this would hardly be the case."[23]

YHWH

According to the documentary hypothesis, the literary sources known as E and P never used the name YHWH for God until it was revealed to Moses (Exod 3:13; 6:2–3). But an examination of the book of Genesis shows that the Yahwist source used it from Gen 2:4 on; in other words, it is as old as Abraham. The combination of the divine name "YHWH" and the general term "Elohim" appears twenty times in chapters 2 and 3 of Genesis and only once in the Torah in Exod 9:30. It is rarely mentioned in the rest of the Bible. The Hebrew term for God, "Elohim," is a generic word while the Hebrew word for Lord, "YHWH," is the proper name. In the story of creation, the name Elohim is used alone. Only afterward is the term YHWH used (2:4). In the midrash we find the interpretation that "the full Name [of God] is employed in connection with a full world."[24] Therefore, more than likely the mentioning of YHWH and Elohim in Gen 2 comes to stress that the God of creation, Elohim, is the same as the God YHWH.

---

23. Mettinger, *In Search of God*, 53.
24. *Gen. Rab.* 13:3.

In Abraham's stories, YHWH is mentioned first with the election of Abraham. YHWH told Abraham to leave his father's house and go to the land that he would show him. The voice of YHWH that appeared in the creation story and ten generations later was heard by Noah. Now the voice of YHWH is heard by Abraham. YHWH is mentioned throughout the Abrahamic stories where it is linked to the promise of the land and many descendants (Gen 12:2-3, 7; 13:15-17; 15:1, 4, 7, 18-21; 18:18; 22:17-18); when Abraham invoked YHWH by name (Gen 12:8; 13:4; 21:33; 24:7); and when Abraham built an altar to YHWH (Gen 12:8; 13:18). Since there is no mention of centralization or established sanctuary, YHWH is mentioned with several places where Abraham worshiped him: Bethel (12:8), Hebron (13:18), Salem (14:18-22), and Beersheba (21:32-3). YHWH also made two major covenants with Abraham: the "covenant between the pieces" (Gen 15:1-21) and the "covenant in the flesh" (17:1-27). The link between the two covenants is reflected in a later biblical prayer that combines verses from the two chapters (Neh 9:7-8).

The association between YHWH and Abraham is also mentioned in the theophany Isaac received in the area near Gerar. YHWH told him to remain in the land and promised to be with him and bless him in fulfillment of the oath that he swore to his father Abraham (26:3). YHWH is also mentioned in the second theophany to Isaac in Beersheba: "That night YHWH appeared to him and said, I am the God of your father Abraham" (Gen 26:24). The epithet "the God of your father" appears here for the first time. It conveys continuity between Abraham and Isaac. The God who spoke to Abraham affirms his promises to Isaac, who is the heir of the blessing. Upon receiving the divine message, Isaac invoked God by the name "YHWH" and he built an altar there as his father Abraham did before.

ELOHIM

Elohim is a longer form of El. It refers to Israel's God more than two thousand times in the Hebrew Bible. It appears frequently with the article "ha Elohim," or "the [true]God." Although Elohim in most cases is the God who was known and worshiped in Israel, the plural Elohim also refers to pagan gods (Exod 12:12; 18:11; 20:3) and sometimes to individual pagan gods (Judg 11:24; 1 Kgs 11:5; 2 Kgs 1:2). Because Elohim is in the plural it led to the thought that we have here traces of polytheism. But it can be explained as signifying "plural of majesty," or more than likely it expresses an abstract idea *zekunim*, or "old age" or *neurim*, "time of youth."

In the Abrahamic stories, Elohim appears when it is linked to the promise of many descendants and the promise of the land (Gen 17:5–8, 16), in a covenant with Abraham and Isaac (17:9–14, 19, 21), and the binding of Isaac (22:1, 3, 8, 12).[25] Universalistic aspects of Elohim are found when it involves non-Israelites, the destruction of the cities of the plain (19:29), Abraham's journey to Gerar (20:3, 6, 11, 13, 17), the expulsion of Hagar and Ishmael (21:12, 17, 20), Abraham's pact with Abimelech (21:21–22), and Abraham's dealing with the Hittites (23:6). In addition, we find an oath that is the combination of "the Lord, the God of heaven and the God of earth" (24:3, 7). This oath is unique in the biblical literature. It gives the Lord God a cosmic dimension. Since Abraham's servant went to a foreign land, it was reasonable to invoke God's universal sovereignty. As noted, Elohim is sometimes applied to the god of other people. Therefore, when it involved Abraham dealing with foreign people, the Bible used the title Elohim. Abraham built several altars for YHWH in different locations, but he built only one altar for Elohim in the story of the binding of Isaac on Mount Moriah.

Our study shows that in the Abrahamic cycles both YHWH and Elohim are mentioned in the narrative framework and the dialogue. It was suggested that originally only one of the terms was used in the traditions and later editors made changes in the narrative and the dialogue. Another suggestion is the existence of different sources. But as pointed out, this solution has many difficulties.[26] The main difference that we can point to is that Elohim is used mainly when Abraham dealt with foreigners.

THE GOD OF MY/YOUR/HIS FATHER

The phrase "the God of my/your/his Father," with the names Abraham, Isaac, or both, is found only in the patriarchal stories, which points to the close relationship between the patriarch and God. This epithet was used first when God appeared to Isaac: "I am the God of your father Abraham"

---

25. In this story, the "angel of the Lord" (22:11, 15) and "Lord" (22:14, 16) are also mentioned.
26. Wenham, "Religion," 164.

(26:24). It came to convey that God would protect Isaac as he protected Abraham (15:1). Later it is mentioned in Jacob's dream at Beth El: "I am the Lord, the God of your father Abraham and the God of Isaac" (28:13). This formula is also mentioned in God's revelation to Moses: "'I am,' he said, 'the God of your father, the God of Abraham, the God of Isaac, and the God of Jacob'" (Exod 3:6). The use of this formula stresses the continuity between the patriarchs and Moses. The God who made the promises of peoplehood and national territory is the God who was revealed to Moses. There are some instances where the formula "the God of my/your father" is mentioned without the name of the patriarch (Gen 31:5, 29; 43:23; 46:3; 49:26). Lewy was the first to point out that the phrase "God of the father" was well known in the ancient Near East over a long period from the nineteenth century BCE.[27] The phrase "god of the father(s)" appears with and without accompanying a personal name. Thus, we find "Ashur god of my father," "Ashur and Amurrum the gods of our father," "Shamash the god of my father," "Ilaprat, the god of your father," and an oath "by the name of the god of my father."[28] Notably, the phrase was not used in reference to Abraham's father. This is because, according to the tradition in Josh 24:2, Terah was an idol worshiper. Abraham's arrival signals a new phase in the history of religion. The phrase "the God of my/your/his Father," which is attested in the patriarchal narrative as well as in the ancient Near East, came to indicate the close relationship between the individual and his god, who was his patron and protector. It was typical for a nomadic society to look for an intimate god who would guide and protect them.

The fact that the patriarchs had personal ties with God is manifested also in titles such as "the God of Abraham"[29] (Gen 28:13; 31:42, 53), the "Fear of Isaac" (31:42, 53), and "Mighty One of Jacob" (49:24).[30] God was the patron deity of the clan.[31] Alt suggested that the patriarchal gods did not bear their own name but were named for their cult founder. To bolster his claims, Alt pointed to the Nabatean and Palmyrean inscriptions

27. Lewy, "Textes Paléo-Assyriens," 29–65.
28. Sarna, *Genesis*, 396.
29. It was suggested that the name was "the Shield of Abraham" on the basis of Gen 15:1. See Hyatt, "YHWH," 130.
30. "Mighty One of Jacob" appears elsewhere only four times and in the poetic text (Isa 49:26; 60:16; Ps 13:2, 5). It is similar to the Akkadian divine title *bel abāriabāri*, "endowed with strength."
31. When Laban and Jacob formed a pact, each side invoked his own deity. Laban swore by the God of Nahor, while Jacob swore by the Fear of Isaac.

I Am YHWH; I Appeared to Abraham, Isaac, and Jacob as El Shaddai

from the first century BCE to the fourth century CE.[32] The inscriptions describe nomadic people who worshiped "the god of [X]," where "X" was the name of the founder of the cult. However, we should note that the patriarchal period is too remote from the Nabatean period to make a valid comparison. Alt further says that the cults of these deities were restricted to certain locals and sanctuaries. He concluded that the cult of the "Mighty one of Jacob" was worshiped among the tribe of Joseph, "the Fear of Isaac" among the tribes of Judah and Simeon, and "the god of Abraham" in the clan of Caleb and the tribe of Judah.[33] As noted by many scholars, there is no basis for this theory.[34] More than likely, the titles that the patriarchs gave to their God were merged by the literary editors into the God of Israel. Their epithets disappeared and they are found under names such as "the God of your fathers," and "the God of Abraham, Isaac, and Jacob."

WORSHIPING ONE GOD

Writing about the religion of the patriarchs, Wenham maintained that the name YHWH was unknown to them. The presence of the name YHWH in Genesis is the result of the insertion of the Yahwist editor.[35] The epithet YHWH was most common in later periods, which led to equating El, the god of the patriarchs, with YHWH. The fact that the Israelites did not know God is based primarily on Exod 6:3, which states that the patriarchs knew God as El Shaddai but not as YHWH. As we pointed out previously, what the verse conveys is that the patriarchs did not experience the power associated with the name YHWH. Furthermore, it appears that the author of Exod 6:3 did not see any contradiction that some of the passages in Genesis suggest that the name YHWH was known to the patriarchs.[36]

According to Cross, the different divine names in the book of Genesis do not point to different gods worshiped by the Hebrews before they adopted Yahwism.[37] He believes they are different titles of "El" through

---

32. Alt, "God of the Fathers," 30–45.
33. Alt, "God of the Fathers," 25–30.
34. Haran, "Religion," 51; Wenham, "Religion," 172–73.
35. Wenham, "Religion," 161–95.
36. Alexander, *Abraham*, 96.
37. Cross, "YHWH," 225–59.

the pre-Mosaic period. He suggests continuity between the patriarchal religion, a form of "El" religion, and the Yahwism, which was accepted later by the Israelites. When the patriarchs and the first Israelites came to Canaan they made "the language of Canaan" their own (Isa 19:8). Thus, not surprisingly, the terms that they used to describe their God were like that of the Canaanites. The patriarchs contextualize their theology to match their situation, so they select a name for God that matches their needs at that moment in time. Each name and phrase had a different meaning and referred to God's different attributes. Abraham had one mighty God to whom he worshiped and attributed to him different characteristics that are found in the different titles of El. In other words, Yahwism was part of the original patriarchal religion. This interpretation is found among the sages who maintained that the ancestors of Israel were true monotheists. Most telling is a midrash that grapples with the different names of God. According to this midrash, the different names of God point to different attributes of God:

> R. Abba. b. Mammel said: "God said to Moses: 'Thou wishest to know My name. Well, I am called according to My work; sometimes I am called "Almighty God," "Lord of Hosts," "God," "Lord." When I am judging created beings, I am called "God," and when I am waging war against the wicked; I am called "the Lord of Hosts." When I suspend judgment for man's sins, I am called "Adonai" for "Adonai" refers to the attribute of Mercy, as it is said: "The Lord, the Lord (Adonai, Adonai), God, merciful and gracious.""[38]

THEOPHANY

In the biblical stories, the purpose of revelation is to make man know God. Revelations show humanity God's power, nature, glory, plans, and his will. The vocabulary that describes God's revelations uses words such as "to see," "hear," "perceive," "to understand," and "to know." In each revelation, God tells man about himself—who he is, about his acts in the past, what he will do, and what he requires them to do. Therefore, God revealed his plans and expectations to Noah and Abraham (Gen 6:13–21; 12:1; 15:13–21; 17:15–21; 18:17). Each revelation was needed because

---

38. *Exod. Rab.* 3:6.

God is transcendent. He is far from man and man can neither see him nor find him.

God spoke and appeared to Abraham. At first, outside of the land of Israel, Abraham only heard God's voice; the divine speech is introduced by "said" (Gen 12:1–2). At the land of Canaan God appeared and "spoke to him" (Gen 12:7). To describe God's theophany, the Hebrew Bible uses the verb "to see." This verb is used three times in the Abrahamic cycle (12:7; 17:1; 18:1). When Abraham arrived at the promised land, he was given a divine vision whose nature is not described. The stress here is on visibility and Ibn Ezra interpreted that God prophetically appeared to Abraham. In Gen 18:1, for a second time "the Lord appeared to him," but it is mentioned without a verbal declaration. In previous theophanies of God, Abraham built an altar and invoked the Lord by name (12:7). In this theophany, the Lord is joined by angels. Maimonides explains that the Torah started with a general statement that *Hashem* appeared to Abraham in a prophetic vision. In verse 2 there is a detailed description of the vision where we read that Abraham lifted his eyes and, in this vision, he saw three angels. According to Maimonides, the whole exchange took place in a vision.[39] Ramban, although he refuted some of Maimonides's assertions, says that whenever seeing or hearing an angel it refers to a vision since human senses cannot perceive an angel.

In the "covenant between the pieces," "the word of the Lord came to Abraham in a vision" (Gen 15:1). The Hebrew word for vision—*maḥazeh*—derives from the root *ḥzh*, "to see," which is found in prophetic experiences.[40] The visions that the prophets experienced included the root *ḥzh* with *davar*, "word" (Isa 2:1; Amos 1:1; Mic 1:1; Hab 1:1), which is like Abraham's experience. According to Radak, Abraham's experience is termed vision because it was more than a speech. He was shown physical things during his prophecy. Ramban says that Abraham now received the word of God in the daytime, for at first it came to him in nocturnal visions.

Even though the Bible describes God's theophany with "to see," "YHWH let himself be seen," and "showed himself," in most cases there is no attempt to describe his form or appearance—only the words that were spoken are mentioned. Evidently, the spoken words were more important than the theophany was.[41] It is also possible that describing

---

39. Maimonides, *Guide for the Perplexed*, 3:43.
40. Num 24:4; Ezek 13:7.
41. Barr, "Theophany," 32.

God's appearance was too difficult for a human to comprehend, thus his appearance is limited to only a few passages. James Barr suggests that "in the teaching of the Old Testament, God is nowhere conceived of as essentially in human form. Rather is he conceived of as pure spirit, able to assume a form rather than as having in himself physical form."[42] However, there is no evidence to support this assertion. The description of God's appearance to the patriarchs is a form of speech and it does not mean that they saw him face to face; it conveys the idea that they received a message from God. According to the Hebrew Bible, the only person who saw God face to face is Moses: "When a prophet of the Lord arises among you, I make myself known to him in a vision, I speak with him in a dream. Not so with my servant Moses, he is trusted throughout my household. With him, I speak mouth to mouth, plainly and not in riddles, and he beholds the likeness of the Lord" (Num 12:6–8). Moses is a unique prophet since, according to this text, he speaks directly to God, "mouth to mouth" or "face to face." There is nothing between them when Moses hears God's voice. Moses sees God's form in clear view. Nevertheless, even though God is close to him, Moses does not see God's face. This is stated in Exod 33:20: "But He said, 'You cannot see my face, for man may not see me and live.'" In other words, by nature, human beings, including Moses, cannot directly observe God.[43]

God is beyond description, yet human nature demands that we attempt to describe God. The Bible does not describe things in terms of objective truths known only to God but in terms of human understanding. This in turn led men to resort to the language of anthropomorphism. God addresses mankind in a manner accessible to their understanding and their own experience; this is what the Talmud means when it says, "The Law speaks with the tongue of man."[44] Accordingly,

> When the Creator wished to describe Himself, He described Himself as provided with eyes, because men are familiar with the sense of sight and know from their own experience that its seat is the member of the body which is the eye, not because He really is provided with bodily members. Likewise, when He wished to let them know that no sound is veiled from Him, He described Himself as provided with ears, because among men

---

42. Rowley, *Faith*, 75–76.
43. See Levine, *Numbers*, 341–42.
44. *B. Meṣ.* 31b.

sounds are perceived by the sense of hearing. The same applies to all matters of this sort.[45]

ANGELOLOGY

Stories about angels' appearances to humans are typical of the patriarchal narrative and the judges' period.[46] In the Isaac and Ishmael stories, angels are mentioned several times. When the Bible needs to describe direct encounters with humans dramatically, it uses angels. After the period of the judges, the appearance of angels diminishes. The last person who received a revelation from an angel was the prophet Elijah. With the development of classical prophecy, the prophet came instead of the angel. Only later, in prophetic visions, not only do we again encounter angels, but a new type of angel. The angels are no longer appearing to humans but are seen in visions. The Hebrew word for an angel is *mal'akh*, derived from the stem *l·'·k*, "to send." In Genesis, it is also used for ordinary humans (32:4). Later, a prophet or a priest might also be called "an angel of the Lord" (Hag 1:13; Mal 2:7).

There is not much we know about them; they are nameless, with no individuality or free will, and no hierarchy among them. Their main function is to deliver God's words and to be emissaries. In Israel, as in the ancient Near East, the angels were part of the royal court; YHWH was envisioned as a king and the angels served in his royal court (Gen 28:12; 33:1–2). There are incidents where angels are perceived in human form; therefore, the people to whom they appear are not aware of their angelic nature. Abraham's three visitors are described as "men" (18:1, 16 22; 19:5, 10, 12, 16). Later, they are described as angels (19:1, 15); but the people of Sodom perceived them to be human (19:5, 9). A similar incident is described in the Samson story where an angel of the Lord appeared to Samson's mother. She describes him as a man of God who "looked like an angel of God, very frightening" (Judg 13:6). Her husband, Manoah, does not recognize him as an angel at first, and does so only after he disappears in flames on the altar (13:20).

When Abraham's visitors arrived at Sodom, the text mentions two angels. This indicates that the third one was different. Indeed, when Abraham spoke to three visitors he spoke and received a response only

---

45. Nemoy, *Karaite Anthology*, 63.
46. Indeed, one of the characteristics of the Jacob cycle is the encounter with angels.

from one of them (18:4, 10). In Gen 19:1 they are referred to as angels before they were referred to as men (18:2). Rashi explains this difference by saying that before, when they were in the presence of God, their superior status faded; they were like mortals. Now, when the divine presence had ascended, they became again angels. Although they are referred to as angels they were perceived by Lot as men, therefore he made a feast for them. More so, the Sodomites also referred to them as men.

> All names that are stated could be understood as the name of God that is stated in the Torah with regard to Abraham are sacred and are referring to God, except for this name, which is nonsacred, as it is stated: "My lords, if I have found favor in your eyes" (Gen 18:3). In this passage, Abraham is addressing the angels who appeared to him in the guise of men, not God.[47]

The arrival of the three heavenly visitors is odd and appears only once in the Hebrew Bible. As mentioned before, adding more to the confusion is the fact that those heavenly visitors bathed their feet, drink, and eat. In the Talmud, we read that they gave the impression of eating.

Another encounter with an angel is mentioned when Hagar ran away from Sarah; afterwards, the angel of the Lord appeared to her (Gen 16:7). This is the first appearance of an angel in the Hebrew Bible. The angel of the Lord is mentioned four times in Gen 16 (verses 7, 9, 10, 11). The angel told Hagar that she would have a son and his name would be Ishmael. The angel speaks to Hagar (Gen 16:7–9, 11), but she responds to God (16:13). There are some texts where the distinction between God and the angels is not clear. In some narratives, the angel appears to be a distinct figure, but later in the narrative, it appears as though it is YHWH and not the angel.

Hagar had a second encounter with an angel; this time after Abraham expelled her and her son Ishmael. In Gen 16, she is in the desert and the water is gone. So, she leaves her son under one of the bushes because she does not want to watch him dying. She sat afar and burst into tears. It was God who heard the cry of the boy, but it was an angel of God who called Hagar from heaven. The angel told her that God heard the boy's cry and would make him a great nation. Then we read that God opened the eyes of Hagar and she saw the well of water. Explaining the appearance of the angel to Hagar, Maimonides says that this happened in a prophetic vision since a messenger of God that is seen or heard is only in a prophetic

---

47. Šebu. 35b.

vision.⁴⁸ Hagar was not a prophetess because the speech she heard was like *bet kol*, "an echo of a divine voice." Alternatively, Hagar saw an angel in the form of a human being, therefore she was not afraid.

The angel of the Lord is also mentioned in the binding of Isaac. At first, God commanded the sacrifice of Isaac, but later Abraham is addressed by the angel of the Lord from heaven (22:1, 11–18). Angels usually travel between heaven and earth (28:12), but the urgency of the moment requires the angel to call from heaven. This is like the call of the angel to Hagar from heaven (21:17). The unclear demarcation between God and the angel is also found in the Moses story. The angel of the Lord appears to Moses in the burning bush (Exod 3:2), but Moses speaks directly with God in the rest of the story. In the Exodus story, it is God who leads the Israelites (13:21), then it is his angel (14:9). So, too, in the Gideon story; sometimes Gideon speaks with God and sometimes with the angel (Judg 6:11). From this, we can infer that the angel was not an independent being but a manifestation of divine power and will. Since the angel is partly identified with God, he is his messenger; therefore, he uses God's name while speaking. Another possibility is that the phrase "angel of God" is an addition. At first, only the name "God" appeared in the stories. But the fear that the stories would be perceived as too corporeal necessitated the addition of the phrase "angel of the Lord." However, since this was not done consistently, there are difficulties. Indeed, this view was held by the *Maghārrīya*, a Jewish sect that flourished in Egypt and among the Karaites.⁴⁹ Accordingly, all the anthropomorphic passages in the Bible refer to angels, rather than to God. Furthermore, it was an angel who created the world and addressed the prophets.

In conclusion, Abraham worshiped El-Elyon, El Olam, El, and Elohim. In addition, from the time of the patriarch Isaac, the God of my Father with the name Abraham started to appear. It was typical for a nomadic society to look for an intimate god as a father figure who would guide and protect them. Abraham selected a name for God that matched his situation and needs. Each name and phrase had a different meaning and referred to God's different attributes; in other words, he worshiped one God, YHWH.

The description of God's appearance to Abraham does not mean that he saw him face to face; it conveys the idea that he received a message

---

48. Maimonides, *Guide for the Perplexed*, 2:42.
49. Man, "Sects Minor," EncJud,14:1088–1089.

from God. God addresses mankind in a manner accessible to his understanding and his own experience. Typical of the patriarchal period is the appearance of angels. These angels appeared as humans and many times there is an unclear distinction between them and God. This led scholars to infer that the angel was not an independent being but a manifestation of divine power and will. The next chapter will examine the death of Abraham and Sarah.

Chapter 12

For Dust You Are, and to Dust You Shall Return

"For he who is reckoned among the living has something to look forward to—even a live dog is better than a dead lion . . . since the living know they will die. But the dead know nothing; they have no more recompense, for even the memory of them has died. Their loves, their jealousies have long since perished; and they have no more share till the end of time in all that goes under the sun" (Eccl 9:4–6).

As in Ecclesiastes, so also in Egyptian texts; death was viewed as something negative and abnormal but part of creation. According to one of the Pyramid Texts, death did not exist in the primeval age before the gods made the world and mankind.[1] In the Mesopotamian Gilgamesh epic we read, "When the gods created mankind, death for mankind they set aside, life in their own hands retaining."[2] Elsewhere, Gilgamesh says that the human cannot scale heaven because their days are numbered.[3]

After Adam disobeyed the divine injunction and ate from the Tree of Knowledge, God punished him: "For dust you are, and to dust you shall return" (Gen 3:19). The same idea—that human beings come from the dust and ultimately return to the dust—recurs in later books of the Bible, e.g., in Job—"All flesh would perish together, and man would

---

1. For Egyptian views on death, see Zandee, *Death*; Žabkar, *Study*, 128; Brunner, *Grundzüge*.
2. Speiser, "Epic of Gilgamesh," 10.3.3–5.
3. Tigay, *Evolution*, 164–65.

return to dust" (Job 34:15)—and in Ecclesiastes—"All go to one place; all are from the dust, and all turn to dust again" (Eccl 3:20).[4] Human life is a journey from dust to dust, ending at the same point it begins, and death is the perpetual nothingness to which all revert when they return to dust. Is death the final station of the human journey from which there is no return, or do the Abrahamic stories allude to some form of continuity after death? To answer this, Sarah's death, which is the first death and burial in the Hebrew Bible, and Abraham's death will be studied. In addition, we will examine mourning customs in that period.

"LIE DOWN WITH ONE'S FATHER"

The Hebrew word for death is *māwet /môt*. The root *m.w.t* is common to the Semitic languages and occurs in Egyptian as well. The "ideal" way of dying was for a man to die when he was old and satisfied with his days and years (Gen 25:8; 35:29), growing and developing until the last day with the mental and physical powers of a lifetime (Deut 34:7). Longevity was regarded as a great blessing, and it was bestowed by God upon his chosen king. Before dying, it was customary for the patriarch to put the affairs of his house in order. He would gather his sons to convey his will and bless them, as noted with Isaac and Jacob.

It was believed that following death a man was reunited with his ancestors. This is expressed in the Bible by idioms such as "lie down with one's father" (Gen 47:30; Deut 31:16; 2 Sam 7:12; thirty-five times in 1 and 2 Kgs and 2 Chr). The Torah employs a similar expression: "He was gathered to his kin," which is found only ten times in the Hebrew Bible and appears only in the Torah. This expression appears with Abraham, Ishmael, Isaac, Aaron, and Moses (Gen 25:8, 17; 35:29; Num 20:24; Deut 32:50) but was never used for women or non-Israelites. All these expressions stem from the idea that a person is buried in the family tomb where he joins his deceased ancestors. However, according to the biblical narrative, Abraham, Aaron, and Moses were not buried with their forefathers. It is noteworthy that in Gen 15:15 God told Abraham, "You shall go to your fathers in peace." Since Abraham was not buried near his fathers this verse refers to spiritual reunification. Or it is possible to say that the spirit of the deceased joined its ancestors in the underworld.[5] The belief

---

4. See also Pss 103:14; 104:29.
5. Lewis, *Cult of the Dead*, 164–65; Westermann, *Genesis 12–36*.

that a man is reunited with ancestors after death can be found in Gen 17:14: "That person shall be cut off from his kin." This suggests that the transgressor will not be reunited with his relatives. It is the opposite of what we read about Abraham: "He was gathered to his kin" (Gen 25:8), which alludes to the afterlife. Despite man's perishability, there is an element that survives his death. In other words, death is a transition to the afterlife where one is united with their ancestors. It was thought that the idea of the afterlife was known in Israel only in a later period, but this is evidently invalid.[6]

Since it was believed that a man was reunited with his ancestors, all the patriarchs and matriarchs, except for Rachel, were buried in the cave of Machpelah, which Abraham purchased from Ephron the Hittite. The patriarchs were buried in the ancestral tomb on family-owned land. Because Jacob lived and died in Egypt, his body was brought back to be interred in the cave of Machpelah (Gen 50:13). From the time of the patriarchs to the end of the biblical period, family sepulchers were the desired form of burial. For the kings of Judah and their families, their wish was to "lie with their father," to "go with their fathers," or to be "gathered to their fathers" (2 Sam 7:12, 2 Kgs 22:20; 1 Chr 17:11; 2 Chr 34:28). The Bible tells us of a second burial in which King Saul and his son Jonathan were buried in the sepulcher of Saul's father Kish (2 Sam 21:14). Being buried with one's ancestors is a theme repeated numerous times with the burial of several kings (1 Kgs 14:31; 15:24; 22:51; 2 Kgs 15:38). The desire to be buried in the same grave site of one's father was so important that Ahitophel went to his city and strangled himself so he would be buried in the sepulcher of his father (2 Sam 17:23). Similarly, when Barzillai asked King David permission to leave, he said, "Turn back, that I may die in my own city, by the grave of my father and my mother" (2 Sam 19:38). On the other hand, it was a curse to not be buried: "Thy carcass shall not come unto the sepulcher of thy fathers" (1 Kgs 13:22).

THE PURCHASE OF THE CAVE OF MACHPELAH

The account of the purchase of the cave of Machpelah is comprehensive. This is unexpected because the Hebrew Bible is terse. However, when there is a wide-range description that relates to events and people there is a reason for it. It is suggested that the complete description of Abraham

6. Sarna, *Genesis*, 174.

purchasing the cave of Machpelah was a sign of the future possession of the land of Israel. R. Judah b. R. Simon said: "This is one of the three places regarding which the nations of the world cannot taunt Israel and say, 'Ye have stolen them.' These are they: the Cave of Machpelah, the [site of the] Temple, and the sepulcher of Joseph. The Cave of Machpelah: And Abraham weighed to Ephron the silver (Gen 23:16). The Temple: So, David gave Ornan for the place six hundred shekels of gold (1 Chr 21:25). And Joseph's sepulcher: And he bought the parcel of ground."[7]

Purchasing the cave of Machpelah was the beginning of the fulfillment of God's promise to Abraham: "I will assign this land to your offspring" (Gen 12:7). Ramban suggests in his commentary that the mention of the cave of Machpelah came to inform us of the place of the burial of the patriarchs. This is because we are obligated to honor the burial site of our ancestors. A different interpretation was offered by the sages who maintained that this was one of the trials of Abraham: "I said to Abraham: "Up, walk about the land, through its length and its breadth, for I give it to you" (Gen 13:17). Ultimately, he sought a place to bury Sarah and did not find one until he purchased it for four hundred silver shekels, and he did not question My attributes and did not protest that I failed to fulfill My promise to give him the land."[8]

It is ironic that Abraham, who received the promise of the land from God, had to ask the Hittites to intercede on his behalf with Ephron son of Zohar to sell him the cave of Machpelah. To purchase it, Abraham had to overcome some hurdles. Abraham was an alien, therefore he needed the permission of the Hittites to acquire land. In addition, according to the Lev 25, which deals with the subject of land tenure in ancient Israel, an alien could not own land in perpetuity (verse 23). Therefore, Abraham had to make sure that future generations could use the cave of Machpelah as a burial site. Another difficulty that the patriarch faced was the reluctance of people in the ancient world to part with their land. The land was looked upon as ancestral trust; most telling are the words of Naboth to Ahab the king of Israel who wanted to purchase his vineyard: "The Lord forbid that I should give up to you what I have inherited from my fathers!" (1 Kgs 21:3). People of the same tribe who share family ties usually lived together in the same area. Transferring the land to an alien meant a possible disturbance of unity and harmony and changing the

---

7. *Gen. Rab.* 79:7.
8. *Sanh.* 111a.

For Dust You Are, and to Dust You Shall Return

demographic balance.[9] Therefore the whole community participated in approving the sale of the land. What Abraham tried to achieve in his negotiations is that "his purchase is final and irrevocable, his ownership absolute and incontestable."[10]

The three patriarchs and three matriarchs were buried in the cave of Machpelah, which is situated in Hebron. The place served as a place of veneration in ancient times and a symbol of national unity. More than likely, this is the reason why David chose Hebron as the first capital of Israel. The cave of Machpelah is the second most sacred place for the Jewish people. It is a place of veneration to this day. The site is also a place of worship for Muslims, who call the place "the sacred precinct of the friend (of God)" (*Harām al-Khalīl*). It is enclosed by a magnificent wall that dates to the time of King Herod. Following centuries of Christian and Muslim control of the place, the cave of Machpelah was liberated by Israel's defense forces in 1967. Since then, Jews, Christians, and Muslims have had the freedom to worship inside the cave.

THE DEATH OF SARAH

The story of the death of Sarah is the first recorded death and burial in the Hebrew Bible. Sarah died at the age of 127 years. Other women's lifespans are not mentioned in the Torah. Usually, the Torah gives the life spans so historical events can be noted. Trying to explain the reason for mentioning Sarah's life span, Rashbam follows the literal meaning of the text suggesting that it was necessary to mention Sarah's death to link it with the purchase of the cave of Machpelah. While Beno Jacob suggested that Sarah's age is mentioned to inform the reader that she died before Rebecca succeeded her.[11] Sarah died at the age of one hundred years, twenty years, and seven years. Strangely, the word years is repeated after every stage: one hundred years, twenty years, and seven years. We would expect to find 127 years or 100 years and 27 years, which usually is found in the Bible. Therefore, it appears that Sarah's life span is described in this manner to tell us that each part of her life is part of the whole, and each part shares some characteristic with its counterparts. "As they are whole [unblemished], so are their years whole: at the age of twenty she

---

9. Sarna, *Genesis*, 157.
10. Sarna, *Genesis*, 157.
11. Beno Jacob, *Genesis*, 149.

was at the age of seven in beauty, and at the age of a hundred she was at the age of twenty in sin."[12] According to another interpretation, 120 years represents the maximum life span and increases by seven fullness.[13]

Another anomaly in the verse is the repetition, "These were the years of the life of Sarah" (Gen 23:1). This is repeated after the enumeration. The LXX and Vulg. omit the last three words of the MT. Speiser and Westermann pointed to scribal dislocation of the word *šenê* from the beginning of the verse where it was supposed to appear before *Ḥayyê*.[14] The expression *šenê Ḥayyê*—"years of the life of"—would be similar to what we read in Gen 25:7; 47:8, 28. The midrash explains the difficulty by suggesting, "To teach you that the life of the righteous is precious before God in this world and the future world."[15] Sarah did not reach the life span of Abraham; she lived forty-eight years less than Abraham. According to the midrash, "She should have reached Abraham's years, but because she said, the Lord judge between me and thee, her life was reduced by forty-eight years."[16] The midrash interprets her dispute with Abraham over Hagar's misdeeds as the main reason for not reaching Abraham's life span. Another interpretation is that her death was caused after learning about the binding of Isaac. In one version it was Satan who appeared to the matriarch and told her that Abraham essentially slaughtered her son Isaac:

> Satan then appeared unto Sarah in the figure of an old man, and said unto her, "Where did thine husband go?" She said, "To his work." "And where did thy son Isaac go?" he inquired further, and she answered, "He went with his father to the place of study of the Torah." Satan said: "O thou poor old woman, thy teeth will be set on the edge on the account of thy son, as thou knowest not that Abraham took his son with him on the road to sacrifice him." In this hour Sarah's loins trembled, and all her limbs shook. She was no more of this world. Nevertheless, she aroused herself, and said, "All that God hath told Abraham, may he do it unto life and peace."[17]

12. *Gen. Rab.* 58:1.
13. Labuschange, "Life Span," 124.
14. Westermann, *Genesis 12–36*, 372; Speiser, *Genesis*, 169.
15. *Gen. Rab.* 58:1.
16. *Gen. Rab.* 45:5.
17. *Sefer Hayysar*, 121.

In another version, we read that it was Isaac himself who told his mother of what took place:

> For Isaac returned to his mother and she said to him: "Where have you been, my son?" Said he to her: "My father took me and led me up mountains and down hills, etc." "Als," she said, "for the son of a hapless woman! Had it not been for the angel you would by now have been slain!" "Yes," he said to her. Thereupon she uttered six cries, corresponding to the six blasts. It has been said that she had scarcely finished speaking when she died.[18]

Sarah was held in such esteem that in the midrash we read that the residents of Hebron closed their places to show their respect for the matriarch.[19] For this act of kindness, they were rewarded: "There was Abraham buried and Sarah his wife. This, however, comes to teach you that all who paid honor to Sarah [by attending her funeral] were privileged to pay the like honor to Abraham." In other words, they did not die before they participated forty-eight years later in Abraham's funeral.[20]

All the matriarchs died before the patriarchs. The deaths of Rebecca and Leah are not recorded in Genesis; the text only indicates they were buried with the patriarchs and the matriarch Sarah. The only matriarch who was not buried in the cave of Machpelah was Rachel, who died while giving birth to Benjamin. She was buried where she died, on the way to Ephrathah in Benjamin. Her death resembles that of Deborah, who was buried where she died near Beth El (Gen 35:8). Later, the leaders of the exodus generation were also buried where they died: Miriam in Kadesh (Num 20:1); Aaron on Mt. Hor or Moserah (Deut 10:6; Num 33:39); and Moses in Moab near Beth-Peor (Deut 34:6).

ABRAHAM'S DEATH

Abraham's death is recorded in Gen 25:7-10. Abraham was 175 years old at the time of his death. In other words, he lived in Canaan for 100 years; his first 75 years passed in silence. He was buried at the cave of Machpelah, the burial site that he purchased from Ephron the son of Zohar the Hittite years earlier for his wife Sarah. In the stories of Isaac and Jacob, we find that the patriarchs blessed their sons before their death. This, however, is

---

18. *Lev. Rab.* 20:2.
19. *Gen. Rab.* 58:7.
20. *Gen. Rab.* 62:3.

not the case with Abraham. Nevertheless, before his death, Abraham put the affairs of his house in order and made sure Isaac was his true heir and successor: "Abraham willed all that he owned to Isaac" (Gen 25:5). The verse is essentially a repetition of Gen 24:36 where the servant stated that Abraham gave all his possessions to Isaac. Ramban, in his commentary on 24:10, says that our verse (25:6) means that Isaac had already taken possession of Abraham's property so that, at the time of his death, the other children would not contest his ownership. We have to remember that in that era the patriarch could designate his successor regardless of the order of his sons' births, which contrasts with later legislation of the Torah (Deut 21:15–17).

Despite the rivalry between Isaac and Ishmael, they buried their father together. This signified that the reconciliation between the estranged brothers had taken place; they buried him in harmony and peace. Isaac is mentioned first because Ishmael was the son of an Egyptian who was a maid of Sarah; he was not equal to Isaac and was not a true heir of Abraham.[21] Trying to explain why Isaac is mentioned first, the Talmud says, "The fact that Ishmael allowed Isaac to precede him demonstrates that he had repented and accepted his authority."[22]

The Bible describes burial with the verb *qbr*, which is common to all Semitic languages. Death and burial often appear together; thus, we find the consecutive forms "he died . . . and was buried." In addition, the name of the subject and the place of burial are common: "And Abraham breathed his last, dying. . . . His sons Isaac and Ishmael buried him in the cave of Machpelah" (Gen 25:8). Abraham died at the age of 175 years, which means that he lived until Jacob was fifteen years old.[23] In other words, Abraham died after the events that are narrated in the following chapters. Examination of the biblical narrative reveals the events are not recorded chronologically. Terah's death, for example, is mentioned at the start of Abraham's story although he lived for another sixty years (Gen 11:32).[24] According to the midrash, "From the point of view of chronology a period of sixty-five years is still required. But first, you may learn

---

21. Beno Jacob, *Genesis*, 165.

22. B. Bat. 16b.

23. This is because Abraham was one hundred years old at the birth of Isaac, and Isaac was sixty when Jacob was born (25:26).

24. Based on Gen 11:26 and 12:4, Terah was 145 years old when Abraham left for Canaan; so he lived for another 60 years after Abraham left.

that the wicked, even during their lifetime, are called dead."[25] But more than likely, the Torah ends stories when there is nothing more to say about the person.

Describing Abraham's death, the Bible says, "Abraham breathed his last, dying at a good ripe age, old and contented" (v. 8). The Hebrew term *vayyigva* is translated as "took his last breath" or maybe "expired"; the term also appears with the death of Isaac (35:29). Ibn Ezra and Radak explain it as a quick death without lengthy sickness. The Talmud says that whenever the term appears with "gathering" (which is mentioned with Abraham), this refers to the death of the righteous people:

> Ravina said to Rav Ḥama bar Buzi: "Is it true that you say that any death about which the word *gevia*, expire is mentioned is the death of the righteous?" Rav Ḥama bar Buzi said to him: "Yes. For example: 'And Isaac expired *vayyigva* and died'" (Gen 35:29). Ravina objected: "But with regard to the generation of the flood it states: 'And all the flesh expired *vayyigva*' (Gen 7:21), and there they died their wickedness." Rav Ḥama bar Buzi said to him: "We say this only when both *gevia* and *asifa*, gathering are used; when these two terms are mentioned together, they indicate the death of a righteous person."[26]

A different interpretation is found in the midrash, which suggests that the term *vayyigva* refers to the righteous who used to suffer from stomach trouble for ten to twenty days.[27] But more than likely this is a stage when a person is in his last final days before death itself. It is possible to link the term to the root *y.g.ʻ.*, which means fatigue. Thus, our term refers to a state of loss of strength that typically happens to elderly people before their death.

Abraham died at a good ripe age, old and content; a similar description appears with Isaac. This is in glaring contrast to Jacob who describes his life to Pharaoh as few and hard; he lived only 130 years (Gen 47:9) while Abraham lived to 175 (25:7) and Isaac to 180 (35:28). Ramban explains the phrase "at a ripe age—old and content" as indicating that he witnessed the fulfillment of all his desires of his heart and was content with all good things. The midrash says that Abraham was content because the "entire reward of the righteous is kept ready for them for the Hereafter, and the Holy One, blessed be He, shows them while yet in this

---

25. *Gen. Rab.* 39:7.
26. *B. Bat.* 16b.
27. *Gen. Rab.* 62:2.

world the reward He is to give them in the future; their souls are then satisfied and they fall asleep."[28] Von Rad pointed out that in ancient Israel life was seen as something limited, therefore when one reached "old and full of days" it was a gracious fulfillment in which the state of satiation was to be reached.[29] Abraham died as God told him in the "covenant between the pieces": "You shall go to your father in peace; You shall be buried at a ripe old age" (Gen 15:15). In other words, he died in peace with no sorrow. The description of Abraham's death ends with "he was gathered to his kin" (25:8). However, as noted above, this is unlikely since Abraham's kin were not buried in the cave of Machpelah. At that time, only Sarah was buried there. Therefore, as we suggested, this more than likely refers to the union of his soul with his forefathers.

MOURNING CUSTOMS

In the account of Sarah's death and burial, Abraham came to mourn and weep for her; only after that did he address the issue of burying her. Many biblical passages, in fact, place the *misped* (lament eulogy) before the interment (Gen 23:2; 50:10, 13; 1 Sam 25:1; 28:3; Jer 22:18; 25:33). In others, the order is reversed—first burial and only then *misped* (1 Kgs 14:8; 13:30; Jer 16:6). The roots *spd* and *bkh*—"cry, weep"—describe mourning practices and occur together frequently (Gen 23:2; 2 Sam 1:12; Isa 22:12; Ezek 24:16; Joel 2:12; Esth 4:3).[30] In Ugaritic, too, the cognate pair describes the mourning for Aqhat the son of Daniel.[31] It appears also in Akkadian and Aramaic.[32] A reading of the Bible, however, indicates that in some places *spd* does not have the same meaning as *bkh*. First of all, *spd* may mean "beating the breast," as in "beat upon your breasts for the pleasant fields" (Isa 32:12).[33] This sense is also found in the Akkadian

---

28. *Gen. Rab.* 62:2.

29. Rad, *Genesis*, 262; Rad, *Old Testament Theology*, 1:390.

30. In some passages, *misped* may also have originally been a bitter cry, as in "for this I will lament" (*espedah*) and a wail: "I will make lamentation like a jackal" (Mic 1:8; Jer 4:8, Joel 1:13).

31. Herdner, *Corpus des tablettes*, 19, 171–72; Pardee, "AQhatu Legend," 1:354.

32. *Bikītu u sipdu/sipittu*; see CAD 223–25; *Targum Sheni on Esther* 1:4.

33. The amora Ulla cited this verse as a prooftext in his distinction among the various expressions of grief associated with mourning: "Ulla said: ['The technical meaning of] a *hesped* is [striking] the breast. . . . [The technical meaning of] *ṭippuaḥ* is clapping one's hands [in grief], and that of *qillus* is [tapping] with the foot [in mourning].'" *Mo'ed Qaṭ*, 27b .

verb *sapādu*, "beat the breast."³⁴ Mourners beat their breasts while performing a funeral dance; this dance is apparently what is denoted by the noun *misped*, as we may infer from two verses: "You turned my lament (*mispedi*) into dancing" (Ps 30:12 [11]); and "a time to mourn (*sefod*) and a time to dance" (Eccl 3:4). Another sense of *spd* may be chanting a dirge or lament, as in "they shall not lament for him (*yispedu lo*), saying, 'Ah my brother!' or 'Ah sister!'" (Jer 22:18; Jer 34:5; 1 Kgs 13:30). Amos refers to those who perform the *misped* as "skilled in lamentation" (5:16).

Abraham is said to rise from beside his dead wife Sarah (Gen 23:3). During the mourning period, the mourners sat (e.g., Ezek 26:16; Job 2:8, 13; Isa 3:26) or lay on the floor (2 Sam 13:31; Lam 2:21), rather than on the usual cushion or carpets. Sitting on the bare floor was a sign of humility and identification with the dead but also proximity to the underworld.³⁵ In extrabiblical texts, when El learns of the death of Baal, he "descends from the throne, sits on the footstool; from the footstool, and sits on the ground."³⁶ The text continues and describes that "he poured dust (*'mr*) of mourning on his head, earth of mortification on his pate."³⁷ According to the account of the death of Nabonidus's mother, kings, princes, and governors "made a great lament, scattered [dust] on their head."³⁸ At the end of the Egyptian "Story of Two Brothers," the grieving elder brother goes to his house "smeared with dust."³⁹ As a mark of their condition, mourners covered their bodies with dust or ashes. After the defeat at Ai, Joshua and the elders put dust on their heads (Josh 7:6; Isa 47:1; Job 2:12; Esth 4:1–3).⁴⁰ By covering themselves with dust or ashes, mourners reminded themselves where they came from and where they would return: "For dust you are, and to dust you shall return" (Gen 3:19). Recall that the Bible identifies dust with the underworld, the place to which people

---

34. *CAD* 150–151.

35. Ward, "Mourning Customs," 3–4; Wensinck, *Semitic Rites*, 12–18.

36. Ginsberg, "Poems," 139.

37. Ginsberg, "Poems," 139. Scholars do not agree about the meaning of the word *'mr*. Gordon says that it means something like "dust" or "ashes." Fenton suggests that the word means "ashes." Gray prefers "turban," Driver opts for "straw" or "hay," and Taylor suggests "straw." See Gray, *Legacy*, 51; Driver, *Canaanite*, 142; Taylor, "First and Last," 163; Fenton, "Ugaritica-Biblica," 69.

38. Oppenheim, "Mother of Nabonidus," 562.

39. Wilson, "Two Brothers," 25.

40. The same custom was part of ceremonies of repentance (Job 42:1; Neh 9:1) and of supplication and entreaty (Job 16:15–17; Dan. 9:3).

descended after death; this may be the explanation of the custom.[41] Another possibility is that it is a reaction to the trauma of bereavement.

One ancient mourning custom that survives to the present is that the bereaved rend their garments. This practice is mentioned for the first time in the Joseph cycle. When Reuben discovers that Joseph has vanished, he tears his clothes (Gen 37:29); Jacob does the same thing after he sees Joseph's bloody cloak (37:34). After the defeat at Ai, Joshua rends his garments (Josh 7:6), and so do Hezekiah, after hearing the Rabshakeh's ultimatum (2 Kgs 19:1), and Mordechai, when he learns of the decree to exterminate the Jews (Esth 4:1). Job tears his robe when he was informed of his children's deaths (Job 1:20). The custom is also documented in extrabiblical texts; during the drought that followed the death of Daniel we read that Anath "rends the garment of Daniel the Rapha-man."[42]

Today at a Jewish funeral, a gash of approximately four inches is cut in the mourner's upper garment, on the left side for parents and the right side for another relative for whom mourning is mandatory (Lev 21:1–3). The mourner stands while tearing the garment (Job 1:20) and recites the benediction that accepts God's justice. In the past, mourners ripped their garments themselves. This act may symbolize a release of tension, or it may be a substitute for cutting oneself. Some believe that it was originally a palliative of self-mutilation.

Wearing sackcloth is another widespread custom that is often associated with rending one's garment. Jacob did so (Gen 37:34), and after Abner's assassination, David told the people to tear their garments and wear sackcloth (2 Sam 3:31). The custom indicated both private and national mourning (Job 16:15; Lam 2:10; Esth 4:1) and sometimes remorse for sin (1 Kgs 21:27; Neh 9:1) or hope for salvation (2 Kgs 19:1, 2; Dan 9:3). The neighboring people also wore sack as a symbol of mourning, remorse, and repentance: in Damascus (1 Kgs 20:31), in Moab (Isa 15:3), in Ammon (Jer 49:3), and in Sidon (Ezek 27:31). Similarly, extrabiblical sources mention that when El, the father of the gods, is mourning the death of Baal, he "puts sackcloth and loincloth," as does Anath.[43]

No information is given for the length of time Abraham mourned for Sarah. The standard mourning period was seven days, as it mentions later in the Joseph cycle where it says that Joseph was mourning for his

---

41. Martin-Achard, *Death to Life*, 27.
42. Ginsburg, "Aqhat," 35, 153.
43. Ginsburg, "Poems," 17, 139.

father: "When they came to the threshing floor of Atad, which is beyond the Jordan, they lamented there with a very great and sorrowful lamentation; and he made a mourning for his father for seven days" (Gen 50:10). The inhabitants of Jabesh-Gilead fasted for seven days after they buried Saul and his sons (1 Sam 31:13). Job's friends "sat with him on the ground seven days and seven nights. None spoke a word to him for they saw how very great was his suffering" (Job 2:13). The seven days of mourning was a custom entrenched in the Second Temple period: "Mourning for the dead lasts seven days, but for a fool or an ungodly man it lasts all his life" (Ben Sira 22:12). Judith was mourned for seven days (Jdt 16:24). When Herod died, Josephus wrote, "Archelaus paid him so much respect, as to continue his mourning till the seventh day; for so many days are appointed for it by the law of our fathers."[44] In fact, the seven-day period of mourning is of ancient origin; Gilgamesh mourns his friend Enkidu for seven days.[45] According to the inscription about the mother of Nabonidus, kings, princes, and foreign governors mourned her for seven days and seven nights.[46]

The time allowed between death and burial is not specified in the Hebrew Bible. However, it is believed that the dead were buried as soon as possible. In a statement about the execution of a criminal by hanging we read, "You must not let his corpse remain on the stake overnight but must bury him the same day. For an impaled body is an affront to God: you shall not defile the land that the Lord your God is giving you to possess" (Deut 21:23). Denial of burial and exposure of the body to predators was considered a curse because it was believed that the unburied could not find rest. According to the current law, the body could not be exposed beyond the day of execution. This verse was the basis of the requirement in the Talmud that all dead should buried on the day of their death unless there is a need for an honorable burial.[47] This custom of burial on the day of death exists to this day among Jews and Muslims.

As our study shows, the only customs that were practiced by Abraham were that he mourned and wept for Sarah and sat on the ground. No information is given as to the length of time Abraham mourned for

---

44. Josephus, *Ant.* 17:8:4.

45. "Day and night I have wept over him. / I would not give him up for burial / In case my friend should rise at my plaint / Seven days and seven nights, / Until a worm fell out of his nose." See Speiser, "Gilgamesh," 5–9, 89–90.

46. Oppenheim, "Mother," 562.

47. *Sanh.* 46a.

Sarah. Abraham is not described as putting dust on his head or rendering his garment and wearing sackcloth. These rites were carried in ancient Israel and are mentioned in extrabiblical sources, which suggest that more than likely Abraham also practiced them.

CULT OF THE DEAD

Providing food to the dead or honoring them with a meal was a common practice in the ancient world. People believed that the dead could influence the world of the living. They could help the living if the latter attended to their needs or harm them if they neglected them. The dead ancestors protected the family and were worshiped by its members. The living were expected to honor them and consult them.

An explicit reference to offerings to the dead is found in the retelling of Israelite history in Ps 106: "They attached themselves to Baal Peor, ate sacrifices offered to the dead" (106:28). This verse apparently expands, and according to the primary account in Num 25:1–5, the Moabite women invited the Israelite men to the "sacrifices for their gods," which the verse in Psalm modifies to "sacrifices to the dead." Scholars also cite Deut 26:12–14 as an example of the custom of offering food for the dead.[48] These verses are part of the declaration to be made when a person finishes removing all the tithes from his house. It concludes with a prayer that the Lord bless his nation and his land. As part of this declaration, the household must state that "I have not eaten of the tithe while I was mourning, or removed any of it while I was unclean, or offered any of it to the dead" (26:14). Lewis conjectures that the ban may refer to "offerings made periodically as part of the continuing death cult as well as those offerings presented after the initial interment."[49] Tigay notes that niches like those found in tombs in Ugarit have been found in tombs excavated in Samaria, the capital of the Northern Kingdom. These niches were used to hold food and drink for the dead. He maintains that the Torah does not ban this practice, but only forbids using tithes for it because contact

---

48. Brichto, "Biblical Complex," 29; Lewis, *Cults of the Dead*, 103–4; Spronk, *Beatific*, 241, 248.

49. Lewis, *Cults of the Dead*, 103.

with the dead is defiling.⁵⁰ Bloch-Smith, too, believes that the prohibition refers to tithes but not to the actual practice of offering food to the dead.⁵¹

As for the patriarchal narrative, it was B. Halevi who suggested that this practice of providing for the dead was prevalent among the patriarchs as well. He points to the non-aggression pact between Laban and Jacob. In this pact, Laban set up a stone as a boundary marker swearing to the God of Abraham and the god of Nahor and their ancestral deities. Jacob, on the other hand, swore by the Fear of his father Isaac. According to him, the word *Elohim* does not only refer to the God of Israel but to gods in general. It also denotes the spirits of the dead, as the woman told Saul: "I see *Elohim* coming up from the earth" (1 Sam 28:13; cf. Isa 8:19). More so, in various extrabiblical texts there is evidence for the use of *Elohim* to refer to the dead.⁵² Thus, Halevi suggested that the sacrifices that Jacob offered were in honor of his dead ancestors. In this way, he also explains the sacrifices in Gen 46:1 when Jacob sacrifices to the God of his father on his way to Egypt.⁵³ However, the treaty between Jacob and Laban was a "non-aggression pact" that was sealed by a meal, which was common in the ancient world. As for the sacrifices before the descent to Egypt, this was part of the incubation ceremony where, indeed, God appeared to Jacob following the sacrifice.

It has been suggested that since the patriarchs and the matriarchs were buried in a family tomb, this points to the cult of the dead.⁵⁴ The cave of Machpelah was originally purchased as a burial place for Sarah, but it later became a family tomb. The dead possessed power and contact with God; thus it was important to visit the burial site to petition the deceased. "Inquiring of the dead" appears on the list of magical practices condemned by the Bible (Deut 18:11). Isaiah refers to this practice when he condemns those "who sit inside tombs and pass the night in secret places" (Isa 65:4). Apparently sitting inside a tomb was part of the rite to raise the spirits of the dead by means of ghost. It is noteworthy that the site of the cave of Machpelah in Hebron is still a holy shrine to this day,

---

50. Tigay, *Deuteronomy*, 144; Sukenik, "Arrangements," 59–65; Bayliss, "Dead Kin," 111–25; Lewis, *Cults of the Dead*, 97.

51. Bloch-Smith, *Judahite Burial*, 123.

52. Spronk, *Beatific Afterlife*, 163; Lewis, *Cults of the Dead*, 49–51, 115. Arnold says *Elohim* "denotes the ancestral dead and not simply ghost or spirit of the dead." Arnold, "Necromancy," 203.

53. Halevi, "Ancestor," 109.

54. Bloch-Smith, *Judahite Burial*, 123.

where people visit and seek guidance and help. Nevertheless, there is no hint in the patriarchal narrative that the dead had any contact with God or that people petitioned at the graves. Thus, according to Albertz,

> While the significance attached to the tombs of paternal and maternal ancestors in the patriarchal narratives and formulas like "gathered to his father" (Gen 25:8, 17; 35:29; 49:29, 33) still indicates that there was emotional solidarity between the living members of the family and their dead ancestors, there are no references whatsoever in the patriarchal narrative to a regular cult of the dead of the kind evident, for example, in kispu ritual of Mesopotamia, and elsewhere they are scanty (Deut 26:14).[55]

To summarize, our study of the book of Genesis reveals that there is already a reference to an afterlife where death is not the last station of a human's life. This was expressed by the biblical idiom to "lie down with one's father." It was believed that the soul of a man is reunited with his ancestors and death is a transition to the afterlife. Therefore, all the patriarchs and matriarchs, except for Rachel, were buried in ancestral tombs on family-owned land in the cave of Machpelah. In the ancient world, people provided food for the dead or honored them with a meal. It was believed that the dead could help the living if the latter attended to their needs or harm them if they neglected them. However, there is no convincing evidence for this practice in the patriarchal narrative. Not much is said about mourning practices, there is only a short note that Abraham came to mourn and weep for Sarah, and he sat on the ground, which was the practice among mourners. Other customs such as putting dust on the head, rending garments, and wearing sackcloth are mentioned in the Hebrew Bible and extrabiblical sources; more than likely they were also exercised by Abraham. The matriarch Sarah's death is the first recorded death and interment in the Hebrew Bible; it is indicative of the great respect for the dead and the importance of proper burial. Abraham died at the age of 175 years, a good ripe age; he witnessed the fulfillment of all his desires. In his death "he was gathered to his kin" (Gen 25:8).

---

55. Albertz, *History*, 81.

Conclusion

The cumulative information that was analyzed suggests that the stories about Abraham contain the historical setting of the end of the third and the beginning of the second millennium BCE. Scrutiny of people's personal names, names of sites, and names of nations showed that they are consistent with earlier period, and in many instances are mentioned also in extrabiblical sources. They fit the origin and geographical setting of the Abrahamic stories. Adding more credibility to the stories is the usage of archaic names for places, supplemented by current names and locations.

Abraham is depicted as a nomad who travels to sites in the central mountain region and the Negeb. Throughout his travels, Abraham stayed close to urban centers so he could participate in small-scale trade for essential products to ensure the survival of his family. When he camped or was on the move, he stayed in a tent. He used the ass as the main animal of burden. Being the head of a small nomadic clan, Abraham had to avoid military confrontation; he kept peaceful relationships with the local inhabitants of the land. This contrasts with a later period when the Israelites were instructed to destroy the seven nations of Canaan.

The Abrahamic narrative shows no regular patterns of worship. It lacked a liturgical calendar and specific places for worship. The religion developed as a reaction to a developing situation. There were no temples and no priests. Abraham built altars to God as a form of worship and invoked his name. No sacrifices are mentioned on the altars except in the story of the binding of Isaac. Prayers and swearing are a simple, spontaneous outpouring of the heart and are not connected to a site or a cult. They were individual and tailored for a specific purpose. Blessings are pronounced by God, but also by individuals. The source of power of a blessing is God. Circumcision, which was carried out by the patriarch, was an ancient custom that is also attested to in extrabiblical sources.

Abraham worshiped El-Elyon, El Olam, El, and Elohim. From the time of the patriarch Isaac, "God of My Father," with the name Abraham started to appear. It was typical for a nomadic society to look for an intimate god as a father figure who would guide and protect them. Abraham selected a name for God that matched his situation and needs. Each name and phrase had a different meaning and referred to God's different attributes. These different attributes of that mighty God were equated with YHWH, the God the Israelites worshiped.

Not much is said about mourning practices. There is only a short note that Abraham came to mourn and weep for Sarah, and he sat on the ground, which was the practice among mourners. Other customs, such as putting dust on the head, rending garments, and wearing sackcloth, are mentioned in the Hebrew Bible and in extrabiblical sources and were also more than likely exercised by Abraham. Abraham died at the age of 175 years, a good ripe age; he witnessed the fulfillment of all his desires. In his death "he was gathered to his kin" (Gen 25:8), which refers to the union of his soul with his forefathers.

The stories about the patriarch Abraham were transmitted orally and were put into writing in the monarchial period. The goal that guided the writers was to create a link between the past and the present. Many events in the life of Abraham were interpreted as foreshadowing the future; the fulfillment of God's promises to Abraham signaled a continuous bond between God and Israel. The rabbis termed it "the deeds of the fathers are signs to the sons." Therefore, Abraham's journeys in the land of Canaan are parallel to Jacob's travels and correspond to a later description of the conquest of land in the book of Joshua. When the Israelites conquered the land, they took the reverse route of Kings Highway, which was used by the four monarchs from the east. They conquered the land and claimed it. Abraham's defeat of the four kings laid his own rights to the land and to his descendants. It gave legitimation to later generations of Israelites to conquer and claim the land. The mention of Melchizedek, the king of Salem, came to emphasize the sanctity of Salem and its role as a city of peace. This foreshadows the future when David conquered it and established his capital there and transformed it into a religious center.

The link between the past and the present is further seen in the covenant between God and Abraham (Gen 15), and it is paralleled with the covenant between God and David (2 Sam 7:4–16; Ps 89:4). This is exemplified by the usage of equivalent language and ideas. The three motifs—many descendants, settlement of the land, and the destruction of its inhabitance—were of immediate concern to the patriarch and King David. The similarities between the two covenants came to strengthen the assertion that the initial covenant is to remain forever and to give legitimation to the Davidic monarchy.

The wife-sister story continues the theme of foreshadowing future events; what happened to Abraham is repeated with his son Isaac and later with the Israelites in Egypt. Abraham and Sarah's migration to Egypt is like the story of the Israelites' descent to Egypt and the exodus. Taking Sarah to Pharaoh's harem is parallel to the taking of the Israelites into slavery. The presents that Abraham received in Egypt are like the silver and gold the Israelites received from the Egyptians when they left Egypt. God interceded in both stories and inflicted plagues on the Egyptians (Gen 12:17; Exod 11:1). What the stories convey is that God, who protected Abraham and Isaac, would later protect his descendants. On the other hand, the story of Sodom and Gomorrah served as a reminder of divine judgment to a sinful community and a warning not to follow the ways of the wicked Sodomites.

In the ancient Near Eastern literature, we find royal inscriptions of myths about gods and purely fictional stories about legendary heroes. No so with the patriarch Abraham, who is portrayed with all his faults and weaknesses along with his triumphs. He is depicted as an obedient man who heard the divine call and without hesitation left his birthplace and his family to follow God's call. His obedience is fully displayed in the binding of Isaac where the patriarch obeyed God's command to sacrifice his son Isaac. By passing the test, it shows Abraham's obedience and love of God; it was a sign of strength for his faith. Abraham's love and trust in God serves as a model to other nations. Despite his separation from his nephew Lot, he came to his aid and rescued him. His act stresses the importance of family ties, and it serves as an archetype for the *mitzvah* of redemption of the captives. He is a compassionate man who cares about the life of other human beings. He pleads with God to save the lives of total strangers, pagans he does not know. He tried to persuade God to change his verdict. Abraham is God's confidant and part of the divine council. Abraham is a model of a God-fearing man.

Bibliography

Aharoni, Yohanan. "The Land of Gerar." *IEJ* 6 (1956) 26-32.
———. "Nothing Early and Nothing Late: Re-Writing Israel's Conquest." *BA* 39 (1976) 55-76.
———. "Tamar and the Roads to Elath." *IEJ* 13 (1963) 30-42.
Ahituv, Shmuel. "'Ashtarot." *EMiqr* 6:404-406.
———. *Canaanite Toponyms in Ancient Egyptian Documents*. Jerusalem: Magness, 1984.
Albertz, Rainer. *A History of Israelite Religion in the Old Testament Period*. Translated by John Bowden. Louisville: Westminster John Knox, 1994.
Albright, William Foxwell, trans. "The Amarna Letters." In *ANET* 483-90.
———. "From the Patriarchs to Moses. I. From Abraham to Joseph." *BA* 36 (1973) 5-33.
———. *From the Stone Age to Christianity*. Garden City, NY: Doubleday, 1957.
———. "The Historical Background of Genesis XIV." *JSOR* 10 (1926) 231-69.
———. "The Kyle Memorial Excavation at Bethel." *BASOR* 56 (1934) 2-15.
———. "New Light on the History of Western Asia in the Second Millennium BCE." *BASOR* 78 (1940) 23-31.
———. "The Northern Boundary of Benjamin." *AASOR* 4 (1922-1923) 150-55.
———. "Some Remarks on the Meaning of the Verb *shr* in Genesis." *BASOR* 164 (1961) 28.
———. "A Third Revision of the Early Chronology of Western Asia." *BASOR* 88 (1942) 28-36.
———. "Western Asia in the Twentieth Century BC: The Archive of Mari." *BASOR* 67 (1937) 26-30.
———. *YHWH and the Gods of Canaan*. Garden City, NY: Doubleday, 1968.
Alexander, T. Desmond. *Abraham in the Negev*. Great Britain: Paternoster, 1997.
———. "Are the Wife/Sister Incidents in Genesis Literary Compositional Variants?" *VT* 42 (1992) 145-53.
———. "The Hagar Traditions in Genesis XVI and XXI." In *Studies in the Pentateuch*, edited by John A. Emerton, 131-48. VTSup 41. Leiden: Brill, 1990.
Alt, Albrecht. "The God of the Fathers." In *Essays on Old Testament History and Religion*, translated by R. A. Wilson, 3-77. Oxford: Blackwell, 1966.
Altmann, Amnon. "On the Question of the Designation of the Land of Israel as *MAT AMMURI* ('The Land of the Emorites')." *Tarbiz* 51(1981-1982) 3-22.

Andrews, David Keith. "YHWH the God of the Heavens." In *Seed of Wisdom: Essays in the Honor of T. J. Meek*, edited by Stewart McCullough, 45–57. Toronto: University of Toronto Press, 1964.

Arnold, Bill T. "Necromancy and Cleromancy in 1 and 2 Samuel." *CBQ* 66 (2004) 199–213.

Astour, Michael C. "Ham." In *ABD* 3:32.

———. "Political and Cosmic Symbolism in Genesis 14 and Its Babylonian Sources." In *Biblical Motifs: Origins and Transformation*, edited by Alexander Altmann, 65–112. Cambridge: Harvard University, 1966.

———. "Salem." In *ABD* 5:905.

———. "Zoar." In *ABD* 6:1107.

Attridge, Harold W., and Robert A. Oden, Jr. *Philo of Byblos: The Phoenician History*. Washington, DC: The Catholic Biblical Association of America, 1981.

Augustine. *The City of God Against the Pagans*. Translated by Eva Matthews Sanford and William McAllen Green. Cambridge: Harvard University Press, 1965.

Avi-Yonah, M. "Ashtaroth, Ashteroth-Karnaim, Karnaim." In *EncJud* 3:737.

Bailey, Lloyd R. "Israelite 'Ēl Šadday and Amorite Bêl Šadê." *JBL* 87 (1968) 434–38.

Bar, Shaul. "Abraham's Trees." *IBS* 28 (2010) 2–20.

———. *Isaac the Passive Patriarch*. Eugene, OR: Wipf & Stock, 2020.

Barr, James. "Theophany and Anthropomorphism in the Old Testament." In *Congress Volume Oxford 1959*, edited by G. W. Anderson et al, 31–38. VTSup 7. Leiden: Brill, 1960.

Beitzel, B. J. "Habiru." In *ISBE* 2:586–90.

Bentzen, A. "Zur Geschichte der Ṣadoḳiden." *ZAW* 51 (1933) 173–76.

Bimson, John J. "Archaeological Data and the Dating of the Patriarchs." In *Essays on the Patriarchal Narratives*, edited by A. R. Millard and D. J. Wiseman, 53–89. Winona Lake, IN: Eisenbraun, 1983. Reprint, Wipf & Stock, 2007.

Bloch-Smith, Elizabeth. *Judahite Burial Practices and Beliefs About the Dead*. JSOTSup 123. Sheffield: JSOT Press, 1992.

Brichto, Herert Chanan. "Kin, Cult, Land, and Afterlife—A Biblical Complex." *HUCA* 44 (1973) 1–54.

Bright, John. *A History of Israel*. 2nd ed. Philadelphia: Westminster John Knox, 2000.

Brunner, H. *Grundzüge der altägyptischen Religion*. Darmstadt: Wissenschaftliche Buchgesellschaft, 1983.

Buccellati, Giorgio. *The Amorites of the Ur III Period*. Naples: Instituto Orientale di Napoli, 1996.

Calvin, John. *Commentaries on the First Book of Moses Called Genesis*. Translated by John King. Grand Rapids: Eerdmans, 1948.

Campbell, E. F. "Shechem Tell Balâtah." In *EAEHL* 4:1345–54.

Cardascia, Guillaume. *Les lois Assyriennes*. Paris: Cref, 1959.

Carr, David M. *Reading the Fractures of Genesis: Historical and Literary Approaches*. Louisville: Westminster John Knox, 1996.

Cassuto, U. "Abraham." In *EMiqr* 1:61–67.

———. *A Commentary on the Book of Exodus*. Jerusalem: Magness, 1967.

———. *The "Quaestio" of the Book of Genesis*. Jerusalem: Magnes, 1990.

Cazelles, H. "The Hebrews." In *People of Old Testament Times*, edited by D. J. Wiseman, 1–28. Oxford: Clarendon Press, 1973.

Černý, J. "Consanguineous Marriages in Pharaonic Egypt." *JEA* 40 (1954) 23–29.

Clements, Roland. *Abraham and David: Genesis 15 and Its Meaning for Israelite Tradition*. Naperville, IL: Alec R. Allenson, 1967.
Clines, David J. A. *What Does Eve Do to Help?* JSOTSup 94. Sheffield: JSOT Press, 1990.
Cohen, Jeffery M. "Was Abraham Heartless?" *JBQ* 23 (1995) 180-81.
Conard, E. W. "The Fear Not Oracles in Second Isaiah." *VT* 34 (1984) 129-52.
Cornelius, Izak. "Genesis 26 and Mari: The Dispute over Water and the Socio-Economic Way of Life of the Patriarchs." *JNSL* 12 (1984) 53-61.
Cowley, A. E. *The Hittites*. London: Oxford University Press, 1926.
Cross, Frank Moore. *Canaanite Myth and Hebrew Epic: Essays in the History of the Religion of Israel*. Cambridge: Harvard University Press, 1973.
———. "A New Qumran Biblical Fragment Related to the Original Hebrew Underlying the Septuagint." *BASOR* 132 (1953) 15-26.
———. "YHWH and the God of the Patriarchs." *HTR* 55 (1962) 225-59.
Cross F. M., and G. E. Wright. "The Boundary and Province Lists of the Kingdom of Judah." *JBL* 75 (1956) 202-26.
Dahood, Mitchell. "The Name Yišmāʿēl in Genesis 16, 11." *Bib* 49 (1968) 87-88.
Delitzsch, Franz. *A New Commentary on Genesis*. 2 vols. Translated by Sophia Taylor. Scribner & Welford, 1889. Reprint, Eugene, OR: Wipf & Stock, 2001.
Dillmann, August. *Genesis: Critically and Exegetically Expounded*. Translated by William B. Stevenson. Edinburgh: T&T Clark, 1897.
Driver, Godfrey Rolles. *Canaanite Myth and Legends*. Edinburgh: T&T Clark, 1956.
Driver, Godfrey Rolles, and John C. Miles, eds. *The Assyrian Laws*. Oxford: Clarendon, 1935.
Driver, S. R. *The Book of Genesis with Introduction and Notes*. London: Methuen, 1904.
Dijkstra, M. "Abraham." In *DDD* 3-5.
Duppont-Sommer, A. "Sur les débuts de l'historie Araméenne." *VTSupp* 1 (1953) 40-49.
Ehrlich, Ernst Ludwig. *Der Traum im Alten Testament*. BZAW 73. Berlin: Topelmann, 1953.
Eichrodt, Walter. *Theology of the Old Testament*. 2 vols. Translated by J. A. Baker. Philadelphia: Westminster, 1961-1967.
Emerton, J. A. "The Origin of the Promises to the Patriarchs in the Older Sources of the Book of Genesis." *VT* 32 (1982) 14-32.
———. "The Riddle of Genesis 14." *VT* 21 (1971) 403-39.
———. "Some False Clues in the Study of Genesis 14." *VT* 21 (1971) 24-47.
Eusebius. *The Onomasticon: Palestine in the Fourth Century A.D*. Translated by G. S. P. Freeman-Grenville. Edited by Joan E. Taylor. Jerusalem: Carta, 2003.
Fensham, F. Charles. "The Son of a Handmaid in Northwest Semitic." *VT* 19 (1969) 312-21.
Fenton, T. L. "Ugaritica-Biblica." *UF* (1969) 65-70.
Finkelstein, J. J., trans. "Additional Mesopotamia Legal Documents." In *ANET* 371, lines 542-47.
———, trans. "The Laws of Ur-Nammu." In *ANET* 523-25.
———. "Mesopotamia." *JNES* 21 (1962) 73-92.
Finkelstein, Israel, and Neil Asher Silberman. *The Bible Unearthed: Archeology's New Vision of Ancient Israel and the Origin of Its Sacred Texts*. New York: Free Press, 2001.
Fishbane, M. "The 'Sign' in the Hebrew Bible." *Shnaton* 1 (1975) 213-34.

Fitzmyer, Joseph. *The Aramaic Inscription of Sefire*. BibOr 19. Rome: Pontifical Biblical Institute, 1967.

Freedman, David Noel. "The Chronology of Israel and the Ancient Near East: An Old Testament Chronology." In *The Bible and the Ancient Near East: Essays in Honor of W. F. Albright*, edited by George Ernest Wright, 203–14. London: Routledge & Kegan Paul, 1961.

———. "Divine Commitment and Human Obligation. The Covenant Theme." *Interpretation* 18 (1964) 419–31.

Gardiner, Alan H. "Adoption Extraordinary." *JEA* 26 (1940) 23–29.

Ginsberg, H. L., trans. "Poems about Baal and Amath." In *ANET* 129–42.

———. "The Tale of Aqhat." In *ANET* 149–55.

Glueck, Nelson. "The Age of Abraham in the Negeb." *BA* 18 (1955) 2–9.

———. "Explorations in Eastern Palestine, 4." *AASOR* 25–28 (1951) 165–66.

———. *Rivers in the Desert*. New York: Norton, 1959.

Goetze, Albrecht, trans. "Plague Prayers of Mursilis." In *ANET* 204–35.

Goldingay John. "The Patriarchs in Scripture and History." In *Essays on the Patriarchal Narratives*, edited by A. R. Millard and D. J. Wiseman, 1–34. Winona Lake, IN: Eisenbrauns, 1983.

Gordon, Cyrus H. "Abraham and the Merchants of Ura." *JNES* 17 (1958) 28–31.

———. "Biblical Customs and the Nuzu Tablets." *BA* 3 (1940) 1–12.

———. "The Patriarchal Narratives." *JNES* 13 (1954) 56–59.

———. *Ugarit and Minoan Crete*. New York: Norton, 1966.

———. *Ugaritic Manual*. Roma: Pontificium Institutum Biblicum, 1955.

———. *Ugaritic Textbook*. Roma: Pontificium Institutum Biblicum, 1965.

———. "Where Is Abraham's Ur?" *BAR* 3 (1977) 20–21, 52.

Gottwald, N. K. "Were the Early Israelites Pastoral Nomads?" *BAR* 4 (1978) 2–7.

———. "Were the Early Israelites Pastoral Nomads?" In *Rhetorical Criticism: Essays in Honor of James Muilenburg*, edited by Jared J. Jackson and Martin Kessler, 223–55. Eugene, OR: Pickwick, 1974.Gray, J. *Legacy of Canaan*. SVT 5. Leiden: Brill, 1957.

Greenfield, J. C. "The Zakir Inscription and the Danklied." In *Proceedings of the Fifth World Congress of Jewish Studies*, edited by Pinchas Peli, 174–91. Jerusalem: World Union of Jewish Studies, 1969.

Greengus, S. "Sisterhood Adoption at Nuzi and the 'Wife-Sister' in Genesis." *HUCA* 46 (1975) 5–31.

Grintz, Yehoshua M. *The Book of Genesis*. Jerusalem: Magnes, 1983.

Gunkel, Hermann. *Genesis*. Translated by Mark E. Biddle. Macon, GA: Mercer University Press, 1997.

———. *The Legends of Genesis*. Translated by William Herbert Carruth. Chicago: Open Court, 1907.

Ha, John. *Genesis 15: A Theological Compendium of Pentateuchal History*. Berlin: de Gruyter, 1989.

Halevi, Benjamin. "Additional Notes on Ancestor Worship." *BethM* 64 (1975) 101–17.

Hamilton, Victor P. *The Book of Genesis, Chapters 1–17*. Grand Rapids: Eerdmans, 1990.

———. *The Book of Genesis, Chapters 18–50*. Grand Rapids: Eerdmans, 1995.

———. "Hānîk." In *TWOT* 1:301–02.

Hakker-Orion, D. "The Role of the Camel in Israel's Early History." In *Early Herders and Their Flocks*, edited by J. Clutton-Brock and C. Grigson, 207–12. Animals and Archaeology 3. Oxford: University Press, 1984.

Hall, Robert G. "Circumcision." In *ABD* 1:1025-31.
Haran, Menahem. "The Religion of the Patriarchs: An Attempt at a Synthesis." *ASTI* 4 (1965) 30-55.
Hartley, J. *Book of Job*. NICOT. Grand Rapids: Eerdmans, 1988.
Hayes, John H., and J. Maxwell Miller, eds. *Israelite and Judean History*. London: SCM, 1977.
Held, M. "Philological Notes on the Mari Covenant Rituals." *BASOR* 200 (1970) 32-40.
Herdner, André. *Corpus des tablettes en Cunéiformes Alphabétiques*. Paris: Imprimerie Nationale, 1963.
Herodotus. *Histories*. Translated by Alfred Denis Godley. Cambridge: Harvard University Press, 1930.
Hiebert, Theodore. *God of My Victory: The Ancient Hymn in Habakkuk 3*. HSM 38. Atlanta: Scholars, 1986.
Hoffmeier, J. K. "The Wives Tales of Genesis 12, 20, and 26 and the Covenants at Beer-Sheba." *TynBul* 43 (1992) 81-99.
Hoffner, Harry A., Jr. "The Hittites and Hurrians." In *Peoples of the Old Times*, edited by D. J. Wiseman, 197-228. Oxford: Clarendon Press, 1973.
———. "Some Contributions of Hittitology to the Old Testament Study." *TynBul* 20 (1969) 27-55.
Hoftijzer, Jacob. *Die Verheissungen an die Drei Erzväter*. Leiden: Brill, 1956.
Holzinger, H. *Genesis*. Leipzig: J. C. B. Mohr, 1898.
Hundley, Michael. *YHWH Among the Gods: The Divine in Genesis, Exodus, and the Ancient Near East*. Cambridge: Cambridge University Press, 2022.
Hyatt, J. Philip. "YHWH as 'The God of My Father.'" *VT* 5 (1955) 130-36.
Irenaeus. *Against the Heresies*. In *The Ante-Nicene Fathers*, edited by Alexander Roberts and James Donaldson, 1:309-567. Grand Rapids: Eerdmans, 1975.
Jacob, Benno. *The First Book of the Bible: Genesis*. New York: Ktav, 1974.
Jenni, Ernst. "'Ōlām." In *TLOT* 2:852-62.
———. "Das wort ''ōlām,' im Alten Testament." *ZAW* 65 (1953) 1-35.
———. "Das wort ''ōlām,' im Alten Testament. *ZAW* 64 (1952) 197-248.
Jirku, Anton. "Ein fall von inkubation im AT (Ex 38:8)." *ZAW* 33 (1913) 151-53.
Kalimi, Isaac. "The Land of Moriah, Mount Moriah, and the Site of Solomon's Temple in Biblical Historiography." *HTR* 83 (1990) 345-62.
Kallai-Kleinmann, Z. "The Town Lists of Judah, Simeon, Benjamin, and Dan." *VT* 8 (1958) 134-60.
Kareling, Emil G. H. "Terach." *ZAW* 40 (1922) 153-54.
Kaufmann, Y. *Toldot ha'Emunah "Yisre' 'elit*. Jerusalem: Bialik Institute, 1956.
Kitchen, K. A. *Ancient Orient and Old Testament*. Downers Grove, IL: InterVarsity, 1966.
———. *The Bible in Its World: The Bible and Archaeology Today*. Downers Grove, IL: InterVarsity, 1978.
———. *On the Reliability of the Old Testament*. Grand Rapids: Eerdmans, 2003.
Koch, Klaus. *The Growth of the Biblical Tradition*. Translated by Susan Marianne Cupitt. New York: Scribner's Sons, 1969.
———. "Šaddaj. Zum Verhältnis Zwischen Israelitischer Monolatrie und Nordwest-Semitischem Polytheismus." *VT* 26 (1976) 299-332.
Kramer, S. N., trans. "Lamentation over the Destruction of Ur." In *ANET* 459.
———. "Lipit-Ishtar Lawcode." In *ANET* 159-61.

Kuenen, A. *An Historical-Critical Inquiry into the Origin and Composition of the Hexateuch.* London: MacMillan, 1886.

Kugel, James L. *The Bible as It Was.* Cambridge: Belknap, 1997.

———. *How to Read the Bible: A Guide to the Scripture, Then and Now.* New York: Free Press, 2007.

Kupper, Jean-Robert. *Les nomades en Mésopotamie au temps des rois de Mari.* Paris: Les Belles Lettres, 1957.

Labuschagne, Casper J. "The Life Span of the Patriarchs." *OTS* 25 (1989) 121–27.

———. "The *Našû-nadānu* Formula and Its Biblical Equivalent." In *Travels in the World of the Old Testament: Studies Presented to Professor M. A. Beek on the Occasion of his 65th Birthday*, edited by M. Heerma van Voss and P. Houwink ten Cate, 176–80. Assen: Van Gorcum, 1974.

Lambdin, T. O. "Egyptian Loan Words in the Old Testament." *JAOS* 73 (1953) 145–55.

Lambert, W. G. *Babylonian Wisdom Literature.* Oxford: Oxford University Press, 1960.

———. "The Domesticated Camel in the Second Millennium: Evidence from Alalakh and Ugarit." *BASOR* 160 (1960) 42–43.

Lapp. P. "Bâb edh-Dhrâ, Perizzites, and Emim." In *Jerusalem Through the Ages. The Twenty-Fifth Archaeology Convention*, edited by J. Aviram, 1–25. Jerusalem: Israel Exploration Society, 1967.

Leibowitz, Nehama. *Numbers 1–20.* AB 4a. New Haven: Yale University press, 1993.

———. *Studies in Bereshit (Genesis) in the Context of Ancient and Modern Jewish Bible Commentary.* Jerusalem: World Zionist Organization, 1976.

———. *Studies in Shemot I.* Jerusalem: World Zionist Organization, 1976.

Lemche, Neils Peter. "Israel, History of (Premonarchic Period)." In *ABD* 3:526–45.

———. *The Israelites in History and Tradition.* Louisville: Westminster John Knox Press, 1988.

Lernau, H. "Faunal Remains, Strata 3–1." In *Early Arad*, edited by Ruth Amiran, 83–111. Jerusalem: Israel Exploration Society, 1978.

Levenson, John D. *The Death and Resurrection of the Beloved Son: The Transformation of the Child Sacrifice in Judaism and Christianity.* New Haven: Yale University Press, 1993.

Levine, Baruch A. *In the Presence of the Lord: A Study of Cultic Terms in Ancient Israel.* SJLA 5. Leiden: Brill, 1974.

Lewis, T. J. *Cult of the Dead in Ancient Israel and Ugarit.* Atlanta: Scholars, 1989.

Lewy, J. "Studies in the Historic Geography of the Ancient Near East." *Orientalia* 21 (1952) 265–92.

———. "Les textes Paléo-Assyriens et l'Anceit Testamnet." *RHR* 110 (1934) 29–65.

Liver, Jacob. "Melchizedek." In *EMiqr* 4:1154–57.

Lods, Adolphe. *Israel from Its Beginnings to the Middle of the Eighth Century.* Translated by S. H. Hooke. London: Routledge, 1932.

Lohfink, N. *Die Landverheissung als Eid: Eine Studie zu Gn 15.* Stuttgart: Katholisches Bibelwerk, 1967.

Loewenstamm, S. E. "The Divine Grants of Land to the Patriarchs." *JAOS* 91 (1971) 509–10.

Lucknebill, Daniel David. *Ancient Records of Assyria and Babylonia.* 2 vols. Chicago: University of Chicago Press, 1926–1927.

Luke, John Tracy. "Abraham and the Iron Age: Reflection on the New Patriarchal Studies." *JSOT* 4 (1977) 35–47.

Lutz, David A. "The Isaac Tradition in the Book of Genesis." PhD diss., Drew University, 1969.
Magen, Itzhak. "Mamre." In *EAEHL* 3:939–42.
Maimonides, Moses. *The Guide for the Perplexed*. Translated by Michael Friedlander. New York: Hebrew, 1881.
Malamat, A. "The Arameans." In *People of the Old Testament Times*, edited by D. J. Wiseman, 134–55. Oxford: Clarendon Press, 1973.
———. "Aspects of the Foreign Politics of David and Solomon." *JNES* 22 (1963) 1–17.
———. "Canaan and the Mari Texts." In *Near Eastern Archeology in the Twentieth Century: Essays in Honor of Nelson Glueck*, edited by J. A. Sanders, 164–77. Garden City, NY: Doubleday, 1970.
———. "Nahor." In *EMiqr* 5:805–9.
Maly, E. H. "Genesis 12:10–20; 20:1–18; 26:7–11 and the Pentateuchal Question." *CBQ* 18 (1956) 255–62.
Margalit, B. *The Ugaritic Poem of Aqhat*. BZAW 182. Berlin: de Gruyter, 1989.
Martin-Achard, R. *From Death to Life*. Translated by John Penny Smith. Edinburgh: Oliver & Boyd, 1960.
Mathews, Kenneth A. *Genesis 11:27–50:26*. The New American Commentary 1b. Nashville: B&H, 2005.
Matt, Daniel C. *The Zohar*. 9 vols. Stanford: Stanford University Press, 2004–2006.
Mattingly, Gerald L. "Kiriathaim." In *ABD* 4:85.
Matthews, Victor Harold. "The Wells of Gerar." *BA* 49 (1986) 118–26.
Mayer, Günter "עָרֵל ʿāral." In *TDOT* 11:359–61.
Mazar, B. "Emori." In *EMiqr* 1:440–46.
———. "The Historical Background of the Book of Genesis." *JNES* 28 (1969) 73–83.
Mazor, Yair "Genesis 22: The Ideological Rhetoric and Psychological Composition." *Bib* 67 (1968) 81–88.
McCarthy, D. J. "Melchizedek: Gen 14:17–20 in the Targums, in Rabbinic and Early Christian Literature." *Bib* 81 (2000) 1–31.
———. *Treaty and Covenant*. AnBib 21. Rome: Pontifical Biblical Institute, 1963.
McConville, J. G. "Abraham and Melchizedek: Horizons in Genesis 14." In *He Swore an Oath*, edited by R. S. Hess, 93–118. Cambridge: Tyndale, 1993.
McEvenue, Sean E. *The Narrative Style of the Priestly Writer*. Rome: Biblical Institute, 1971.
McNamara, M. "De populi Aramaeorum Primordiis."*Verbum Domini* 35 (1957) 129–42.
Meek, Theophile J., trans. "The Code of Hammurabi." In *ANET* 369, lines 163–80.
Mendenhall, G. E. "Covenants Forms in Israelite Tradition." *BA* 17 (1954) 50–76.
Mettinger, T. N. D. *In Search of God: The Meaning and Message of the Everlasting Names*. Translated by F. H. Cryer. Philadelphia: Fortress, 1988.
Mihelic, J. L. "Shur, Wilderness of." In *IDB* 4:342.
Millard, Allan R. "Arameans." In *ABD* 1:345–50.
———. Methods of Studying the Patriarchal Narrative as Ancient Texts." In *Essays on the Patriarchal Narratives*, edited by Allan R. Millard and Donald J. Wiseman, 35–51. Winona Lake, IN: Eisenbrauns, 1983.
Miller, J. Maxwell. "The Patriarchs and the Extra-Biblical Sources: A Response." *JSOT* 2 (1977) 62–66.
———. "Sin and Judgment in Jeremiah 34:17–19." *JBL* 103 (1984) 611–13.

Miller, Patrick D. *The Divine Warrior in Early Israel*. Cambridge: Harvard University Press, 1973.

Milevski, Ianir. *Early Bronze Age Goods Exchange in the Southern Levant: A Marxist Perspective*. London: Routledge, 2014.

Milgrom, Jacob. *Cult and Conscience*. Leiden: Brill, 1976.

Moore, Carey A. *Judith*. AB 40. Garden City, NY: Doubleday, 1985.

Moran, William L. "The Scandal of the 'Great Sin' at Ugarit." *JNES* 18 (1959) 280–81.

Morgenstern, Julian. "The 'Bloody Husband' (?) (Exod. 4:24–26) Once Again." *HUCA* 34 (1963) 35–70.

———. *Rites of Birth, Marriage, Death, and Kindred Occasions Among the Semites*. Cincinnati: Hebrew Union College Press, 1966.

Moscati, S. *The Semites in Ancient History*. Cardiff: University of Wales Press, 1959.

Muffs, Yochanan. *Love and Joy, Law, Language, and Religion in Ancient Israel*. Cambridge: Harvard University Press, 1992.

Muilenburg, J. "The Birth of Benjamin." *JBL* 75 (1956) 194–201.

Naaman, Nadav. "The Shihor of Egypt and the Shur That is Before Egypt." *TA* 7 (1980) 95–109.

Nebo, Yehoshaphat. *Perushe Rabbi Yosef Bekhor Shor 'al ha-Torah*. Jerusalem: Mosad Harav Kook, 1994.

Neff, Robert Wilbur. "The Annunciation in the Birth Narrative of Ishmael." *BR* 17 (1972) 51–60.

Nemoy, Leon. *Karaite Anthology: Excerpts from Early Literature*. New Heaven: Yale University Press, 1952.

Nikaido, Scott. "Hagar and Ishmael as Literary Figures: An Intertextual Study." *VT* 51 (2001) 219–42.

Noth, Martin. *The History of Israel*. Translated by Stanley Godman. New York: Harper & Brothers, 1958.

———. *A History of Pentateuchal Tradition*. Translated with an introduction by Bernhard W. Anderson. Englewood Cliffs, NJ: Prentice Hall, 1972.

———. *Die Ursprünge des Alten Israel im Lichte Neuer Quellen*. Köln-Opladen: Sozialwissenschaften, 1961.

Obermann, Julian. "How Daniel Was Blessed with a Son: An Incubation Scene in Ugaritic." *Supplement to the Journal of the American Oriental Society* 66 (1946) 1–30.

O'Callaghan, R. T. *Aram Naharaim*. Rome: Pontificium Institutum Biblicum, 1948.

Oppenheim, A. Leo, trans. "The Mother of Nabonidus." In *ANET* 560–62.

Oren, Eliezer D. "Gerar." In *ABD* 2:989–91.

Ouellette, Jean. "More on ʾĒl Šadday and Bêl Šadê." *JBL* 88 (1969) 470–71.

Pagolu, Augustine. *The Religion of the Patriarchs*. JSOTSup 277. Sheffield: Sheffield Academic, 1998.

Pardee, Dennis, trans. "The ʾAQhatu Legend (1.103)." In *COS* 1:343–56.

Parrot, André. *Abraham and His Times*. Translated by James H. Farley. Philadelphia: Fortress, 1968.

Petersen, D. L. "A Thrice-Told Tale: Genre, Theme, and Motif." *BR* 22 (1973) 30–43.

Pfeiffer, R. H., trans. "Akkadia Oracles of Prophecies." In *ANET* 449–50.

Pinker, Aron. "The Expulsion of Hagar and Ishmael (Gen 21:9–21)." *Women and Judaism* 6 (2009) 1–24.

Pitard, Wayne T. "Before Israel: Syria-Palestine in the Bronze Age." In *The Oxford History of the Biblical World*, edited by Michael D. Cogan, 33–77. Oxford: Oxford University Press, 1998.
Polzin, R. "The Ancestress of Israel in Danger." *Semeia* 3 (1975) 81–98.
Price, Randall. *The Stones Cry Out: What Archaeology Reveals About the Truth of the Bible*. Eugene, OR: Harvest House, 1997.
Pritchard, James B. ed., *Ancient Near Eastern Texts Relating to the Old Testament*. 3rd ed. Princeton: Princeton University Press, 1969.
Pury, Albert de. "EL-OLAM." In *DDD* 288–91.
Rabinowitz, Jacob. "The 'Great Sin' in Ancient Egyptian Marriage Contracts." *JNES* 18 (1959) 73.
Rad, Gerhard von. *Genesis: A Commentary*. Translated by John H. Marks. Philadelphia: Westminster, 1961.
———. *Old Testament Theology*. Philadelphia: Westminster John Knox, 2001.
Rainey, A. F. "Chaldea, Chaldeans." In *ENJud* 5:330.
———. "Royal Weights and Measures." *BASOR* 179 (1965) 34–36.
Rast, Walter E. "Bab-Edh-Dhra'." In *ABD* 1:559–61.
Rattner, R. "Three Bulls or One: Reappraisal of 1 Sam 1:24." *Bib* 68 (1987) 98–102.
Reif, S. C. "Dedicated to חנך." *VT* 22 (1972) 495–501.
Rendtorff, R. "Genesis 15 im Rahmen der Theologischen Bearbeitung der Vätergeschichten." In *Werden und Wirken des Alten Testaments: Festschrift für Claus Westermann*, edited by R. Albertz, 74–81. Göttingen: Vandenhoeck and Ruprecht, 1980.
———. *The Problem of the Process of Transmission in the Pentateuch*. JSOTSupp 89. Sheffield: JSOT Press, 1990.
Rosenthal, Franz, trans. "Building Inscriptions." In *ANET*, 653–54.
———. "Yehavmilk Byblos." In *ANET* 656.
Rowley, Harold Henry. *The Faith of Israel*. London: SCM, 1956.
———. "Melchizedek and Zadok (Gen 14 and Ps 110)." In *Festschrift, Alfred Bartholet zum 80 Geburtstag*, edited by W. Baumgartner, 461–72. Tübingen: Mohr, 1950.
———. "Zadok and Nehushtan." *JBL* 58 (1939) 113–41.
Rowton, M. B. "The Topological Factor in the Habiru Problem." In *Studies in Honor of Benno Landsberger on His Seventy-Fifth Birthday*, edited by H. G. Güterbock and Th. Jacobsen, 375–87. Assyriological Studies 16. Chicago: The University of Chicago, 1965.
Rudin-O'Brasky, T. *The Patriarchs in Hebron and Sodom (Gen 18–19): A Study of Structure and Composition of the Biblical Story*. Simor: Jerusalem, 1982.
Sarna, Nahum. "Abraham in History." Biblical Archeological Review 3 (1977) 5–9.
———. *Exploring Exodus: The Heritage of Biblical Israel*. New York: Schocken, 1986.
———. *The JPS Torah Commentary: Genesis*. Philadelphia: Jewish Publication Society, 1989.
———. *Understanding Genesis*. New York: Schocken, 1996.
Sasson, Jack M. "Circumcision in the Ancient Near East." *JBL* 85 (1966) 473–76.
Schmidit, N. "Kadesh-Berna." *JBL* 29 (1910) 61–76.
Schneider, N. "Patriarchennamen in Zeitgenössischen Keilschrifturkunden." *Bib* 33 (1952) 521–22.

Schuab, R. Thomas, and Walter E. Rast. *The Southeastern Dead Sea Plain Expedition: An Interim Report of the 1977 Season*. AASOR 46. Boston: American Schools of Oriental Research, 1979.

Schunck, K. D. "Benjamin." In *ABD* 1:671-73.

Scott, R. B. Y. "Weights and Measures of the Bible." *BA* 22 (1959) 22-40.

Segal, Moses Hirsch. "The Religion of Israel Before Sinai." *Tarbiz* 30 (1961) 215-30.

Selman, Martin J. "Comparative Customs and the Patriarchal Age." In *Essays on the Patriarchal Narratives*, edited by Allan R. Millard and Donald J. Wiseman, 91-139. Winona Lake, IN: Eisenbrauns, 1983.

Skinner, John. *A Critical and Exegetical Commentary on Genesis*. ICC. New York: Scribner's Sons, 1910.

Snijders, L. A. "Genesis 15: The Covenant with Abraham." *OTS* 12 (1958) 261-79.

Soden, W. von. "Zum akkadischen Wörterbuch 89-96." *Orientalia* 26 (1957) 127-38.

Soggin, J. A. "Abraham and the Eastern Kings: On Genesis 14." In *Solving Riddles and Untying Knots: Biblical, Epigraphic, and Semitic Studies in Honor of Jonas C. Greenfield*, edited by Ziony Zevit, Seymour Gittin, and Michael Sokoloff, 283-91. Winona Lake, IN: Eisenbrauns, 1995.

Speiser, E. A. *Genesis*. AB 1. Garden City, NY: Doubleday, 1982.

———. "The Wife-Sister Motif in the Patriarchal Narratives." In *Biblical and Other Studies*, edited by Alexander Altmann, 15-28. Cambridge: Harvard University Press, 1963.

Speiser, E. A., trans. "The Epic of Gilgamesh." In *ANET*, 772-99.

Sperling, David S. *The Original Torah*. New York: New York University Press, 1998.

Spronk, Klass. *Beatific Afterlife in Ancient Israel and in the Ancient Near East*. Kevelare: Butzon & Bercker, 186.

Stamm, Johann Jacob. "Der Name Isaac." In *Festschrift für A. Shädelin*, edited by Hans Dürr and Wilhelm Michaels, 33-38. Bern: Herbert Lang, 1950.

Strange, Guy le. *Palestine Under the Moslems: A Description of Syria and the Holy Land*. London: Alexander P. Watt, 1890.

Talmon, Shemaryahu. "'The Comparative Method,' in Biblical Interpretation: Principles and Problems." In *Congress Volume: Gottingen 1977*, edited by John A. Emerton, 320-56. Leiden: Brill, 1977.

Taylor, J. Glen. "A First and Last Thing to Do in Mourning: *KTU* 1.161 and Some Parallels." In *Ascribe to the Lord: Biblical and Other Studies in Memory of Peter C. Craigie*, edited by Lyle Eslinger and Glen Taylor, 151-57. JSOTSup 67. Sheffield: JSOT Press, 1988.

Thompson, Henry O. "Hobah." In *ABD* 3:235.

Thompson, John Alexander. "Shur." In *ISBE* 4.497-98.

Thompson, John L. "Hagar, Victim or Villain? Three Sixteenth-Century Views." *CBQ* 59 (1997) 213-33.

Thompson, Thomas L. *The Origin Tradition of Ancient Israel 1: The Literary Formation of Genesis and Exodus 1-23*. JSOTSup 55. Sheffield: JSOT Press, 1987.

Tigay, Jeffery H. *The Evolution of the Gilgamesh Epic*. Philadelphia: University of Pennsylvania Press, 1982.

———. *The JPS Torah Commentary: Deuteronomy*. Philadelphia: The Jewish Publication Society, 1996.

Towner, W. Sibley. "'Blessed Be YHWH,' and 'Blessed Art Thou, YHWH': The Modulation of a Biblical Formula." *CBQ* 30 (1968) 388-89.

Tsevat, Matittiahu. *The Meaning of the Book of Job and Other Biblical Studies*. New York: Ktav, 1980.

Udd, Kris J. "Bab Edh-Dhra', Numeira, and the Biblical Patriarchs: A Chronological Study." PhD diss., Andrews University, 2011.

Vaux, Roland de. *The Early History of Israel*. Translated by David Smith. Philadelphia: Westminster Press, 1978.

Van Seters, John. *Abraham in History and Tradition*. Brattleboro, VT: Echo Point, 1975.

———. "Confessional Reformulation in the Exilic Period." *VT* 22 (1972) 448–59.

———. *Prologue to History*. Louisville: Westminster John Knox, 1992.

———. "The Religion of the Patriarchs in Genesis." *Bib* 61 (1980) 220–33.

Vawter, Bruce. *Old Testament Theology*. 2 vols. Translated by D. M. G. Stalker. New York: Harper & Row, 1962–1965.

———. *On Genesis: A New Reading*. Garden City, NY: Doubleday, 1977.

Wagner, Max. "Beiträgezur Aramaismenfrage im Alttestamentlichen Hebräisch." In *Hebräische Wortforschung: Festschrift zum 80. Geburtstag von W. Baumgartner*, edited by Benedikt Hartmann, Ernst Jenni, E. Y. Kutscher, et al., 355–71. VTSupl 16. Leiden: Brill, 1967.

Ward, Eileen F. de. "Mourning Customs in 1, 2 Samuel." *JJS* 23 (1972) 1–27.

Warner, Sean M. "The Patriarchs and Extra-Biblical Sources." *JSOT* 2 (1977) 50–61.

Weinfeld, M. "The Covenant of Grant in the Old Testament and in the Ancient Near East." *JAOS* 90 (1970) 184–203.

———. "The Loyalty Oath in the Ancient Near East." *UF* 8 (1976) 400–401.

Weisberg, David B. "Loyalty and Death: Some Ancient Near Eastern Metaphors." *Maarav* 7 (1991) 253–67.

Wellhausen, J. *Die Composition des Hexateuchs und der Historischen Bücher des Alten Testaments*. Berlin: Reiner, 1899. Reprint, de Gruyter, 1963.

———. *Prolegomena to the History of Israel*. Translated by Allan Menzies and John Sutherland Black. Edinburgh: Adam & Charles Black, 1885.

———. *Der Text der Bücher Samuelis*. Göttingen: Vandenhoeck and Ruprecht, 1871.

Wenham, Gordon J. *Genesis 1–15*. Grand Rapids: Zondervan, 1987.

———. *Genesis 16–50*. WBC 2. Nashville: Thomas Nelson, 2000.

———. "The Religion of the Patriarchs." In *Essays on the Patriarchal Narratives*, edited by A. Millard and D. J. Wiseman, 161–95. Winona Lake, IN: Eisenbrauns, 1983.

———. "The Symbolism of the Animal Rite in Genesis 15: A Response to G. F. Hasel." *JSOT* 22(1982) 134–37.

———. "The Symbolism of the Animal Rite in Genesis 15: A Response to G. F. Hasel." *JSOT* 19 (1981) 61–78.

Wensinck, A. J. "Abban and Alalakh." *JCS* 12 (1958) 124–29.

———. *Some Semitic Rites of Mourning and Religion*. Amsterdam: J. Müller, 1917.

———. "They Lived in Tents." In *Biblical and Near Eastern Studies: Essays in Honor of William Sanford Lasor*, edited by Gary A. Tuttle, 195–200. Grand Rapids: Eerdmans, 1978.

———, trans. "The Vassal Treaties of Esarhaddon." *Iraq* 20 (1958) 59–72.

Westermann, Claus. *Genesis 12–36*. Translated by John J. Scullion, S.J. Minneapolis: Fortress: Minneapolis, 1995.

———. *The Promises to the Fathers*. Translated by D. E. Green. Philadelphia: Fortress, 1980.

———. "The Way of the Promise Through the Old Testament." In *The Old Testament and Christian Faith*, edited by B. W. Anderson, 200–224. New York: Harper, 1963.

Williamson, P. R. *Abraham, Israel, and the Nations: The Patriarchal Promise and Its Covenant Development in Genesis*. JSOTSup 315. Sheffield: Sheffield Academic, 2000.

Wilson, John A., trans. "From the Lists of Ramses III." In *ANET* 260–62.

———. "The Journal of a Frontier Official." In *ANET* 258–59.

———. "List of Asiatic Countries under the Egyptian Empire." In *ANET* 242–43.

———. "The Story of Si-Nuhe." In *ANET* 18–22.

———. "The Story of Two Brothers." In *ANET* 23–25.

Wiseman, Donald J. "Abraham Reassessed." In *Essays on the Patriarchal Narratives*, edited by A. R. Millard and D. J. Wiseman, 141–60. Winona Lake, IN: Eisenbrauns, 1983.

———. "Ration List From Alalakh 7." *JCS* 13 (1959) 19–33.

Wood, Bryant G. "The Discovery of the Sin Cities of Sodom and Gomorrah." *Bible and Spade* 12/3 (1999) 67–80.

Woolley, C. Leonard, and T. E. Lawrence. *The Wilderness of Zin*. PEFA 3. London: Jonathan Cape, 1915.

Yaron, R. "*Kā'eth Hayyah* and *Koh Leḥay*." *VT* 12 (1962) 500–501.

Yelvin, Samuel. "Benjamin." In *EMiqr* 2:263–81.

———. "Ur." In *EMiqr*, 1:170–75.

Žabkar, L. V. *A Study of the Ba Concept in Ancient Egyptian Texts*. Chicago: University of Chicago Press, 1968.

Zadok, R. "On Five Iranian Names in the Old Testament." *VT* 26 (1976) 246–47.

Zandee, J. *Death as an Enemy According to Ancient Egyptian Conceptions*. Leiden: Brill, 1960.

Zarnis, J. "Camel." In *ABD* 1:824–26.

Scripture Index

HEBREW BIBLE

Genesis

Reference	Pages
1:22	162
1:28	162
2	173
2:4	167, 173
2:20	75n9
2:21	65n35
3	105, 173
3:9	89, 106
3:19	185, 195
3:24	112
3:29	193
4:1	92
4:3	133
4:9	95, 106
4:14	112
4:20	26
6:8–9	2
6:11	105
6:13	105
6:13–21	178
7:21	193
8:20	133
9:13	80
9:16	78
9:21	26
10:9	117
10:15	34
10:19	21
10:21	49
10:25	49
11:2	40n18
11:6	49
11:26	8, 103, 192n24
11:29	149
11:30	103
11:32	8, 192
12	39, 47, 83, 136, 137–38, 139, 152
12:1	14, 121, 167, 178
12:1–2	179
12:1–3	2, 82
12:2	59n5, 60, 76, 83, 103, 179
12:2–3	174
12:4	192n24
12:4–5	138
12:5	29
12:6	17, 25, 29, 78, 159
12:6–7	24
12:7	59n5, 83, 126, 155, 174, 179, 188
12:8	17, 18, 24, 25, 26, 126, 155, 158, 174
12:9	17, 20, 24
12:10	17, 138, 151
12:10–13	145
12:10—13:1	140
12:10–20	27, 133, 134, 136, 137, 148
12:11	120

Genesis (continued)

12:11–13	138
12:11–15	138, 145
12:12	151
12:13	9n19
12:14–16	138
12:16	29, 31, 104, 151
12:17	152
12:17–20	138
12:18	146
12:19	138
13	38, 39, 138
13:1	17, 20
13:2	28n38, 29, 147, 152
13:3	17, 26
13:4	155, 158, 174
13:5–11	39
13:8	97
13:10	92
13:12	26, 97
13:13	92
13:14–16	59n5
13:15	83
13:15–17	174
13:16	60, 83
13:17	17, 188
13:18	17, 26, 39, 45n43, 126, 155, 159, 174
13:18–19	38
13:24	45n44
14	37, 38, 39, 39n14, 40, 41, 44, 45, 48, 54, 55, 99, 168
14:1–11	38
14:1–12	38
14:3	44
14:6	43
14:7	6n11, 43
14:8–20	38
14:10	81
14:11–12	38
14:12	97
14:12–17	38
14:13	19, 39, 45n43, 48, 59n6, 159
14:13–16	39n15
14:14	45n43, 46
14:15	15, 47n53, 59n6
14:16	38, 59n6
14:17	50
14:18	52
14:18–20	50, 51, 54
14:18–22	168, 174
14:19	53
14:19–20	168
14:20	59n6
14:21	50, 59n6
14:21–24	38, 50
14:22	161, 163, 168, 173
14:24	19
15	39, 39n14, 57, 58, 58n4, 59, 59n6, 61, 63n25, 64, 66, 67, 68, 70, 71, 73, 81, 82, 83, 103, 118
15:1	58, 59, 59n6, 68, 82, 140, 174, 176, 176n29, 179
15:1–5	58
15:1–6	58n2
15:1–6 E	58n1
15:1–21	174
15:1b	58n1, 60
15:2	15, 59, 59n6, 60, 94
15:2–3	60
15:3	59, 82
15:3–4	108
15:3a	58n1
15:4	59, 69, 82, 109, 174
15:4–5	60
15:5	58, 58n1, 59, 61, 83, 103
15:6	67, 69
15:7	12, 59, 61n17, 82, 174
15:7–8	59
15:7–21	58, 58n2, 61, 67
15:7–21 J	58n1
15:8	59, 82, 94
15:9	59, 61
15:11	58n1
15:12	58
15:12a	58n1
15:12b	65
15:13	59
15:13–14	83

Scripture Index

15:13–16	65, 69	17:1c–8	73
15:13–21	178	17:2	78, 82, 83n32, 103, 106
15:13a	58n1		
15:14	58n1	17:2–3	83
15:15	65, 186, 194	17:3	77, 82
15:16	39n15, 58n1	17:3a	74
15:17	58	17:3b–8	73
15:18	82, 83	17:4	75, 78, 82, 83n32
15:18–21	174	17:4–6	109, 118
15:19–21	39n15	17:4–8	73, 74
15:20	41	17:4b–6	74
16	69, 83, 108, 115, 117, 118, 133, 182	17:5	76
		17:5–8	175
16:1–4	115	17:6	77, 78, 79, 83, 171
16:1–14	116	17:7	74, 75, 82, 83n32, 94, 118
16:1–16	115		
16:1a	116	17:7–8	79, 83
16:2	116	17:8	82, 83
16:2–3	105	17:9	75, 83n32
16:3	34, 116	17:9–11	82
16:4	112	17:9–14	72, 73, 74, 164, 175
16:6–7	59n5	17:10	83n32
16:7	21, 106, 182	17:11	83n32
16:7–9	182	17:12	111, 164
16:8	106	17:13	83n32
16:9	106, 116, 182	17:13–14	82
16:10	89n18, 106, 118, 182	17:14	75, 83n32, 187
16:11	106, 115, 116, 182	17:15–16	73, 74
16:12	117	17:15–21	73, 178
16:13	168, 173, 182	17:15–22	73, 81
16:15–16	108, 116	17:16	74, 77, 78, 79, 175
16:16	116	17:16–17	83
16:19	108	17:16–21	109
16:22	181	17:16a	79
16:45	34	17:16b	79
17	72, 73, 74, 75, 79, 81, 82, 83, 84, 165	17:17	74, 77, 78, 82
		17:17–18	74
17:1	83, 86, 103, 168, 170, 179	17:17b	74
		17:18	74, 79, 82, 109
17:1–2	74, 82	17:18b	75
17:1–8	73	17:19	74, 75, 79, 82, 83n32, 102, 108, 111, 164, 175
17:1–27	174		
17:1a	74, 75		
17:1b	75	17:19–21	73, 74
17:1b–3a	73	17:20	78, 114
17:1ba	74	17:21	75, 79, 84, 110, 163, 175
17:1bb	74		
17:1bc–2	74	17:21a	75

Genesis (continued)

17:22	73, 75, 86
17:22a	74
17:22b	74
17:23	118
17:23–27	73, 75
17:24–25	74
17:24a	75
18	39, 84, 85, 86, 87, 90, 96, 97
18:1	17, 19, 26, 39, 86, 96, 159, 179, 181
18:1—19:23	85
18:2	86, 182
18:3	86, 87, 182
18:4	182
18:4–5	87
18:6	26
18:9	26
18:9–15	84
18:10	26, 79, 84, 89, 109, 110, 182
18:12	78, 90, 96, 102, 108
18:13	77, 96
18:14	79, 84, 89
18:15	96
18:17	178
18:17–21	91
18:18	174
18–19	38
18:19	84
18–19	85
18:20	93, 95
18:20–21	92
18:20–32	85
18:23	96, 141
18:23–32	96
18:24	96
18:25	91, 96, 120
18:26	95, 96
18:28	95, 96
18:29	95
18:30	95
18:31	95
18:32	95
19	39, 51, 85, 87, 90, 92, 96, 97
19:1	90, 96, 182
19:1–3	96
19:1–8	96
19:2	120
19:5	181
19:8	98
19:9	181
19:10	181
19:12	181
19:13	87, 92, 96
19:14	96, 97, 98
19:15	96
19:15–23	99
19:16	181
19:17	96
19:18–22	96
19:19	96
19:21	96
19:24	98
19:24–25	98
19:25	98
19:28	98
19:29	85, 175
19:32–35	97
20	110, 135, 136, 137, 138–42, 152
20:1	17, 20, 21, 27
20:2	138, 139, 143
20:2–18	137
20:3	139, 140, 141, 175
20:3–7	139, 160
20:4	141
20:4–5	140
20:6	139, 175
20:6–7	140
20:7	141, 157
20:8	141, 144
20:9	143, 146
20:11	139, 143, 144, 175
20:12	149
20:13	139, 145, 175
20:15	144
20:16	28n38
20:17	140, 157, 175
21	39, 69, 115, 117, 118
21:1	89, 109
21:1–21	115, 116
21:2	102, 110

21:5	xviin2, 116	22:14b	134
21:6	77, 78, 102, 108	22:15	106, 175n25
21:6b	111	22:16	69, 175n25
21:7	111	22:17	60n12, 106, 162
21:8	97n46	22:17–18	174
21:8–21	115	22:19	17, 22, 132
21:9	78n19	22:20–22	8
21:9–21	106	22:22	5
21:10–19	116	23	24, 27
21:12	116, 118, 175	23:1	190
21:13	113–14, 115	23:2	194
21:14	113, 116	23:3	195
21:15	116	23:6	39, 175
21:16	116	23:16	188
21:17	116, 127, 175, 183	23:17	19
21:18	115, 116	23:19	19
21:19	116	24	29, 35
21:20	115, 116, 117, 175	24:3	161, 175
21:21–22	175	24:4	6
21:22–32	21n15	24:7	6, 59n5, 143, 174, 175
21:22–34	145	24:10	9n19, 192
21:23	33, 160	24:12	157
21:24	160	24:12–14	157
21:26	160	24:16	142
21:27	29, 160, 161	24:26–27	157
21:28	160	24:27	157
21:30	22	24:35	28n38, 29, 31
21:31	145	24:36	192
21:31–33	22	24:40	69
21:32	161	24:60	162, 163
21:32–33	174	24:62	107
21:33	20, 22, 158, 168, 169, 170, 174	24:67	26
		25	143
22	122, 127, 134	25:1	78
22:1	120, 175, 183	25:5	192
22:1–19	122	25:6	xviin2, 114, 192
22:2	121, 122, 155	25:7	190, 193
22:3	29, 175	25:7–10	191
22:5	29	25:8	186, 187, 192, 193, 194, 200
22:6	126		
22:7	120, 128	25:11	163
22:8	126, 128, 134, 175	25:12–18	106
22:10	130	25:17	186, 200
22:11	106, 120, 123, 175n25	25:18	21, 107
22:11–18	183	25:19	110
22:12	69, 120, 122, 175	25:20	9, 9n19, 35
22:13	134, 156	25:26	192n23
22:14	128, 175n25	25:27	26

Genesis (continued)

26	136, 137, 142–43, 152
26:1–11	136
26:1–13	136
26:3	148, 174
26:3–4	59n5, 68
26:4	60n12
26:5	69
26:7	143
26:8	78n19, 143
26:9	143, 146
26:10	143, 146
26:12–13	148
26:18	23
26:23	22
26:24	68, 106, 174, 176
26:25	22, 158
26:26–31	145
26:29	33
26:31	161n20
26:33	22, 145
26:34	34
27:2	117
27:46	34
28:1–4	156
28:3	168, 170
28:3–4	59n5
28:5	9, 35
28:10–22	107
28:12	181, 183
28:12–19	173
28:13	176
28:13–14	59n5
28:13–15	68
28:18	25
28:19	18
29	35
29:1	67
31:5	176
31:13	168
31:17	29
31:18	166
31:20	9, 35
31:22	124
31:24	9, 35
31:25	26
31:29	176
31:33	26
31:34	26, 29
31:42	176
31:47	9, 11, 35
31:53	176
32:4	181
32:16	29
33:1–2	181
33:7	24
33:13–14	24
33:17	26n27
33:18	52n69
33:19	27
33:20	24, 168
33:21	24
33:27	24
34:10	28
34:14	165
34:16	28
34:18	64n30
34:21	28
34:25	86, 105
34:28	29
35:1	155
35:2	25
35:4	24
35:7	168
35:8	191
35:11	78, 168, 170
35:21	26
35:27	19
35:28	193
35:29	186, 193, 200
36	78
36:2	34
36:20	42
36:32	41n26
37:25	29, 29n42
37:29	196
37:34	196
41:25	151
42:26	29, 31
42:34	28
43:1	151
43:13	168
43:14	170
43:18	29
43:23	176

44:3	29	11:1	152
44:13	29	11:2–3	152
45:23	29	12:12	174
46:1	22, 199	12:13	80
46:3	176	12:25–27	92
47:8	190	12:35–36	152
47:9	193	12:40	xviin1
47:28	xviin2, 190	12:44	165
47:30	186	12:48	165
48:3	168, 170	13:9	80
48:9–20	156	13:16	80
49:3–28	156	13:21	66, 183
49:5	105	14:9	183
49:22	21	15:22	21, 124
49:24	176	15:22f	114
49:25	168, 171	15:25	120
49:26	176	16:4	120
49:29	200	17:8	42
49:33	200	17:14	42n29
50:5	27	17:15	156
50:10	194, 197	18:11	174
50:13	187, 194	19	122
50:24–25	109	19:18	66
		20:3	174
Exodus		20:5	95n40
		20:7	151
1:16	151	20:18	66
2:23	92n28	22:21–22	92n28
2:24	69	22:28	156
3:2	183	22:29	80
3:6	176	23:23	32
3:7	92n28	23:33	160
3:8	34n60, 88	24:5	156
3:9	92n28	24:8	62
3:13	173	28:10	166
3:17	88	28–29	156
3:18	124	29:45	79
3:21–22	152	31:12	80
4:24–26	164	31:16	78
4:25	80, 164	31:17	80
4:31	109	31:18	166
6:2–3	167, 173	32:13	60n12
6:3	170, 172, 177	33:2	32
6:5	69	33:20	180
6:8	161, 161n21	34:11	32
6:12	166	34:12–16	32
6:30	166	34:26	156
9:30	173	34:34	142n23

Exodus (continued)

39:43	163

Leviticus

1	61n18
1:14	61n19
1:17	61
5:7	61n19
5:11	61n19
8–10	156
11:45	79
12:3	72
14:19	141n19
14:20	122
17:8	122
18:6	141n19
18:9	140
18:11	140
18:21	133
18:22	92n30
18:24	92n30
20:2	133
20:13	92n30
20:17	140
20:18–20	80
20:23	92n30
21:1–3	196
21:7	112
22:13	112
22:27	80
22:33	79
25	188
25:23	188
25:38	79
26:42	69
26:45	69, 79

Numbers

6:24–26	163
8:2–26	156
8:18	156
12:6–8	180
12:13	140, 157
13:23	45n44
13:24	45n44
13:26	6n11
13:27	88
13:29	42
14:30	161, 161n21
15:41	79
20:1	191
20:13	6n11
20:17	44
20:24	186
21:22	44
24:4	170, 171, 179n40
24:6	170
24:16	171
24:17	6n11
25:1–5	198
31:25–41	53
32:8	6n11
33:39	191
34:5	66

Deuteronomy

1:4	42
1:10	60n12
1:44	42
2–3	44
2:8	43
2:11	41
2:12	42
2:14	43
2:20	41
2:22	42
3:1	42
3:10	42
3:11	41
6:1–3	92
6:3	88
6:6–7	92
6:8	80
6:20–25	92
7:1	32, 34n60, 46, 66n39
7:1–2	32
7:2	32, 160
7:3–4	32n55
8:2	120
8:16	120
10:6	191
10:8	163
10:22	60n12

11:18	80	8	19
11:23	32	8:9	25
12:2	20, 122, 159	8:12	25
12:31	133	8:30	25
14:21	89n12	9:1	34n60
14:22–29	53	10	25
18:11	199	10:1	51
18:13	83	11	25
20:17	46	12:22	6n11
21:15–17	192	15	21
21:19	97	15:4	66
21:23	197	17:15	41
22:14	141n19	20:4	97
22:19	112	20:7	6n11
22:22	139	22:23	122
22:29	112	24:2	176
23:5	51	24:2–3	2
23:8	32	24:14	84
24:1	112	24:23	25
24:3	112	24:26	25
24:10	9	34:3	49
24:16	95n40		

Judges

25:17–19	42n29
25:20	9
26:5	9, 35	3:5	34n60
26:12–14	198	4:6	6n11
26:12–15	53	6:5	29n42
26:14	198, 200	6:11	183
26:15	90	6:24	156
27:22	140	6:26	122
28:62	60n12	7:8	46
29:22	99	7:16	46
31:16	186	9:4	48
32:11	61n19	9:26	48
32:40	161, 161n21	11	134
32:50	186	11:3	48
33:27	170	11:24	174
34:6	191	11:31	122
34:7	186	13:2–5	59n8
48:7	9	13:6	181
		13:20	181
		15:1	110
		19:29	125

Joshua

3:10	34n60
5:2	80, 164, 165

1 Samuel

5:2–9	165		
7:2	25	1:22–24	112
7:6	195, 196	1:24 MT	62n21

1 Samuel (continued)

1:25	62n21
6	152
13:9	122
14:6	165
15:2–8	42n29
15:3	29n42
15:10	59n7
15:17	21
16:20	31
17:26	165
17:36	165
22:2	48
24:15	141n20
25:1	194
25:18	31
27:8	21
27:9	29n42
28:3	194
28:13	199
28:24	88n11
30	45
30:17–19	42n29
31:4	165
31:13	197

2 Samuel

1:12	194
3:31	196
6:18	163
6:20	163
7:4	59n7
7:4–16	69
7:12	69, 186, 187
7:16	78
7:24–29	78
8:5–6	48
8:18	55
13:13	149
13:31	195
14:26	28n37
17:23	187
17:27–28	51
19:38	187
21:14	187
22:30	21

1 Kings

3:6	69
5:1	66
5:4	66
6:1	xviin1
8:23	69
9:20	34n60
9:26	43
10:2	29n42
11:5	174
12:22	59n7
13:22	187
13:30	194, 195
14:8	194
14:23	20, 159
14:31	187
15:24	187
16:1	59n7
16:31	52
17:2	59n7
17:8	59n7
17:20–22	140
18:24	158
18:31	59n7
19:8	43n37
20:31	196
21:3	188
21:17	59n7
21:27	196
22:51	187

2 Kings

1:2	174
3:27	134
4:8–17	59n8
4:14	110
4:16	89
4:17	89
4:33–35	140
5:11	158
7:1	97n45
7:18	97n45
8:9	29n42
15:38	187
16:3	134
19:1	196
19:2	196

19:12	6n8	**Jeremiah**	
22:20	187	2:20	20, 159
23:10	133	4:8	194n30
23:34	76	5:1	95
24:7	66	6:10	166
24:17	76	9:25	166
		11:5	88
Isaiah		14:6	106n11
2:1	179	14:12	123
2:1–4	55	16:6	194
2:3	121n6	22:18	194, 195
3:26	195	23:5	91
5:6	91n27	23:14	92
6:8	91	23:18	91
8:3	141n19	23:22	91
8:19	199	24:5	5
9:6	52, 91n26	25:12	5
11:14	67n39	25:33	194
12:4	158	29:10	109–10
13:6	170	31:28	95n40
13:19–22	99	34	63n25
15:3	196	34:5	195
16:5	91n26	34:9	112
19:8	178	34:16	112
22:12	194	34:17–19	61
29:1–8	134	34:18–20	64
29:10	65n35	49:3	196
30:24	31	49:29	29n42
30:29	121n6	50:1	5
32:12	194	50:8	5
32:14	106n11		
32:17	52	**Ezekiel**	
41:8	130	1:3	5
41:13	68n47	1:24	170
43:1	68n47	8:3	61
47:1	195	12:13	5
48:18	52	13:7	179n40
49:26	176n30	16:16	5
51:9	170n11	16:49	92
52:1	165	17:3	65n32
55:3	69	18	95n40
60:16	176n30	20:5	161
60:17	52	20:12	80
64:6	158	20:20	80
65:4	199	20:23	161n21
		24:16	194
		26:16	195

Ezekiel (continued)

27:18	47
27:23	6
27:31	196
33:20	95n40
43:24	123
44:7	165
44:9	165, 166
47:19	43n38
48:28	43n38

Hosea

1:8	112
8:9	106n11

Joel

1:13	194n30
1:15	170
2:12	194
3:5	158

Amos

1:1	179
1:5	12
3:7	91
5:10	97n45
5:16	195
6:13	42n31

Jonah

1:9	50

Micah

1:1	179
1:8	194n30
4:1–4	55
4:2	121n6
6:6–7	134

Habakkuk

1:1	179
1:12	170n11
3:5	87

Zephaniah

2:9	99
3:9	158

Haggai

1:13	181

Zechariah

5:9	65n32
5:11	40n18
8:3	121n6
13:9	158

Malachi

2:7	181
2:16	112

Psalms

3:4	68n46
13:2	176n30
13:5	176n30
18:30	21
24:3	121n6
30:12 [11]	195
68:15	170
72:17	70
73:11	169
74:12	170n11
76:3	52
76:3–4	55
78:35	52, 168
80:19	158
81:6	76
85:11	52
89:3	69
89:4	69
89:13	8
89:29–30	78
89:37	78
91:1	170
103:14	186n4
104:29	186n4
105:1	158
106	198
106:28	198

107:11	169	3:55	158
110	54		
110:1	163	**Ecclesiastes**	
110:4	51, 52, 54, 55, 163	3:4	195
116:13	158	3:20	186
116:14	158	9:4–6	185
116:17	158		
132:12	78	**Esther**	
136:13	66	4:1	196
		4:1–3	195
Proverbs		4:3	194
8:23	170n11		
9:8	160	**Daniel**	
30:14	125	2:5	5
		2:10	5
Job		2:14	40n19, 40n20
1:3	29n42	2:15	40n20
1:9	120	9:3	195n40, 196
1:17	5	12:7	161
1:20	196		
2:8	195	**Ezra**	
2:12	195	4:12–13	21
2:13	195, 197	9:1	34n60
4:12–14	65		
4:13	65n35	**Nehemiah**	
8:3	120	9:1	195n40, 196
16:15	196	9:7	12
16:15–17	195n40	9:7–8	82, 174
24:15	142n23	9:8	34n60, 67
33:15–16	65n35	9:23	60n12
34:15	186	13:15	31
39:5–8	106n11		
42:1	195n40	**1 Chronicles**	
42:8	157	1:18–19	49
42:12	29n42	1:28	111
		1:34	111
Ruth		5:21	29n42
1:6	109	5:27–29	xviiin2
1:20–21	171	6:57	6n11
2:19–20	163	7:20–27	xviiin2
4:2	95	17:11	187
		21:25	188
Lamentations			
2:10	196		
2:21	195		

2 Chronicles

3:1	121
8:4	43n37
8:7	34n60
9:1	29n42
14:14	29n42
20:2	43
20:16	134
34:28	187

ANCIENT NEAR EASTERN TEXTS

Alalakh Tablets

58	48

Alalakh treaty

11:39–42	63

Egyptian Execration Texts

42, 52

El-Amarna tablets

EA 197, 256	42

El-Augarna texts

52

Epic of Aqhat

89

Esarhaddon, prophecies

15, 20	68, 68n48

Esarhaddon vassal treaty

63n27

Gilgamesh

	87n6, 185, 197, 197n45
10.3.3–5	185n2

Keret

89

Le Palais royal d'Ugarit (PRU)

	IV
139–140	141n21

List of Thutmose III

	42
no. 118	43n33

Maqlû

II, line 19	66n36

Middle Assyrian Laws

Tablet A

section 22	142

Naga ed-Der stella

164–65

"Story of Two Brothers"

195

Ugarit

Canaanite epics	172n22

DEUTEROCANONICAL BOOKS

Judith

	81
1:6	40n19
4:4	47n53
5:6	12
15:4	47n53
15:5	47n53
16:24	197

2 Maccabees

7:27	112n32

Sirach (Ben Sira)

22:12	197
39:26	88

PSEUDEPIGRAPHA (HEBREW BIBLE)

2 Enoch

33:11	40n19

Jubilees

	112
12	12
12:1–4	3
13	12
13:11–13	150n38
15:30	81
17:4	112
17:15–16	129n35
18:13	121
19:8	14n43

DEAD SEA SCROLLS

1QapGen

19:14–19 ar	150
21:29	41
22:10	47n52
22:13	52

ANCIENT JEWISH WRITERS

Josephus

Antiquities of the Jews

1:10:1	46n46
1:181	52
1:232	129n36
1.12.2	123n13
11:1	93n31
17:8:4	197n44
154–157	4n1
186	19n8

Against Apion

1:123	52n70

Jewish Wars

	46
4	99n50
4:533	20n9
5:9:4	46n47
482	99n50

Pseudo-Philo

Biblical Antiquities (Liber aniquitatum biblicarum)

	130
32:2–4	130n41

RABBINIC WORKS

Midrash

'Abot de Rabbi Nathan

34	93n34

Genesis Rabbah

13:3	173n24
38:13	3
39:7	193n25
39:9	14nn44–45
39:16	158n10
40:6	xxiiin25
42:5	41nn24–25
42:8	49–50, 50n61, 80n23, 164n29
44:17	61n19
45:1	104n1
45:4	105n7
45:5	105n9, 190n16
46:3	171n15
48:14	89n13
48:19	90n21
50:5	92n29
50:9	98n48
54:3	160n18
55:4	130n38

Genesis Rabbah (continued)

55:6	124n16
55:7	120n3, 121nn4–5
56:1	124n17
56:2	125n21
56:3	125n23
56:4	126n25
56:8	129n35, 130n40
56:11	128n33, 132n46
58:1	190n12, 190n15
58:7	191n19
61:6	162n24
62:2	193n27, 194n28
62:3	191n20
79:7	188n7

Exodus Rabbah

1:1	113n38
3:6	178n38

Leviticus Rabbah

2:10	130n39
20:2	191n18

Deuteronomy Rabbah

11:3	101n61

Tanḥumah Genesis

	91n25
3:9	xxiiin26

Lech Lecha (Gen 12:1—17:27)

9	25n26

Pirqe Rabbi Eliezer

	126
31	125n18, 126n26

Sefer Hayysar

121	190n17

Pesikta Rabbati (Pesiqta Rabbati)

	127
40	127n29

Sechel Tov

	107
11	107n16

Sifra Emor

14:4	80n25

Sifre

Deuteronomy

32	130

Talmudic Literature

Baba Batra

16b	192n22, 193n26
82b	159n15

Bava Metzi'a

31b.	180n44
86b	86n2, 89n14
87a	88n10, 111n27

Berakhot

13a	76n13, 77n16

Beṣah

32b	94n37

Giṭṭin

75b	112n33

Ḥullin

60b	21n15

Ketubbot

60a	112n33

Kiddushin

29a	164n30

Megillia

16a	60n13
23b	95n41

Middot

2:5	124n15

Mo'ed Qatan

27b	194n33
28a	80n25

Nedarim

32b	164n27

Pesaḥim

4a	123n11

Roš Haššanah

16b — 77n18

Sanhedrin

46a — 197n47
89b — 120n3
105b — 123n12
109b — 93nn32–33
111a — 188n8

Šebuʿot

35b — 86n4, 182n47

Shabbat

54a — 127n27
127a — 86n4

Soṭah

3:11 — 98n47
14a — 86n3

Yebamot

64a — 104n2

Targums

Onkelos — 107

Sheni on Esther

1:4 — 194n32

Commentaries and Rabbis Mentioned

Abba b. Mammel — 178

Abraham Ibn Ezra
— 58, 179, 193

Baḥya ben Asher — 132

Bekhor Shor, Joseph ben Isaac
— 107

Judah b. R. Simon
— 188

Maimonides (Rambam)
— 80, 132, 133n49, 158, 179, 182

Guide for the Perplexed
— 86, 170

1:63 — 172n19
2:13 — 159n12, 170n12
2:42 — 183c48
3:24 — 132n47
3:29 — 159n12, 170n12
3:43 — 86n5, 179n39
3:49 — 80n22

Yad, Hilkot Zeraim

8.10 — 47n55

Malbim (Meir Leibush ben Yehiel Michel Wisser)
— 78

Rabbi Akiba — 124
Rabbi Elazar — 88

Radak (David ben Joseph Kimhi)
— 58, 93, 105, 107, 128, 149, 159, 179, 193

Genesis 15:5 — 61
Genesis 15:12 — 61
Ralbag — 112

Ramban (Moses ben Nahman or Nachmanides)
— 12, 25, 83, 86, 87, 88, 92, 97, 109, 121, 127, 149, 150, 151, 158, 164, 179, 193

Rashbam (Samuel ben Meir)
— 58, 189

Rashi (Rabbi Salomon ben Isaac)
— 12, 105, 107, 109, 111, 120, 122, 124, 126, 127, 172, 182

Rav Hama bar Buzi
— 193

Sforno — 124

Kabbalah

Zohar

2:1:104a — 90nn22–23
2:1:104b — 91n24
2:1:106a — 101n61

Scripture Index

NEW TESTAMENT

Luke
1	59n8
1:7	110
2	59n8

Acts
7:2	12

Romans
	131
8:31–32	131n43

1 Corinthians
10:11	xxiii

Galatians
4:29	112

Hebrews
7:1	163
11:17–19	125

EARLY CHRISTIAN WRITINGS

1 Clement
	129
31:2–4	129n37

Augustine
	131

City of God
16:32	132n45

Epistle of Barnabus
	131
7:3	131n42

Irenaeus
	131

Against Heresies
4:5:4	131n44

GREEK AND ROMAN LITERATURE

Eusebius

Onomasticon
	19
8:6	43n38
70	19nn6–7

Praeparatio evangelica
1:10	52n73

Herodotus

Histories
	164
1:181, 5	5n5
2:37	164n31

Homer
Odyssey — 87
37:485–487	87n8

Ovid
	90

Fasti
5:494	90n19

Philo of Byblos

Phoenician History
1:33–34	165n32

Strabo
	131
739	5n5

www.ingramcontent.com/pod-product-compliance
Lightning Source LLC
Chambersburg PA
CBHW050848230426
43667CB00012B/2195